Getting the
College EDGE

Second Edition

Mona Casady

Design Coordinator and Typesetter: Laura Brady
Photographer: Niki Quasius
Project Manager: Stephen Almeida
Publishing Manager: Paul Kennedy
Webpage Manager: Irene Francka

Printed by Webcom Limited, Toronto, Canada

ISBN: 0-9752661-0-1

ORIENTING YOURSELF TO college is much like new employees' orientation to their company. After being hired by a company, new employees have a competitive edge if they know the procedures, services, and benefits as well as management's expectations of them as employees. After being admitted to college, new students have an edge if they know the academic procedures, available services (campus resources), benefits of higher education, and their professors' expectations of students. Good study skills and communication skills will hone this edge. *Getting the College Edge* will help you get the most from your campus and from yourself.

What are the most critical needs of new college students in order to succeed not only in the first year but beyond to graduation?

After 35 years of college teaching experience and countless discussions with professors and peer leaders, I realized that busy students and teachers needed a practical, efficient approach to college success. *Getting the College Edge* addresses this need with its unique 3-in-1 design—combining a textbook, a workbook, and a reference manual. The textbook material includes information that will enable you to maximize your college experience and to improve your study skills and communication skills. The workbook material enhances your learning and provides opportunities to practice your skills. The reference manual allows you to create your own personalized guide to your campus, professors, fellow students, and even the surrounding community. This manual will be invaluable to you as a resource throughout your college career.

Getting the College Edge is a unique student success text in that it emphasizes school-to-work skills while at the same time giving strong coverage of academic skills like note taking and time management. The chapters focus on practical strategies to help students—both traditional and nontraditional—progress from college to career through the discussion of topics such as working in groups, making presentations, conducting meetings, and listening.

How does *Getting the College Edge* improve student performance and retention rates?

Seven years of administering the Survey of Freshmen and having the results analyzed by a professional statistician have guided me in improving the college success course. Summarized data and statistical analysis of approximately 2,500 freshmen each year have pinpointed significant factors of college success. These important success factors have been incorporated throughout *Getting the College Edge*.

Getting the College Edge has been used successfully at Southwest Missouri State University for the past eight years by over 24,000 first-year students. Retention studies exist for the course success rate, showing a significant increase in retention for all student categories tracked. Information on these retention studies may be found on my website: http://www.casadyenterprises.com/collegesuccess/retention.htm

This edition of *Getting the College Edge* is based on conscientious and thorough input from 10 reviewers representing various sizes and types of colleges and universities across the nation. In addition, 28 teachers and 49 peer leaders at my university provided comments, criticisms, and suggestions on how the previous edition could be improved. Many diligent professionals have been invaluable in developing this textbook.

How can a textbook actually teach students to "get a competitive edge"?

Special effort was made to provide helpful features that can enhance learning. Easy-to-read content is written in a positive, supportive tone. The topics are applicable to all students regardless of age or experience. You will find many forms, illustrations, and samples to use or to modify for your personal needs throughout college and beyond.

With *Getting the College Edge* as the base for our student success course, two awards have been received. My university was recognized by *The Templeton Guide: Colleges That Encourage Character Development* in 1999, and I was presented one of the Outstanding First-Year Student Advocate Awards by the National Resource Center for the First-Year Experience in 2002.

Retained and Improved Features

Chapter Objectives Each chapter begins with a set of objectives, which lay the foundation for the upcoming lesson and provide focus. The major section headings of the chapter parallel the objectives.

Self-Assessments Each chapter has a self-assessment opportunity so you can check on yourself. What are your thoughts? What do you already know about yourself? What is your knowledge base or skill level on the respective topic? Self-assessments enable you to assess your level of understanding.

Focus on Communication Skills The ability to communicate effectively is one of the hallmarks of success both in college and in business. Writing, speaking, and listening all are identified by the US Department of Labor as foundation skills necessary for success in the workplace. The early introduction of communication skills in Chapter 2 provides the tools which are practiced in subsequent chapters in the Communication Exercises and the writing/journaling exercises—Sharing Reactions and My Reflections Journal.

Communication Exercises The communication exercises use specific language directing you to further develop your skills in communicating with others. You will gain practice in writing, interviewing, telephoning, e-mailing, and speaking. Interpersonal communication skills will be further developed as you speak with or write to one person, work in small groups, or present to the entire class. Implementing strategies from *Getting the College Edge* will help you feel more comfortable when speaking and writing to your professors, peers, co-workers, and employers.

Sharing Reactions These writing exercises invite you to share ideas, thoughts, decisions, and new information with your instructor and/or classmates. Your instructor might have you further process your reactions in small groups or with the entire class, which will help you gain insights from others.

My Reflections Journal At the end of each chapter you have an opportunity to reflect on the respective topics you have read and to think about how you will apply the suggested strategies to your course work and your life. Your written response is a confidential writing that is read by only your instructor and/or a peer leader or peer mentor (should your class have a peer leader or mentor). Guides for journal writing are given inside the back cover of *Getting the College Edge*.

Focus on School-to-Work Skills Every chapter introduces skills that will enhance college success as well as success beyond college. Chapter 15, "Becoming Involved on Campus," which is unique to *Getting the College Edge*, is key to this focus. Research shows that involvement in campus organizations and extracurricular activities contributes to college success and to career success. Getting involved in leadership positions on campus provides opportunities to practice business skills such as organizing and running meetings. Also, this kind of involvement is considered by employers to be a competitive advantage in the workplace. Another important work-related skill is problem solving.

Solve This Case exercises help you develop problem solving skills. *Solve This Case*, at the conclusion of each chapter, is a case study that presents a realistic scenario for which you can apply decision making and critical thinking skills. Working alone or with your peers in group discussions, you can apply the concepts presented in the chapter to solve a college student dilemma.

Focus on Campus Orientation and Resources In addition to providing strong coverage of communication and study skills, *Getting the College Edge* will help you to tap into the wealth of resources available in your own college community. With the new *Personal References* section, this edition has enhanced this focus.

Practice Tests On the website for *Getting the College Edge* you can access a practice test for each chapter to check your understanding of the concepts presented: http://www.casadyenterprises.com/collegeedgebook/practicetests.htm. You may print the results of the self-test to review before taking the respective in-class exam.

New Features

Self-Assessment Exercises have been expanded and enhanced so each chapter has at least one opportunity for students to assess their understanding of respective concepts and/or skills.

Personal References Section To strengthen the campus orientation and resources focus described, this new reference section consists of blank forms and documents that will be filled in as you read about the relevant topics in the text. You will be prompted to go to the *Personal References* section to answer questions in the margins that appear throughout the text as well as to complete some of the exercises. Once this section is completed, you will have your own reference manual that will include invaluable information such as phone numbers and locations for essential resources (on campus as well as relevant off-campus resources); phone numbers and e-mail addresses of your professors, your academic advisor, and classmates; term calendars; life goals; descriptors about your learning style; your college's academic rules, regulations, and procedures; your career planning data; contacts at campus organizations; and your budget worksheet.

For easy access, this *Personal References* section is found at the end of your book; it can be removed and placed on your shelf for reference throughout your college career. The *Front Cover* of your book can be copied as the front cover of your *Personal Reference Manual.*

On the inside of the front cover, you can personalize your text. You can record key information for this term including your contact information and schedule of courses. In the event your book inadvertently is misplaced, it can be returned to you easily.

Communication Chapter Moved Up For students to get off to a positive start and have the tools to do the communication exercises early in the text, the communication chapter (Communicating Effectively) was moved to Chapter 2.

Journal Writing has been expanded and reformatted. In *My Reflections Journal*, which appears at the end of each chapter, various questions are presented from which your instructor and you can choose the most appropriate ones to answer. *Journal Writing Guidelines* are provided inside the back cover of the textbook for easy reference.

Modular Format You may select any of the chapters in the order of your choice. From the database of 17 chapters, a customized text can be produced. For more information contact Mona Casady at the website http://www.casady enterprises.com/collegeedgebook/customizing.htm.

College Success Consulting

Committed to promoting and supporting college success courses and peer leadership, I can help your school establish or improve your first-year experience course or freshman seminar. Sharing expertise, support services, and materials with others is a pleasure. Ten years of teaching and administering a student success course as well as a peer leadership program have prepared me to help you with course design, implementation, recruitment, instructor training, teaching strategies, assessment, and much more. You may contact me by visiting my website at http://www.casadyenterprises.com/consulting.htm.

Ancillaries

In using the textbook *Getting the College Edge*, you have many supportive materials available. These items will save you preparation effort and time.

Instructor's Resource Manual The *Instructor's Resource Manual* (IRM) that accompanies *Getting the College Edge* will guide professors through integrating the textbook with supplemental aids and campus resources to provide a strong first-year experience for the students in your program. Various strategies are offered to target different learning styles. Discussion guides will help you connect the chapter content, exercises, transparencies, case study, personal reference section, and supplemental in-class activities. Additional aids are provided on the Class Prep CD-ROM.

Getting the College Edge Website The *Getting the College Edge* website, which can be accessed at http://www.casady enterprises.com/collegeedgebook.htm, provides students and teachers with additional resources to accompany the main text. The student site provides Practice Tests for end-of-chapter review—perfect for studying before an in-class exam. Instructors can access research findings on college success factors and retention rates.

PowerPoint Slides Accompanying each of the chapters in the text, PowerPoint slides review the major concepts of the respective chapter. These slides are available for individual or classroom use via the Class Prep CD-ROM.

Class Prep CD-ROM A *Getting the College Edge* Class Prep CD-ROM provides instructors with electronic support to accompany the *Instructor's Resource Manual (IRM)*. This CD-ROM provides a sample of course objectives, chapter exams, answer keys, a comprehensive final exam and its answer key, and PowerPoint slides—all of which can be customized to suit the needs of your course. The Survey of Freshmen and the Course Evaluation questionnaires are included to facilitate course assessment.

Acknowledgments

Many valued professionals deserve acknowledgment for the development and production of this book. Terry Brennan, Pearson Custom Publishing, launched me in writing this book for my campus. With Shani Fisher as editor, Houghton Mifflin Co published the previous edition. Conscientious reviewers devoted time and effort in the formal critique process, and valued adopters provided specific feedback to help shape this new edition.

From the 400+ teachers and 250+ peer leaders who have served under my leadership throughout the last nine years, I have learned invaluable information about college student success. They have been creative and generous in sharing effective methods.

Special thanks go to Sylvia Shepard for her developmental editing, to Niki Quasius for photographic services, to Laura Brady for typesetting and graphic art design, to Paul Kennedy for his publication guidance, and to Irene Francka for her website expertise. Appreciation goes to my Creator for giving me ability and to my family (Rolin, Gertrude, Janet, Ron, and Cleo) for their steadfast encouragement and love.

Best wishes are extended to teachers, peer leaders, and students of college success courses. Much commendation goes to the marvelous people on campuses who are kind and helpful to each other. Together we are making a difference in the lives of our first-year students, which radiates throughout our campus communities.

MONA CASADY

CONTENTS

Contents Overview

5 Enhancing Reading, Listening, and Note Taking 71

6 Taking Tests 89

7 Making Academic Decisions 105

8 Maintaining Health and Wellness 125

ORIENTING YOURSELF TO COLLEGE

Objectives

Upon completing this chapter, you should be able to:

- Begin the transition to college with realistic expectations
- Establish a support system
- Prepare to work efficiently
- Identify and locate campus resources
- Enhance your self-concept and self-awareness

ENROLLING IN COLLEGE for the first time is much like moving to a new city or being a new employee of a company. Regardless of age or experience, newness brings with it mixed feelings that range from excitement to fear. Whether you have just graduated from high school or are continuing your education after employment, military service, or parenthood, you are experiencing a transition in your life. Your orientation course and this book will help you make the transition smoothly.

Colleges and universities offer more than academic programs. They provide ways for students to interact with a variety of personalities, to assess themselves, and to improve their lives. In the college community you will make new friends and learn to appreciate the diversity of our society. Positive experiences and friendships will bolster your confidence. In facing academic or personal challenges, you have many campus resources and services available to help you. New doors will be open to you. In choosing the ones to enter, you will discover tools that enable you to make wise decisions and to continue learning throughout life.

In becoming oriented to college, you want to get off to a good start. Successful students have realistic expectations and establish a strong support system. They are prepared to work efficiently, and they become acquainted with campus resources for help. To overcome feelings of doubt or fear and to boost confidence, they review basic ways to enhance their self-concept.

By following the basic suggestions of this chapter, you can establish a firm foundation for college success. Your enjoyment and satisfaction with college will be strengthened if that foundation is cemented with a positive attitude, a willingness to work, flexibility in adjusting to change, and a determination to succeed.

■ Begin the Transition to College with Realistic Expectations

The transition to college life usually feels uncomfortable at first. You have stepped out of your comfortable daily routine and home environment. Both recent high school graduates and those who are reentering the education realm are anxious about developing better study habits and test-taking skills. International and single students away from their families and close friends might feel homesick. Those who live in apartments or residence halls might encounter incompatibility with their living mates, whereas those who live at home with their families might be distracted or pulled away from college effort by loved ones.

As you make the transition to college life, you will experience many changes. Compared to high school, college requires more reading and schedules exams less frequently (thus covering more material). You will have to get yourself up and to classes on time. If you have quit full-time employment to attend college, you will miss the regular paycheck and will have to adjust to a new daily schedule. If your transition is from full-time homemaker and parent to student, you will have to juggle multiple roles and perhaps make child care arrangements.

Upon entering college, you will have long-term and short-term goals. Long-term goals focus on general plans for the next five or six years. They would include your expected degree date, career choice, desired standard of living (quality of housing, car, and so forth), and personal relationships (such as marriage or parenthood). Short-term goals are aimed at the first year of school and are more specific. Among your immediate goals might be your course load per term, your desired grade-point average (GPA), and the number of employment hours per week you need to meet expenses.

Consider all aspects of your life, and be realistic in setting goals. Here are some first-year students with realistic goals:

Terry, 18 years of age Since he was in junior high, Terry has known that he wants to be a science teacher and track coach. He excelled in math, science, and athletics in high school. With the goal of graduating in four years, Terry plans to carry 17 credit hours each term and work during the summers. His parents pay for most college expenses.

Sandra, 26 years of age As a wife and mother of two children, Sandra plans to become an elementary teacher. Until her youngest child begins school, she plans to take 9 credits a term. Then Sandra will enroll as a full-time student, relying on her husband's financial support. Her estimated degree date is May or August of the sixth year.

Kristin, 19 years of age Kristin participates in music, theater, and dance. Being undecided about a major, she plans to work during the summers in theme parks or tent theater to explore a career in entertainment. Limiting her course load to 15 credits a term and working 15 hours a week, Kristin plans to graduate in five years.

Roberto, 18 years of age An international student, Roberto attends college on a tennis scholarship. Because of rigid practice and game schedules as well as language difficulty, he will take only 12 credits a term and attend summer school to graduate in five years. Roberto would like to become a professional tennis player.

Margaret, 55 years of age Upon being laid off from her job of twenty-two years, Margaret has decided to get more education. She never attended college after completing high school but has found that in order to earn enough money to support her family she needs to obtain a degree. Margaret is committed to working part time and attending classes full time. She plans to study management information systems.

Bill, 35 years of age In Bill's full-time job a promotion would depend on his learning computer technology. Though the company pays tuition for career development, Bill can take only one computer class this first term because he and his wife are active in the community and in their children's school events. Bill knows a degree is more than six years away.

Exercise 1 Stating Goals

Write about your long-term goals–what you plan to be doing five years from now. Include information about (1) when you plan to complete your degree requirements, (2) what career you plan to pursue, and (3) your choice of major. If you are undecided about career choice or major, describe two options you are considering.

_____

_____

_____

_____

From your statements of long-term goals, fill in lines 14, 15, and 16 of your Personal Profile sheet, found as Figure 1 at the end of this chapter.

■ Establish a Support System

Successful students typically are not self-made; they receive help from others, and they help each other. You can become oriented to new surroundings faster, more smoothly, and with greater enjoyment if you have a support system. Your teacher and classmates in this course will be one support group. More support will come from your roommate(s), family, friends, other teachers, and staff personnel.

> _A support person is a friend who cares,_
> _Who offers you help when a problem glares._
> _A support person is one who listens,_
> _Who neither judges nor asks for reasons._
> _A support person is a star no less,_
> _Who shares key moments and praises success._
>
> —Mona Casady

In each of your courses you might choose at least one classmate to get to know. As partners, you can help each other. For example, if your partner is absent, you could call or e-mail him or her to see if he or she is okay, and you could provide information on what was covered in class. If you in turn do not understand part of a lecture or an assignment, you could ask your partner for help.

Questions located in the margins, like the one below, appear throughout the chapters and ask you to identify information and resources specific to your campus. Record the answers to these questions on the respective forms in the Personal References section at the end of this text.

Identify two classmates in this course to get to know for support.

Exercise 2 Exchanging Names and Phone Numbers

For each course, exchange names, phone numbers, and e-mail addresses with two or more classmates. Prepare a reference sheet in your course notebook with these names and the contact information, and place a copy near your phone. You will appreciate this handy reference, especially in an emergency. Also, fill out the Classmates form in the Personal References section at the end of this text. College students are responsible for knowing what was covered in class.

Another part of your support system is the person or persons with whom you live. Establishing a positive relationship and a supportive environment requires open communication. Some challenges can be expected, for no two people are alike.

Living in a Residence Hall

In a residence hall you will get to know many new people who will vary by race, religion, financial strength, maturity, talents, interests, family support, lifestyle, and values. Some of these new acquaintances will become lifetime friends, and others you will choose to exclude from close association. The conversation noise on your floor and interruptions by visitors might challenge your ability to concentrate on studies. If you have a car, you need to know the lot(s) for which your parking permit is valid and the regulations of campus parking to avoid parking tickets.

Upon moving into a residence hall, you will need to establish a personal routine that is compatible with that of your roommate(s). This will include deciding where you will study, when you will take study breaks, when you will eat, and with whom you will share social events.

You will want to discuss certain items of concern with your roommates. Examples of topics to cover include cleaning the room, wearing each other's clothes, lending money, dividing expenses, designating quiet study times, handling phone calls, and establishing visitor rights. If you share the bathroom, you might decide who uses it first in the mornings.

Where is the office of residential life and services?

?

If you have a problem about residence life, first talk with your roommate(s) to try to resolve the situation. The next step would be to see your resident assistant (RA), then the residence hall director, and finally the director of residence life and services.

Living Near Campus but Away from Home

If you share housing near campus, your housemate probably will be one of your closest support persons. Though you might have been good friends in high school or at work, you could encounter new challenges in an apartment setting.

You might discuss grocery shopping, menus, meal preparation, eating times, and computer or furniture use and care. Phone expenses, including long-distance charges, need to be addressed. Bills for rent, utilities, and trash service are assumed to be divided; but which person is designated to pay the bill? When is the partner expected to pay his or her share? Studying times and visitor rights must be agreed upon. House cleaning and possibly yard care need to be decided.

On a campus map that shows the designated parking lots, note where you can park legally near your classes, laboratory or library work, and other activities. Carefully review the parking regulations for on-campus and off-campus streets to avoid fines.

Where is the parking administration office?

Living at Home and Commuting to Campus

If you live at home, your immediate support system will be your family. Discuss how tasks will be divided among family members, and decide on levels of responsibility. If you live with your parents, establish an understanding about your freedom to come and go without checking in.

If you have young children or an ailing member of the family, you will be making arrangements for care. If the care can be divided among family members, each person's responsibilities need to be decided upon.

Does your student union have an area where commuters can meet?

All Living Situations

In any housing situation, you need at least one person with whom to discuss your college work. Support each other, negotiate your differences, and make mutual agreements. Let each other know about your standard schedule of attending classes, working, or going to meetings. For courtesy in taking messages and for ease in handling emergencies, inform each other about where you are going and when you plan to return. Neither age nor relationship matters.

If you share housing, a number of items need to be discussed and negotiated to the satisfaction of both parties. You might begin with your own list. Then view the factors listed in the following exercise, and develop a Living Agreement form around which to focus discussion.

Exercise 3 Preparing a Living Agreement

To discuss important factors that relate to your housing situation, prepare a Living Agreement form. A Living Agreement form appears in the Personal References section at the end of this text. Begin by deleting the irrelevant items listed; then add those pertinent to your living arrangement. Come to an agreement on how each will be handled. Meal preparation, for example, might state: *Each prepares own breakfast and lunch; dinner is shared–Chris prepares it on M & W and Lynn on T & R nights.* Save the Living Agreement as a form, and make copies of the signed agreement for all parties. Consider revisiting the agreement periodically and making necessary revisions.

Living Agreement

- Alarm clock wake-up
- Time to use bathroom
- Wearing each other's clothes
- Use of each other's supplies
- Meal preparation
- Kitchen clean-up
- Laundry
- House cleaning
- Quiet hours for studying
- Lights-off hours for sleeping
- Use of computer equipment

- Radio, TV, and stereo time
- Phone messages
- Phone bills
- Rent and utility bills
- Appliance rentals
- Visitors of same sex
- Visitors of opposite sex
- Child care
- Lawn care
- _____
- _____

■ Prepare to Work Efficiently

Successful college students commit themselves to work. They integrate academic studies, extracurricular activities, and perhaps employment as major activities. As responsible adults, they want to *make a difference* in the lives of others to improve society.

Some students can learn quickly with little mental or physical effort, and some have financial support from parents, an employer, or a scholarship. Most students, however, have to work hard, both mentally and physically, to achieve their goals.

Many students are employed to help support their education. They are thrifty in their lifestyle, and their standard of living is moderate. Withholding immediate pleasures for long-term happiness, they plan upon graduating from college to get a better-paying job that will support a higher standard of living.

If you earned A's and B's in high school without having done much homework or having attended classes regularly, you need to prepare for much more rigorous work in college. You will have to do most of the assigned work, including small-group projects, outside class. Some courses will require that you use a computer lab, the library, or the writing center. You will be challenged to analyze cases, research topics, and apply logic to take a stand on issues. Then you will be expected to express the results clearly in writing or by speaking to a group.

In preparing to do your best, follow the model of professional office executives. Set up an efficient desk management system, get necessary supplies, organize materials, obtain reference items, and develop a records management system. You will have course folders or notebooks, reference items, and files to organize. You will use your computer to enhance efficiency.

Get Office Supplies

Equip your desk and backpack or briefcase with office supplies so you will be ready for typical in-class and homework assignments. The shopping list in Table 1 can be modified for your needs.

Your backpack or briefcase needs to include #2 pencils to use for math problems and computer-scanned exam sheets as well as pens (with black or blue ink) to use for taking notes and doing in-class writing assignments. Highlighting markers and pens with colored ink are needed as you read your textbooks and review class notes.

Table 1 Office Supplies

____	Pocket calendar and organizer	____	Tape dispenser and tape
____	Notebooks (one per course)	____	Ruler
____	File folders or filing pockets	____	Scissors
____	Paper for printer	____	Sticky notes
____	Toner cartridge for printer	____	Envelopes
____	Pens and pencils	____	Postage stamps
____	Highlighting markers	____	Rubber bands
____	Liquid cover-up/white-out	____	Rubber cement, glue, or paste
____	Stapler, staples, staple remover	____	Letter opener
____	Paper clips	____	_____

For an efficient desk management system, the most frequently used supplies (such as pens, letter opener, and paper clips) would be in the center drawer or on the top of the desk. If you are right-handed, your top left drawer would have paper supplies (paper, envelopes, sticky notes, and stamps) and the top right drawer would have supplies such as liquid cover-up, staples, tape, scissors, rubber bands, and glue. If you are left-haded, your paper supplies would be in the top right drawer and your other supplies would be in the top left drawer.

Where is the bookstore?

Where is the post office?

Where can you buy office supplies off campus?

Organize Materials

Each course needs a separate folder or notebook. If you use one notebook for all courses, you run the risk of losing important materials for all courses if your notebook gets lost or stolen. In front will be the policy statement and syllabus, which should include dates on which major assignments are due and exam dates. Use dividers to distinguish one section from another. Depending on the course, you might label the sections by unit topic, subtopics, textbook chapters, or exam dates. In the pocket of the folder or notebook, have supplies that you will need for the class.

General supplies for all courses will be in your backpack or briefcase. If you live on campus, you can go home during the day to get supplies; but commuter students do not have that option.

Obtain Reference Items

You will need handy access to these reference items:

Calendar (month at a time)   Campus map
Dictionary   College catalog
Pocket-size spelling book   Term class schedule booklet
Thesaurus   Address book with names, addresses,
Documentation style manual(s)   phone numbers, and e-mail addresses
Files   of family, friends, and businesses

Position these items within arm's length when seated at your desk or computer. Your files could fit within your side desk drawer or could be placed in a file box or cabinet.

Develop a Records Management System

Save important documents pertaining to your academic work and personal business. In order to retrieve information quickly, set up separate file folders for each type of document. You might develop a records management system similar to Table 2.

Table 2 Records Management System

FILE LABEL	CONTENTS
Contracts	Housing and insurance contracts; Living Agreement
Correspondence	Letters, memos, and announcements received
Degree Progress	Advisement forms, approved course substitution or waiver, degree audit, and transcript
Employment	Applications, withholding tax forms, job history
Financial Aid	Grant, loan, and scholarship papers
Grades	Midterm and end-of-term grade sheets
Organizations	Agendas, programs, and committee work
Portfolio	Best papers, achievements, awards, and résumé
Receipts	Receipts of expenditures, including textbooks and supplies
Registration Papers	Placement test results, registration form, add/drop slips, and change to Pass/Not Pass or Audit
Term Schedule	Schedule of classes, work, and standing meetings; list of professors with their campus addresses, phone numbers, and e-mail addresses

In a separate folder for each course, file all papers of a unit after the respective unit exam. This way your backpack or briefcase will be lighter to carry; and if you lose a folder or notebook or your carrying case, all papers will not be lost—only the recent ones. Arrange files in alphabetical order by subject title.

Take Advantage of Computer Aids

Many courses in college require the use of a computer. For this course, the computer aids include word processing to key and print assignments, e-mail to communicate with others and to submit assignments to your instructors, self-assessment software, Internet and library searches, and text-computer interactions. Take advantage of these computer aids, which enable you to interact with the textbook and your instructor.

■ Identify and Locate Campus Resources

Your college offers many services, which your tuition helps to cover. Campus resources can help you with course work, health, physical fitness, advisement, registration, financial aid, counseling, employment, career guidance, and other needs. The sooner you get acquainted with these facilities, the easier and more enjoyable college life will be.

For Course Work Assistance

Analyze your skills and abilities to do course work. Circle any of the following skills that you could improve with help from experts. Write them on line 18 of your Personal Profile sheet, found as Figure 1 at the end of this chapter.

Where are the tutorial centers or labs that assist students with these courses and skills?

Reading speed and comprehension   Computer applications
Math   Writing
Science   Foreign language

If you need help, get assistance promptly. First, go to the respective department office, which could refer you to a service center or lab or to outstanding majors or graduate assistants who offer tutorial services. Next, go to the student affairs office to see if someone coordinates tutorial services.

Should you have a disability for which you need special services, you would seek assistance from disability services. Your campus also might have a learning diagnostic clinic.

Where is the disability services office?

For Personal Business

You will conduct personal business at various offices. Initial needs include getting an ID card, applying for financial aid, locating housing, buying a meal plan, seeking academic advisement, registering for classes, paying tuition and fees, and getting a parking permit.

Where can you get an ID card?

After the term begins, you might need to add or drop a course. For some courses, you can change from a graded basis to a pass/not pass or to an audit basis. Later you may need to declare or change your major, request an exception to a requirement, and order a transcript (a history of your courses and grades). Should an emergency prevent you from finishing a term, you would withdraw from college; then you would not receive an F in any courses of your current enrollment. Your academic advisor can help you in making these decisions.

Where is the academic advisement center?

Exercise 4 Identifying Campus Resources

Working with a classmate, use your catalog, campus directory, and college website to identify campus resources that can help you in course work and personal business. Fill out the Campus Resources sheets at the end of the book in the Personal References section. Fill in the first line for each resource or service. The blank spaces for notes will be filled in later as you learn more about the resources. You will have a handy reference.

For Health and Physical Fitness Needs

The health center or clinic offers general health care. If your health needs cannot be served there, a physician will refer you to a specialist at a nearby clinic. Typically, campus health centers offer prescriptions and services at reasonable rates.

Health centers also sponsor special events for students. At health day events you can learn how to become healthier and can also get your cholesterol checked, body fat measured, and blood pressure taken.

Being physically fit helps you to function at your best. You might want to know where you can work out, get a locker, and perhaps play intramurals. The physical fitness center(s), the sports complex, and the athletic field(s) on campus will enable you to reduce stress and meet new friends who share your interests.

Where is the health and wellness center?

Where is a physical fitness center?

For Leadership and Social Skills

The office of student activities sponsors a variety of programs and provides many services to help enhance your enjoyment of college. You will be able to hear nationally known speakers and entertainers throughout the year. This office also sponsors homecoming and holiday events.

Participating in student organizations helps students develop leadership and social skills. Your choices might include honor and professional groups, sororities and fraternities, religious groups, sports clubs, and service groups. Visiting meetings and observing activities sponsored by organizations can help you decide on one to join.

Where is the office that coordinates student activities?

■ Enhance Your Self-Concept and Self-Awareness

The way we see ourselves affects how we function in new surroundings and how we face challenges. People who have healthy self-concepts get along well with others. They recognize their own strengths and weaknesses. They take pride in their abilities and achievements, and they know which weaknesses or deficiencies can be improved. At the same time, they overcome negative influences by applying effective ways to improve their self-concepts. Enhancing your self-concept can help you not only as you enter college but throughout life.

Recognize Your Strengths, Abilities, and Positive Characteristics

We have many more positive qualities than we recognize or admit. Perhaps we are modest or do not take the time to reflect and appreciate the potential within ourselves. Among the positive factors that college freshmen have listed are those in the following self-assessment opportunity.

Self-Assessment: Assessing Your Positive Characteristics

For each of these positive characteristics, which include your strengths and abilities, put a check next to the ones that describe you:

Outgoing	____	Have done well in a certain subject area	____
Patient	____	Athletic—have excelled in sports	____
Helpful to others	____	Empathetic	____
Sense of humor	____	Easy to get along with	____
Friendly	____	Enjoy reading—am an avid reader	____
Cheerful	____	Talented in music	____
Good leader	____	Self-disciplined	____
Artistic abilities	____	Responsible	____
Good listener	____	Loyal to friends	____
Reliable	____	Kind	____
Optimistic	____	Open-minded	____

Count the number of check marks, and write the total here: _____

What are your additional strengths, abilities, and positive characteristics?

On your Personal Profile sheet, found as Figure 1 at the end of this chapter, fill in lines 17, 19, and 20.

Overcome Negative Influences

To build a healthy self-concept, we must overcome negative influences. In talking with professors and in writing journal papers, college students have expressed these concerns:

- Having been criticized or ridiculed by family, teachers, or employers

- Comparing their worst features with the best features of someone with a stronger background or more experience

- Setting unrealistic goals or expectations for themselves

- Associating with cynical or pessimistic people

- Suffering from the trauma of divorce, death, accident, or job loss

- Feeling homesick, lonesome, or unfamiliar in a new environment

- Lacking financial support (from family, financial institution, or scholarship)

Where is the counseling center?

Where would you go to see a chaplain on or near your campus?

- Being fearful about certain required courses

- Suffering from chronic illness, permanent disability, or life-threatening disease

- Lacking emotional support from family or partner

- Maintaining a long-distance relationship

- Being forced to go to college by parents, partner, or employer

- Being indecisive in choosing a major

Perhaps you share some of these challenges. If so, consider going to the counseling center or to a chaplain for confidential support. In overcoming negative influences and conquering challenges, we mature and develop empathy for others who are undergoing similar problems. By the time you have read this book and completed the college orientation course, you should be able to handle most challenges or to seek assistance from professionals.

Build a Healthy Self-Concept

Students without a healthy self-concept have difficulties in college. They might be critical of others, condescending, resentful of constructive criticism from teachers, uncomfortable when alone or inactive, jealous, or apathetic. They might place high value on material possessions, make excuses, or leave projects unfinished. They blame everyone else but themselves for their problems.

With diligent efforts you can improve your self-concept. Motivational experts like Dale Carnegie, Patrick Coombs, Norman Vincent Peale, Hal Urban, and Zig Ziglar have described successful ways to build a healthy self-concept. By applying their suggestions in the following list to college life, you can overcome obstacles in your academic or social path and have a better chance at succeeding.

- *Smile and be pleasant.* Being pleasant with a smile initiates a contagious, positive reaction.

- *Be thankful.* Express gratitude for gifts, kindnesses, good teaching, reference letters, and awards.

- *Maintain a good personal appearance.* When we look sharp, we improve confidence and self-esteem.

- *Learn people's names.* Learn names of teachers, administrators, and classmates; address them by name.

- *Take an interest in others.* Ask classmates and teachers questions about themselves, and listen carefully.

- *Make others feel important, and show respect for their expertise.* We can learn from others and enhance our communication skills.

- *Inform teachers and support persons about yourself.* They can provide individualized attention to your needs.

- *Choose positive reading and listening topics from recognized leaders.* Select leaders who have made major contributions to society; they are role models.

- *Make eye contact.* Look people in the eyes as you converse or speak to groups.

- *Set realistic goals.* Enroll in the number of credits you can complete successfully.

- *Use discretion in developing friendships.* Choose friends who have a positive attitude and who share your values.

- *Learn from failures, but do not dwell on them.* If you get a low grade, find out how to improve on the next exam or paper.

- *Join an organization with worthwhile goals and service projects.* You will meet new friends, share similar interests, and develop leadership skills.

- *Commend people; give sincere compliments.* Everyone wants to feel appreciated, needed, and worthwhile.

Exercise 5 Sharing Your Personal Profile and Schedule

To help your instructor get to know you, complete your Personal Profile (Figure 1) and Personal Schedule (Figure 2) at the end of this chapter. The Personal Schedule will be a handy reference for you and your support persons, including your roommate(s), family, and the teacher of this course.

Detach the pages; the original is for your teacher. Make as many copies as you need for yourself and other support persons.

Motivational experts on self-concept express value in knowing oneself, communicating effectively, and solving problems as ways to build self-confidence. This textbook is committed to helping you further develop these attributes of a successful student.

Knowing yourself Your self-awareness will be enriched as you do a variety of assignments. Self-Assessments help you to describe who you are, to identify your strengths, and to be aware of weaknesses to overcome. Sharing Reactions exercises are to be done as you are reading the text; these immediate and short writing opportunities can be processed as a reaction paper to be shared with classmates or as a quick journal to be shared confidentially with your instructor. You will take more time to share personal thoughts in each chapter's My Reflections Journal, which is a confidential writing to be read only by your instructor.

Communicating effectively Communication skills are extremely important for building self-confidence as well as for achieving success in college and throughout life. Your communications skills will be enhanced by the various Communication Exercises that involve talking with another person, e-mailing, listening, writing, and speaking to a group. Because these skills are so important, the next chapter is devoted to communicating effectively–providing the tools to do the exercises that are distributed throughout the book and giving you opportunities to practice these skills.

Solving problems Meeting challenges and overcoming obstacles in college will enable you to succeed in attaining your goals. To further develop your ability to think critically, to make sound decisions, and to solve problems, you will get to practice on Solve This Case at the end of each chapter.

With greater self-confidence and self-esteem, you will be able to meet your goals and surpass your expectations of college. Better yet, you will be equipped with important attributes that are sought by employers.

Exercise 6 Building Self-Concept

Selectively give a *sincere compliment* to three individuals. As you do so, *smile, make eye contact*, and *address them by name*. Notice how each person reacts and responds.

	PERSON	COMPLIMENT	HIS OR HER REACTION
1			
2			
3			

Using the computer, write a short essay on the topic "Complimenting People Affects Self-Concept." Be sure to include your reaction to how the individuals responded to your compliments.

Getting off to a good start in college is as important as a firm foundation in building construction. Successful students have realistic expectations of college rigor and their own potential. They establish a support system with others and prepare to work efficiently. Campus resources and services are investigated and used to maximize the college experience. By enhancing self-concept and self-awareness, these students build self-confidence and expand human relations skills. Success is related also to self-awareness, self-confidence, and good human relations skills. This book and the exercises in it are designed to help you become this kind of student and to develop these skills, which are so important in college and beyond.

Solve This Case—Roommate Challenges

Sam and Ted are roommates in a residence hall. In the second week of the term, they are experiencing challenges in their relationship.

Having graduated in the upper 15 percent of his class, Sam is a diligent student who devotes most of his time to attending classes and studying (for which he wants total quiet). His schedule is to go to bed by 11 PM and get up at 6 AM. Sam keeps his side of the room neat and clean, and his desk is well organized with school supplies at hand. Since he wants to do well on his first exams, Sam limits his social time to visiting with students during meals and while walking to classes. His roommate, Ted, annoys him. Ted is sloppy, does not clean his side of the room, often borrows supplies, and blares music until midnight. Worst of all, Ted changed the alarm clock setting so it would not go off at 6 AM; Sam was almost late for class.

Ted was an above–average student in high school but was able to get B's without studying. With an outgoing personality, Ted enjoys

meeting new people and wants to get involved on campus. He usually does not get to bed before 1 AM and likes to sleep until 8 AM. At home his mother did the cleaning, but they liked the more casual "lived-in" appearance. He thinks Sam is dull, obsessed with neatness, and lacking in social skills. Playing his favorite music helps Ted cope. Because Sam's alarm goes off so early and interrupts his sleep, Ted changed the setting once to see if Sam would wake up by his "inner alarm clock." Ted is disappointed that college is not what he so enthusiastically anticipated.

1 What strengths does each roommate have to offer the other?

2 Which patterns need to be adjusted to promote better compatibility?

3 Which problems are the least likely to jeopardize the college success of either Sam or Ted?

4 How can Sam and Ted improve their relationship as roommates?

My Reflections Journal

Journal writing is an opportunity to express your feelings and experiences in a confidential manner with your instructor. In writing a journal entry, you will be reflecting on the content of the chapter as it applies to you. In return, you can expect comments from your instructor.

For each of the following questions, write a one- or two-sentence reflection. Using your computer, you can compose at your fingertips and then either print the page or e-mail it to your instructor. Review the instructions on journal writing inside the back cover of this textbook, and follow your instructor's specific guidelines.

1 Why did you decide to go to college?

2 Why did you choose this college?

3 How is college different from what you expected?

4 What do you like most about being in college?

5 Which aspects of college life are most challenging?

6 How does your family feel about your going to college?

Website Practice Test

On the website at http://www.casadyenterprises.com/collegeedgebook/practicetests.htm you can access a practice test to check on your understanding of the chapter concepts. You may print the results of this self-test to review before taking the respective in-class exam.

Figure 1—Personal Profile

PERSONAL PROFILE

1. Name _____ Birth Date _____ Soc Sec #_____-_____-_____

2. Local Address _____ Telephone: (____) _____
   Building/Room #

   _____   _____   _____
   Street   *City, State*   *Zip*

3. Permanent Address   Telephone: (____) _____

   _____   _____   _____
   Street   *City, State*   *Zip*

4. E-Mail Address_____

5. Contact for Emergency_____ Relationship_____

6. Telephone and Address if different from Permanent   Telephone: (____) _____

   _____   _____   _____
   Street   *City, State*   *Zip*

7. Housing: ❑ Residence Hall   ❑ Fraternity/Sorority House   ❑ Apartment   ❑ Rent   ❑ Homeowner

8. Commuting Time: ❑ Within 20 minutes   ❑ 21-40 minutes   ❑ 41-60 minutes   ❑ Over 1 hour

9. Housing Mate(s): ❑ Live With Parents ❑ Live alone ❑ Live with others; how many? _____

10. Do you have children?   ❑ Yes   ❑ No Their ages: _____ Other dependents?   ❑ Yes   ❑ No

11. Currently employed?   ❑ Yes   ❑ No   Hours per week? _____   Circle Days: S   M   T   W   R   F   S

12. List recent work experience (30 days duration or more)

Job/Position	Company Name and Address	Dates	Description of Responsibilities/Tasks

13. High School: _____ City/State: _____

14. Credit Hours this Semester_____ Major _____ Check if undecided ❑

15. What career do you plan to pursue upon graduation? _____

16. If uncertain, what occupations are you considering? _____

17. What are your strengths as a college student? _____

18. What areas are you particularly interested in strengthening? _____

19. Describe achievements of which you are most proud: _____

20. Favorite activities/hobbies/interests: _____

21. Have you had military service?   ❑ Yes   ❑ No   If so, describe: _____

22. International student?   ❑ Yes   ❑ No   If yes, which country? _____

23. Travel: Outside of State?   ❑ Yes   ❑ No   Where?_____

24. Travel: Outside of Country?   ❑ Yes   ❑ No   Where?_____

PERSONAL SCHEDULE OF:

Please record your class times, work schedule, and standing commitments.

	8:00–8:50	9:00–9:50	10:00–10:50	11:00–11:50	12:00–12:50	1:00–1:50	2:00–2:50	3:00–3:50	4:00–4:50	5:30	6:30	7:30	8:30
MONDAY													
TUESDAY	8:00–9:15	9:30–10:45		11:00–12:15		12:30–1:45	2:00–3:15		3:30–4:45				
WEDNESDAY													
THURSDAY	8:00–9:15	9:30–10:45		11:00–12:15		12:30–1:45	2:00–3:15		3:30–4:45				
FRIDAY													
SATURDAY													

2 COMMUNICATING EFFECTIVELY

Objectives

Upon completing this chapter, you should be able to:

- Realize how actions speak

- Cultivate face-to-face communication

- Improve your e-mail and telephone communication

- Enhance your relationships with positive written messages

- Write letters of inquiry or request

- Request special consideration or an appeal

IN COLLEGE AS WELL AS in the employment world you will accomplish your goals most efficiently and with greatest satisfaction if you communicate effectively. Your body language, first of all, speaks loudly; so you need to realize how it is interpreted by professors and classmates. For informal, spontaneous, and urgent messages, you will depend on e-mail and the telephone. Written communication in the form of a letter or memo is your choice when you want the message to be documented on paper and to be read at the recipient's convenience. For all these forms of communication, the tips and suggestions in this chapter should help you express yourself well.

■ Realize How Actions Speak

Without saying a word you communicate about yourself through your actions. Even silence or lack of action has meaning. You also communicate through your personal appearance (clothing, jewelry, and makeup) as well as by eye contact, facial expressions, and gestures.

Communicating Through Body Language and Actions

Body language can be positive, negative, or questionable. If you walk briskly and stand erect, you communicate positive messages; if you slouch, negative messages. Similarly, if you habitually look down, you appear to have a bad attitude. Scratching your head may indicate you are bewildered. When the pupils of your eyes enlarge, you are probably observing a pleasant experience; when the pupils become smaller, you appear to be displeased in some way. If you look at the clock and put materials into your backpack, you are communicating that the class period is over and you want to leave.

Body movement can be misunderstood by others. For example, crossing your arms in front of your chest could be interpreted as indicating resistance or that you are cold. Removing your jacket could be interpreted as an act of flirtation or being too warm.

Professors, too, communicate through their body language and movements. If during an appointment the professor begins to shuffle papers or stand up, probably the time for discussion is up and it is time to leave. Looking at a clock or watch as students enter the class late indicates that the professor wants the students to know they are late and that he or she disapproves of their tardiness.

Being Absent or Late to Class

Because of some situations, you may be absent from classes. Examples of legitimate reasons would be an accident, an illness, the death of a close friend or relative, and college-sponsored events—athletic games, debate tournaments, and music performances. Typically the coach or faculty sponsor will prepare an explanatory memo for students to show their professors. The memo explains the college event at which the students are participating and authorizes absence from classes.

What are the phone numbers of the secretaries in the departments where you are taking classes?

The proper way to handle a necessary absence is to contact the professor in advance, turn in assignments ahead of the absence, and get the next assignment. Ask a classmate to take notes for you. If an exam is scheduled, make arrangements for taking the exam.

In emergency cases for which you cannot reach the professor by e-mail or phone, you can contact the professor's department secretary. In a crisis you could contact the dean of students office, which at many colleges would notify your professor. As soon as possible you would contact your professor.

Unacceptable reasons for missing class include oversleeping (forgetting to set the alarm or not hearing it; you could set two alarm clocks), not having the assignment done, and needing to study for another course's exam. By setting priorities and managing time effectively, you can avoid acting irresponsibly in these ways.

Being late to class, walking in front of the professor as he or she is speaking, and letting the door slam are inappropriate actions. They are disruptive and show disrespect to others. If your tardiness is unavoidable, quietly shut the door and walk behind people to find a seat.

In each of the following cases the professor probably would interpret the student's action as a negative or questionable message. The professor probably would think the student has not accepted responsibility for college work.

STUDENT'S ACTION	PROFESSOR'S POSSIBLE INTERPRETATION
Drumming of fingers on the desk	Student is bored with my lecture.
Whispering or passing notes; talking with another student	Student is not listening; other business at hand is more important than the class.
Absent from class frequently without and explanation.	The course is a low priority of the student. The student is not dependable.
Not showing up for an appointment or personal conference.	The student's time is more important than the professor's time.
Student brings beverage and snack to a designated NO FOOD OR DRINK lab.	Student chooses to ignore college's rules and is careless of school property.
Student wears a cap to class.	Student is disrespectful.
Cell phone rings or pager buzzes.	Student is important and wants attention; interruptions take precedence over class.
Turning in homework torn out of a notebook (with ragged edge) and in loose sheets (not stapled).	The student is neither responsible nor detail-minded, and is disorganized and messy.

■ Cultivate Face-to-Face Communication

The manner by which you speak to your professors and others conveys a distinct message. To cultivate effective face-to-face communication:

- Look the other person in the eyes.
- Smile; have a pleasant expression on your face.
- Speak clearly (loud enough to be heard and slowly enough to be understood).
- Be courteous, positive, and tactful.
- Use correct grammar (a grammatical error might get more attention than the idea being expressed).

Zooming into some of the typical questions and statements students direct to their professors, you will discover how many professors interpret the face-to-face communication.

Asking About Class, Homework, and Turning In Assignments

Homework is assigned to give you practice in learning new material so you can develop competency. Professors then must process your assignments (evaluate, summarize, respond to you, and so forth). Thus, assigning homework ultimately requires work for the professor. If professors wanted easier lives, they would not assign homework.

The best time to ask questions about assignments or lecture notes is during class if the professor allows time for them. If not, check the professor's scheduled office hours and request an appointment. Do not try to see the professor just before or after class. Before class a professor needs time to either get materials in order or to establish a friendly atmosphere by informally talking with the students. After class the teacher needs to get materials in order, exit the room so the next class can enter, and prepare for the next hour's appointments or class.

If you have a situation for which you request special consideration, see the professor privately; do not ask in front of classmates. Desiring to be fair to all students, a professor likely will not say "Yes" to an exception publicly. You have a better chance if you go to the professor's office.

Be courteous and tactful in communicating a positive attitude about the course. The following questions and statements are inappropriate to the eyes and ears of most professors:

STUDENT'S ACTION	PROFESSOR'S POSSIBLE INTERPRETATION
"Why do we have to learn this? They don't use this in the real world."	Lack of respect for the course, the professor, and the teaching style.
Raising a hand during class lecture and asking, "Will this be on the test?"	The student wants to learn only what is necessary to pass tests; the value of a college education is ignored.
In response to an assignment, "You know, some of us have to work; and we have other classes."	Lack of respect for the course and the professor; lack of commitment to college as a priority over employment.
"You give us too much busy work."	The student does not see any value in the assignment.
Turning in an assignment late and saying, "I'm sorry this is late, but I had to work so I can pay for my new car."	Material possessions and employment are higher priorities than a college education. Lack of time management.
"I missed class yesterday. Would you go over it with me?"	Student thinks the course is not important and 50 minutes of class can be summarized in 5 minutes.
"I am going to miss our next class. Will we do anything important?"	The course is a low priority. Lack of respect for the course and the professor.
"May we get out early today?"	Other activities have higher priority.
"When may I take the test I missed last class period?"	Inappropriate handling of the absence not to have notified the professor promptly; false assumption that a make-up exam is permitted.

Responding to Graded Work

When you get back an assignment or a test with comments, you can appreciate that the professor took an interest in your progress enough to give feedback. If the feedback and grade are positive, you are glad. If the results are below par because you did not understand the material or did not know how to study, meet with the professor to get help.

If your grade is less than what you feel you deserved, make an appointment to talk with the professor. Avoid illogical comments such as "I worked too hard to get a C on that paper. You need to look at it again." Hard work in itself does not earn a high grade; you must apply the right *kind* of work. Also illogical is "Why did you give me a C? I was in class every day and took notes." Grades are not given; they are earned. Attendance and note taking are important but do not guarantee high grades; quality of effort overrides quantity of time spent on a task. Finally, it shows misunderstanding to say, "Why do we need to know grammar, spelling, and punctuation? I will have a secretary to do that for me." Even if you have a secretary, you (the author and boss) ultimately are responsible for the document. Knowledge of your language is important in every aspect of a job.

When you have good reason to feel that your grade is not deserved or not fair, use a positive and tactful approach: "Would you check . . . ?" or "Would you explain why this response earned only 10 of the possible 15 points?" or "What could I have done to earn at least a B on this project?" If the professor made an error, he or she likely will be willing to raise your grade—especially if you were courteous in your communication.

Asking a professor to reevaluate a paper may also have a certain risk. In scrutinizing your paper, the professor could discover some overlooked errors that could lower your grade, offsetting any added points you might have acquired.

Exercise 1 Communicating Face to Face

Assume you have the following situations for which you need to talk with your instructor. For each situation describe when and where you would see the instructor; then write what you would say.

a With three exams scheduled the same day, ask to reschedule the one for this course.
When: _____ Where: _____
What to say: _____
_____

b Having to drive 150 miles for a wedding, you will miss Friday's class.
When: _____ Where: _____
What to say: _____
_____

c Having studied late for a test, you do not have today's homework completed.
When: _____ Where: _____
What to say: _____
_____

■ Improve Your E-Mail and Telephone Communication

What are the full names of your teachers?

Both e-mail and the telephone enable you to get important messages to others promptly. The recipient does not have to be home when you key the message or call (provided the phone has a voice message system).

In communicating with your professors, you will choose the tool that best meets the professor's needs. Find out his or her preference.

An advantage of e-mail is that you can print the communication, providing proof of your contact. Sometimes telephone messages get lost or are not delivered. If you choose e-mail for classmates and friends, you must be sure the recipient is a person who uses e-mail regularly and accesses his or her mail at least once a day. Because some students have more than one e-mail address, you need to be sure you are sending to the e-mail address he or she uses regularly.

An advantage of using the telephone is that you can have immediate and live two-way conversation, providing the recipient is at his or her desk when you call. Problems with telephoning include the inability to reach people who are not home and who do not have a telephone message system.

Exercise 2 Knowing How to Contact Your Teachers

At a moment's notice you want to be able to contact any (and perhaps all) of your teachers. In the Personal References section at the end of this text, locate and fill in the Teacher Information form.

Using Proper E-Mail Etiquette

E-mail was designed for short messages: making announcements, seeking input and replying, and exchanging informal notes. The recipient does not have to be present to receive the message at the time you send it. E-mail is ideal for notifying professors of an emergency that prevents your attending class and for setting up an appointment with your academic advisor. You can e-mail a classmate or your professor if you have a question about your notes or an assignment. If you are working on a team project, you can notify all members about an upcoming meeting.

Certain risks are involved in using e-mail. Because the recipient cannot hear the tone of your voice or see your face, e-mail easily can be misinterpreted. Long documents are not appropriate and are not easy for recipients to read, especially when the format is irregular. Many people have the message printed on paper for ease of reading, for documentation of the message, and for the convenience of reading later (perhaps away from their computer). Some users frequently send poems and stories to friends and relatives on their address list. These messages are time consuming for the recipients to read and print. Computer viruses are passed via messages with attention-getting subject lines. Be cautious before opening e-mail with an unusual subject.

Practice the following guidelines of proper e-mail techniques:

1 Maintain an accurate and up-to-date address list.

2 Keep the message short.

3 Use correct grammar, spelling, capitalization, punctuation, and word usage. Even for informal messages, your language skills are a reflection of your intelligence.

4   Include the following in your signature block: your first and last name, mailing address, phone number, fax number (if applicable), and e-mail address.

5   Check for incoming mail each day at least in the morning and late afternoon or evening.

6   Use the attachment feature (attaching a document that was produced by word processing software) only if you are sure the recipient or all recipients have the same software. Or, attach both a Word document and a WordPerfect document. Attachments put the burden (cost and time) of printing on the recipient; use this feature with discretion. Before sending an assignment to your professor, be sure this method is acceptable.

7   Use a distribution list or the listserv feature only when each person on the list needs to receive the message.

Exercise 3 E-Mailing Your Instructor

Send an e-mail message to your instructor of this course. In one paragraph describe what you like most about this class and a positive characteristic of the teacher you appreciate. Below your signature include your local address, phone number, and e-mail address.

Using Proper Telephone Etiquette

The telephone is so much a part of our lifestyle that we take it for granted and may be unaware of using it incorrectly. In addition to conversing socially with friends, we conduct personal business on our home phones. Whether in person or by a messaging system, we give an impression of ourselves to callers. To make a positive impression, telecommunication consultants recommend the following procedures in using the telephone both at work and at home.

Answering the Phone

☎   Answer the phone by the second ring.

☎   Identify yourself. At home: "Hello. This is Chrystie Wolf. How may I help you?" At work: "Administrative Services, Chrystie Wolf speaking. How may I help you?" This kind of greeting establishes confidence with the other party, creates a professional and friendly tone, eliminates guess work and saves time, indicates you are a responsible person, and prompts the caller to identify himself or herself.

☎   If the caller wants to speak to another person and that person is unavailable, offer to help (if applicable) or to take a message: "Sam is not here (or is not available). May I take a message for you or ask him to return your call?" Do not tell where the third party is, for you might not know the possible consequences. Message forms are helpful when taking messages (as shown in Figure 1).

Figure 1—Important Message

IMPORTANT MESSAGE				
For: *Sam*		Date: *Oct 27*	Time: *2:15 PM*	
Caller: *Randy*				
Phone Number: *888-7777*				
Location Call From: *at work*			✓	Phoned
Message: *He can be reached at work until 4 PM.*				Returned Call
After 5 PM call 864-6666.			✓	Please Call
				Will Call Again
				Came to See You
				Needs to Meet You
Message Taken By: *Sandra*				

Placing a Call

☎ Be sure the number is correct before placing the call.

☎ Allow time for the person receiving your call to answer (five to six rings).

☎ Address the party being called, identify yourself, and state the purpose of your call: "Dr Adamson, this is Leonard Drake, from Section 14 of your Math 135 class. I have a question about our assignment . . ."

During Conversation

☎ Express yourself clearly, and use normal tone and volume.

☎ Address the other party by name.

☎ Smile as you speak, and visualize the other party.

☎ Be pleasant, natural, distinct, and expressive.

☎ Be a good listener; concentrate on the caller's message; be interested.

☎ To confirm main points, repeat key phrases or ask questions.

☎ Jot down notes.

☎ Be businesslike and efficient.

☎ If you must leave the line to get information, ask the caller if he or she has time to wait or prefers that you call back. Never put someone on hold for longer than a minute.

☎ Avoid slang, such as: "Okay, Yeah, Uh-huh, Bye-bye." Instead, say: "Yes, Certainly, Of course, Good-bye."

Ending the Call

☎ Let the caller initiate ending a call.

☎ Say "Good-bye" pleasantly.

☎ Replace the receiver gently.

Self-Assessment: Assessing Your Telephone Skills

Evaluate your telephone communication procedures and skills. Do you . . .

	ALWAYS	SOME-TIMES	NEVER
1 Answer the phone within 2 to 3 rings?	____	____	____
2 Have a message pad and pen near the phone?	____	____	____
3 Identify yourself and the purpose of making a call?	____	____	____
4 Address the other party during the conversation?	____	____	____
5 Offer to call back if you must leave the line more than 1 minute?	____	____	____
6 Tell living mate(s) you are leaving and when you will return?	____	____	____
7 Offer to take a message or have living mate return the call?	____	____	____
8 Make sure the number is correct before placing the call?	____	____	____
9 Allow the person receiving your call 5 to 6 rings to answer?	____	____	____
10 Speak on the phone without food or gum in your mouth?	____	____	____
11 Speak clearly and distinctly?	____	____	____
12 Smile while speaking?	____	____	____
13 Visualize the person with whom you are speaking?	____	____	____
14 Speak directly into the transmitter?	____	____	____
15 Take the initiative to end the call if you placed it?	____	____	____
16 Listen carefully?	____	____	____
17 Repeat key phrases or ask questions to confirm main points?	____	____	____
18 Let the caller initiate ending the call?	____	____	____
19 Say "Good-bye" at the close of the call?	____	____	____
20 Replace the receiver gently?	____	____	____
Totals	____	____	____

Scoring Your Telephone Communication Procedures and Skills

For each "Always" give yourself 5 points. For each "Sometimes" give yourself 2 points. No points are given for "Never" answers. Figure your total score.

90-100 points	Excellent
80-89	Good
70-79	Fair
0-69	Unsatisfactory

Write your message as recorded on your telephone messaging system:

_____

_____

Using a Messaging System to Receive Incoming Calls

Where can you get an answering machine?

To receive messages when you are away from your phone, you may have an answering system with your recorded greeting—a good way to alleviate phone tag. Studies show that only 25 percent of business calls (between 8 AM and 5 PM) are completed on the first try. Because students are away from their phones most of the working hours, phone tag is more extensive on college campuses than in businesses.

Where can you find out if voice mail is available?

A pleasant and short recording like this is appropriate: "You have reached 444-5555. Please leave your name, date and time of call, and message. If you would like one of us to call back, include your phone number." Some people record humorous or unusual greetings on their messaging system. Such recordings are risky, for you never know who will call. The caller might be a professor, a financial aid officer, an employer, a person interested in dating you, or a parent. "Cutesy" recordings can be offensive and damaging to relationships.

Courtesy and professionalism are among the hallmarks of effective communication. Using proper media etiquette, receiving messages when you are away from your desk, and returning calls or messages are important communication skills to practice.

■ Enhance Your Relationships with Positive Written Messages

Where would you go to buy paper and envelopes?
Where on campus can you buy stamps?

Messages are written rather than spoken when you want the recipient to have a printed record of what you say. Letters and memos can be read at a time convenient to the reader, and they are more formal than e-mail. College years present many reasons for writing letters—for example, you may be asking someone to be a reference on your behalf, applying for a job or internship, or writing an editorial for the college newspaper. In all such cases, there are certain guides to keep in mind. You should have supplies on hand to write notes, memos, and letters. Your supplies should include at least a dozen envelopes and first-class stamps.

Reviewing the Basics of Written Messages

Correspondence falls into four categories:

- *Social Correspondence*—to family and friends; may be handwritten on stationery.

- *Personal Business Letter*—to organizations with which you do business; should be typed or printed; personal letterhead or plain paper is used. On plain paper the writer's return address should be included.

- *Business Letter*—to a person outside your organization; about the business of your employer; should be typed or printed; letterhead paper is used.

- *Memorandum*—to a person or group within an organization; about its business; is typed or printed; memohead or plain paper is used; organization name and address are not keyed because all correspondents have the same; name of the department is part of the memo address when writer and recipient are from different departments.

Two recommended letter styles, in which all parts begin at the left margin, are *block* and *modern simplified*. These formats are the easiest to key and to read.

- *Block Style*—a traditional format; a salutation and complimentary close are used.

- *Modern Simplified Style*—a contemporary format; day, month, and year dateline; letter address is in all caps and is positioned for a window envelope; requires a subject line; in place of a salutation and complimentary close, the name of the recipient is included in the first and last paragraphs; periods are used at the end of sentences and in decimal amounts but <u>not</u> after abbreviations or numbered items. All personal letters and memos shown as examples in this book illustrate the modern simplified style.

You can enhance your composition of letters and memos by following these guides offered by communication consultants:

1 ***Organization*** Outline the body of the message, including the main points of each paragraph, before you begin to write. Each paragraph should cover only one main idea.

2 ***Shortness*** Use short words, sentences (an average of 17 words), and paragraphs (no longer than 7 to 8 lines). Do not repeat what the reader already has said or knows.

3 ***Simplicity*** Write to express a message, not to impress the reader with technical, sophisticated words. Write naturally as you talk. Use simple, familiar words.

4 ***Strength*** Use specific words. Vary sentence beginnings. Each paragraph should begin with a unique word. Avoid repeating adjectives; use a thesaurus to vary vocabulary.

5 ***Sincerity*** Strive for a courteous and friendly tone. Be human. Admit mistakes.

6 ***"You" Approach*** Adapt the message to the reader. Be positive. Explain how the reader will benefit or why it is to his or her advantage to do what you are suggesting. Avoid using "I" more than once in a paragraph or to begin a paragraph. Show interest in the reader.

7 ***Mechanics*** Use correct grammar, spelling, punctuation, capitalization, and word usage.

Extending Thanks and Commendation

Goodwill messages are written by successful professionals and students. When people do special things for you, your class, or an organization of which you are a member, an important courtesy is to write a thank-you message. You would express thanks in the following situations:

- ✉ A professor, peer leader, or classmate helps you with a difficult assignment.

- ✉ A professor or employer or supervisor writes a reference letter for you.

- ✉ Your academic advisor has discussed extensively your degree program with you.

- ✉ Your employer or parents provide financial support for your college fees.

- ✉ You receive an award or scholarship.

- ✉ A friend takes extra time to listen and to encourage you when you are "stressed out."

- ✉ You receive a gift.

- ✉ You have been a weekend guest at the home of a friend, perhaps your roommate.

- ✉ A guest speaker in your class gives an outstanding presentation.

A thank-you letter can be only three paragraphs. You might follow this helpful outline:

¶1 Express thanks for *something specific*. Explain the significance of that person's help so he or she can visualize your benefiting from it.

¶2 Commend the person for being *thoughtful, generous, empathetic, and helpful* to others.

¶3 Take an interest in that person's life (job, family, education, health, and so forth).

In writing thank-you notes, neither thank in advance nor say "Thank you again" for the same courtesy in the same letter. An example of a thank-you note to the parents of a friend who hosted a weekend visit is shown in Figure 2.

Figure 2—Thank-You Note

Dear Mr and Mrs James

Thank you for the pleasant and relaxing weekend we spent together. Your family possesses a special quality that makes friends feel welcome and at home.

I enjoyed your delicious meals, Mrs James. The lasagna dinner was tasty, and lemon pie is one of my favorite desserts. You were thoughtful to make cookies for Ted and me; they seemed to disappear within a couple days. You must be comforting to the hospital patients you help.

Thanks for taking us fishing, Mr James. You were patient with me when my lure got caught in the weeds. I have never seen anyone clean fish as fast as you do. Having been outside in the fresh air, I can study much better this week. Good luck in the upcoming bass tournament.

With appreciation

Paul

An example of a thank-you letter to a professor for help on a report is shown in Figure 3.

Figure 3—Thank-You Letter

APPRECIATION FOR YOUR HELP

Thank you, Dr Blanco, for giving me extra help with my report yesterday. You helped me to organize the paragraphs better. The handout on formatting reference notes will help me in preparing other research papers as well.

Your history class is interesting because you share accounts of your travels and slides of significant historical events. You must be looking forward to the international conference in Toronto. The audience will enjoy your presentation.

The time you devoted to me and your research expertise are appreciated, Dr Blanco.

Bertha Starwick

Bertha Starwick
Woods House, Room 308

Commendation letters are written for professors, sponsors, classmates, friends, and relatives to acknowledge special accomplishments. People appreciate congratulatory letters upon being awarded (Figure 4), elected to office, promoted, or featured in the newspaper.

Exercise 4 Thanking an Advisor or Teacher

Write a letter of appreciation for one of these situations. Check a directory or catalog to be sure the name is spelled correctly and the address is accurate.

- To your academic advisor, who has devoted time and shown interest in your future.
- To a former teacher, coach, scout leader, or director who has had a positive impact on you.
- To a current teacher who has helped you with a difficult assignment, met with you for a personal conference or problem, or done something special for your class.

    Address an envelope. If the recipient is on campus, mark it **CAMPUS MAIL**. If the letter is being sent off campus, put a stamp on the envelope. See the example shown in Figure 5.

Figure 4—Letter of Commendation

Congratulations on Your Teaching Award

How delighted I was to see your picture in *The Tribune* today, Miss Angster. You are most deserving of the Outstanding Teaching Award.

Your word processing class was one of my favorites in high school. You presented new features and concepts in an easy-to-understand method. My keyboarding and word processing skills are used every day in college. Not having to depend on another person's time schedule or skill, I save time and money by keying my own papers.

What classes do you teach this semester? Are you still sponsoring FBLA? You are appreciated as a special teacher, Miss Angster. You are caring, and you go the extra mile to give students help outside of class. Best wishes for a rewarding school year!

Lynn Wright

Lynn Wright
2400 Rocky Branch Road
Vienna VA 22181-1143

Figure 5—Envelope Format

Ms Arnie Troy
Riverview Apartments—C53
2210 Nye Drive
Fremont NE 68025-2114

MR ROLIN CARLBERG
RIVERVIEW APARTMENTS
2109 NYE DRIVE
FREMONT NE 68025-2114

■ Write Letters of Inquiry or Request

Should you move, you will need to notify the college records office and all businesses with which you have an account (including the bank, telephone, and insurance companies) that your address will change. If you need information for a report or research paper, you might write to a company or government agency. If you plan to pursue graduate work, you will write to various universities to inquire about their graduate programs. As chair of a program committee, you will be inviting guest speakers. Since there are no obstacles or risks involved in these situations, they call for direct inquiries or simple requests. Your goals in writing are to let your reader know *what* you want and to make it *easy to reply*, for you want to get the action or results you need. Enclosing a self-addressed and stamped envelope facilitates a prompt reply.

Why would you write rather than call the person? By writing a letter, you have a permanent record of your message. The recipient, too, has a visual reminder of your request so the response can be accurate and complete. Keep these points in mind when you write direct inquiries or simple requests:

1 Begin with a direct question or identify the subject.

2 Be as specific as you can.

3 Tell why you need or want it, and (if applicable) stress the reader's benefit.

4 If you have several questions to be answered or items to be sent, number them.

5 Ask for a reply by a certain date—allowing about two weeks.

6 Express gratitude but do not thank in advance: "I would appreciate . . ."

The examples shown in this book are to request information for a report (Figure 6) and to notify the records office about a change of address (Figure 7). By following the letter format illustrated (Figure 6), you can fold and position the letter in a window envelope (Figure 8). Window envelopes save you from addressing an envelope and possibly mismatching envelopes and letters when you are preparing several letters.

Figure 6—Modern Simplied Letter Format

Set Top Margin at 1.8 inches

27 October 2004

E3—Press ENTER or RETURN key 3 times

MR DALE GUMZ   *Letter Address = Envelope Address*
INDUCTIVE ENGINEERING   *All caps and no punctuation*
803 MAIN STREET
CEDAR FALLS IA 50613-1146

                    E3

REQUEST FOR CAREER INFORMATION

                 E3
      Addressee's name in body to personalize letter

For my College Seminar, Mr Gumz, I am obtaining information about a career in engineering. Your nephew, David, suggested I write to you. Would you please answer these questions?

1 Which type of engineer are you—mechanical, industrial, or chemical?

2 What do you like most about your job? What is most satisfying?

3 What is most dissatisfying, challenging, or frustrating about your job?

4 How would you describe the job market for young engineers just out of college in Cedar Falls, Waterloo, Cedar Rapids, and Des Moines?

5 Which general ed courses (during freshman and sophomore years) would you recommend to prepare me for transferring to an engineering school?

Because my report is due November 22, your reply by November 15 would be helpful. Your advice and information will be appreciated, Mr Gumz.   *E4*
      Addressee's name in body again to close

Jan Carlson

Mr Jan Carlson
624 Green Valley
Oro Valley AZ 85737-1036   *No periods after abbreviations or numbered items*

Exercise 5 Requesting Information for a Report

Write a letter to someone who is in a career or occupation you are considering. Inquire about the most satisfying aspects of the job, its challenges and frustrations, college courses recommended, job market conditions, descriptions of entry-level positions, and advancement opportunities. Ask for a reply within two weeks.

Compose, print, and sign the letter. Fold the letter for a window envelope. Enclose a stamped and self-addressed envelope. Stamp and mail the letter. Consider sending the letter to three people so you can get three perspectives.

Figure 7—Letter to Change Address

---

21 October 2004

RECORDS OFFICE
SOUTHWEST MISSOURI STATE UNIVERSITY
901 SOUTH NATIONAL AVENUE
SPRINGFIELD MO 65804

CHANGE OF ADDRESS

Please change your records to reflect my new mailing address (both local and permanent).

Old Address—Until November 1	*New Address—After November 1*
3165 Belhurst Springfield MO 65804	5368 South Roanoke Springfield MO 65804

My phone number will not change. Please mail my end-of-the-term grades to the new address. Your promptness in correcting my address will be appreciated.

Holly Crandell

Miss Holly Crandell
Phone 887-5555
Student ID #555-66-8888

■ Request Special Consideration or an Appeal

If your grade report shows what appears to be an error, you might want to contact the professor to check (Figure 9). If you fall short of general education, residency, or degree program requirements, you might appeal to the administrative unit (department head, dean, or committee) responsible for the decision (Figure 10). You might apply for awards and scholarships. If you live in an apartment, you might need to persuade the owner or manager to repair or redecorate your room. You might want to invite a well-known speaker to address your organization, but no money is available to pay expenses or an honorarium. In each of these cases you have an obstacle or challenge:

- Convincing a teacher to reevaluate your work or records and to raise your grade

- Avoiding enrollment in a 3-credit-hour course to fulfill a 1-credit-hour shortage

- Competing with many other well-qualified students for an award or scholarship

- Getting the apartment owner to repair something, repaint, or install new carpeting

- Persuading a well-known speaker to give a presentation free (without an honorarium)

Figure 8—Instructions on Folding Letter for Window Envelope

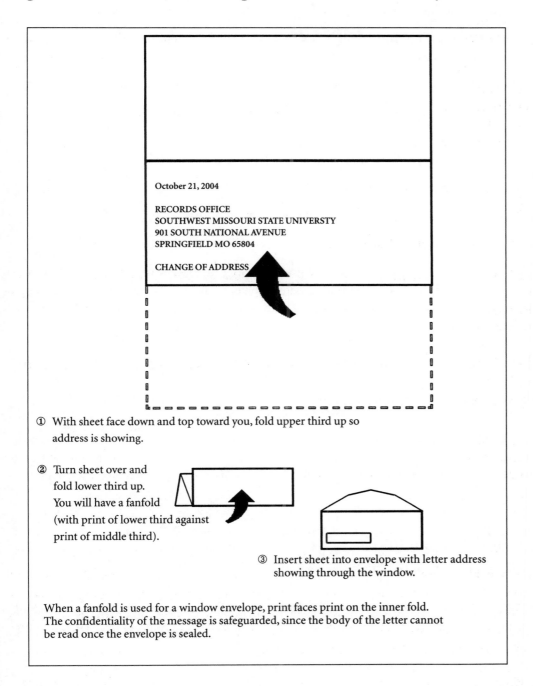

October 21, 2004

RECORDS OFFICE
SOUTHWEST MISSOURI STATE UNIVERSTY
901 SOUTH NATIONAL AVENUE
SPRINGFIELD MO 65804

CHANGE OF ADDRESS

① With sheet face down and top toward you, fold upper third up so address is showing.

② Turn sheet over and fold lower third up. You will have a fanfold (with print of lower third against print of middle third).

③ Insert sheet into envelope with letter address showing through the window.

When a fanfold is used for a window envelope, print faces print on the inner fold. The confidentiality of the message is safeguarded, since the body of the letter cannot be read once the envelope is sealed.

The strategy of writing persuasive requests is similar to that of writing simple, direct requests; but a few more techniques might apply if they are appropriate for the situation:

1 Offer something in return—apply the *"you" approach* (explaining how the reader would benefit or why it would be to his or her advantage to do what you are requesting).

2 Address the letter to a person—not to a professional position, department, or company.

3 Provide facts and evidence (copies of letters, your transcript, the invoice, etc) to prove your case.

4 Appeal to the reader's fairness.

5 Explain how you were inconvenienced.

6 Help the reader to reply; enclose a stamped envelope addressed to yourself.

7 Follow up with a phone call if necessary.

In the letter requesting reevaluation of a grade (see Figure 9), the student provided facts that showed careful records of class performance had been kept. The tone of the letter is polite (beginning with positive aspects of the instruction), and the student is tactful by saying "if an error inadvertently was made."

Figure 9—Letter Requesting Re-evaluation of a Grade (Subject Line and Body)

MY FINAL GRADE IN ACCOUNTING 201

As a student in Sec 17 of your ACC 201 class last term, Dr Evans, I appreciated the way you explained new material and provided realistic examples. The homework was relevant and helped me understand new concepts. Your evaluation of assignments and exams seemed to be fair.

When my final grades arrived, I was disappointed to see my ACC 201 grade was a C. With an understanding of the concepts, I was pleased my test grades (85, 90, 92, and 88) averaged 89%. According to your syllabus, 89% is a B and exams weighed 60% of the final grade.

My homework (20% of the grade) was complete and on time to earn an A. Quizzes (20% of the grade) averaged a C. Do your records of my work match these figures? If so, shouldn't my final grade have averaged a B?

Would you please check to see if an error inadvertently was made, Dr Evans? Your reevaluation of my ACC 201 grade will be appreciated. Please call me at 777-555 if you have questions. Could you let me know your decision by January 15?

Should you have to appeal to a degrees committee, you might follow some of the techniques shown in Figure 10. You will notice the student provided facts and an explanation about her circumstances. In addition, she tells how she plans to meet the degree program requirements the next term.

Figure 10—Letter Appealing for a Degree Check (Subject Line, Body, and Closing Lines)

APPEAL FOR A DEGREE CHECK

Since entering UCSB, Dr Cortez, my goal has been to get a Bachelor of Science degree with a major in Management (Comprehensive). Though 61 hours have been completed with a 2.8 GPA, I have not completed these requirements yet: QBA 237, ACC 211, and MTH 135.

As my transcript shows, I had to begin the math series at the level of MTH 3. Thus, I was unable to complete all the COBA lower-division requirements before reaching 75 hours.

Next semester I will be enrolling in the three courses listed in the first paragraph and would like to file my degree program. Would you please give me special permission to file my degree program this spring?

I will appreciate the conscientious review by your committee, Dr Cortez.

Stacey Edgeworth

Miss Stacey Edgeworth (ID #666-77-111)
818 Eucalyptus Avenue
Santa Barbara CA 93101-4166

Exercise 6 Deciding What to Do and Say

For each of these situations, decide what you would do and say. Identify the most appropriate means of communication and the most effective words.

a To Professor: You missed class yesterday.

_____

_____

b To Professor: You will miss the next class for an out-of-town debate tournament.

_____

_____

c To Classmate: You will miss next class; please take notes and get assignment.

_____

_____

d To Professor: You feel the grade on a paper returned is less than what you deserve.

_____

_____

If you practice effective communication skills in college, you will have many satisfying personal experiences. Moreover, as you pursue advanced courses, leadership positions in organizations, and ultimately full-time employment, you can present yourself in the most professional manner. Exemplary communication skills are fundamental to a successful future.

Solve This Case–Requesting In-State Residency Status

Formerly from another state, Dan enrolled in college upon having completed his military service. Before leaving the military, he changed his state of residence and started paying taxes in this state, where he has lived over a year. An off-campus job and personal savings support all his financial needs. Dan is a registered voter and licensed driver in this state.

Dan plans to register for next fall's term in April. He phoned the registration office on March 20 to request in-state residency status.

1 Why was Dan's request by telephone an inappropriate means of communication?

2 Should the written request be sent by an e-mail message or by a letter?

3 Compose a persuasive request that should help Dan gain in-state residency status.

My Reflections Journal

For each of the following questions, write a short two- to three-sentences reflection on your communication experiences. Your instructor might want this journal writing experience to be sent by e-mail (sometimes called e-journaling) or printed and turned in on paper.

1 What nonverbal behavior (body language) in others do you perceive to be negative?

2 Are there any suggestions on telephone etiquette you plan to incorporate?

3 For what purposes do you use e-mail?

4 What has been your experience in writing letters?

5 How do you feel about your communication skills after having studied this chapter?

Website Practice Test

On the website at http://www.casadyenterprises.com/collegeedgebook/practicetests.htm you can access a practice test to check on your understanding of the chapter concepts. You may print the results of this self-test to review before taking the respective in-class exam.

3 SETTING PRIORITIES AND MANAGING TIME

Objectives

Upon completing this chapter, you should be able to:

- Prioritize goals
- Identify activities and time requirements
- Establish a calendar system and organizer
- Prepare a weekly schedule
- Improve time management skills

AT THE END OF A recent term 2,113 freshmen were asked, "What advice do you have for next year's incoming freshmen?" The most frequently cited response was "Get your priorities straight, and improve your time management." When 62 peer leaders (mostly juniors) were asked to identify their biggest challenge as freshmen, the majority emphatically said "time management."

Regardless of age, economic status, or experience, most people are challenged to re–think priorities and to improve time management skills. Even business and professional conferences include sessions that address this need.

The amount of time we spend on an activity and the order by which we choose to do activities indicate our priorities. If our priorities do not support our goals, it is like "the tail wagging the dog." Successful people first establish goals, then set their priorities to achieve those goals, and finally manage their time according to the priorities.

One freshman, Traci Burns Pattison, said in a letter of advice to new freshmen at the end of her first semester. "Planning your time appropriately will save you many headaches and cram sessions. Allow two to three hours of study for every hour of class time. Remember why you came to college—to get an education that will benefit you the rest of your life." Traci became a business teacher and continued her education to earn the master's and specialist's degrees.

■ Prioritize Goals

Most institutions and organizations have goals that support their mission statement. Perhaps your college has a theme or descriptive statement that makes it unique among other institutions in the region. It may put a special emphasis on public affairs, international affairs, environmental conservation, or technology. Budget decisions are based on prioritizing its goals.

What is your life's mission?

As a student, you will prioritize your goals according to your life's mission. You will make decisions about expending money and time according to the priorities you have set for long-term and short-term goals. Begin with your long-range plans; then you can focus on this term's goals.

Long-Term Goals

Long-term goals are influenced by your dreams and values. What motivates you to become better educated? How do you see yourself being successful? What factors or possessions are most important to you? What accomplishments in life would please you the most? Look ahead to the next five or six years–what you want to be doing and how you plan to live. Among the long-term goals stated by many freshmen are to:

- Earn a bachelor's degree
- Get a good job
- Be promoted to a better job
- Buy a new car
- Go to graduate school
- Get married
- Rent a nicer apartment
- Be healthy
- Raise a family
- Buy a house

Exercise 1 Prioritizing Long-Term Goals

Identify and rank your three major long-term goals:

1 _____ (first priority)
2 _____
3 _____

Which of your long-term goals is the most important? Focus on your first priority as you set short-term goals for this term (semester, quarter, or trimester).

_____

On the Goals Worksheet in the Personal References section at the end of this text, transfer this list to Major Long-Term Goals Ranked in Order of Priority.

Goals of This Term

Your goals this term will be stepping stones to attaining the long-term goal you ranked as your first priority. Assume your goal is to earn the bachelor's degree within four years. Various factors will affect the ease with which you reach that long-term goal.

How your expenses are being paid—whether you will be working If a scholarship or your family pays for most of your expenses, getting a job will not be a high priority. You might get a part-time job, however, to earn extra spending money or to gain experience in work that relates to your career goal. In either case, your goal this term might be to work no more than ten to fifteen hours a week.

What are the obstacles you face to meet your goals?

If you have to pay for most or all of your expenses, your term goals likely will include being employed at least twenty to twenty-five hours a week and attending summer school. Or, you might get a full-time summer job that pays enough to support your taking a full load at college during the fall and spring terms.

How well your high school education prepared you for college courses You are well prepared for college courses if your high school education included:

- Advanced English, mathematics, science, and foreign language courses
- High grades matched by high standards
- Daily homework (approximately an hour per course) outside class
- Strict attendance expectations

If your placement test, ACT scores, or SAT scores indicate a lack of readiness to enroll in entry-level courses, you will be guided to take preparatory courses first. Should preparatory courses not count toward the degree requirements, you may have to take a heavy course load some terms to graduate within your designated time limit or go an extra term.

If you took mostly easy courses that were outside the "college prep" category, were awarded high grades without having to do homework, or were allowed to skip classes regularly, you will have major adjustments to make in college. Compared to high school, college-level courses are more rigorous and require more homework. Regular attendance is expected.

Whether you have care-giving responsibilities at home If you are single and have no care-giving responsibilities, you can set priorities and manage time as you wish. On the other hand, if you are a care-giver in your family or are married, you have limits on your time schedule and will need cooperation from others at home.

What kind of impression you want to make In applying for awards, jobs, and scholarships, you probably will ask teachers and employers to write reference statements. They will write about your ability to accept responsibilities, your dependability, your interpersonal skills, and your leadership potential. Therefore, it is important to make a good impression.

Your ability to manage time Once you establish a time management plan, you will make adjustments as conditions change. Much effort and self-discipline are needed to carry out the plan and to improve time management skills. Establishing a calendar system is the first step. A functional system enables you to see at a glance the term, each month, and each week. Carrying a planner (pocket organizer) enables you to check important dates as you make new appointments.

If you have handicaps or weaknesses related to college preparation, you can anticipate having to exert extra effort to earn your degree. Be realistic about your preparation, and make appropriate adjustments.

How can you overcome the obstacles you face?

The student Stephen Hess, in a letter to new freshmen that was written at the end of his first semester in college, said, "Can you remember being able to work a 30-hour-per-week job, not studying, having fun with your friends, and still getting A's and B's in high school? That isn't going to 'fly' in college. Trust me; I tried it, and my grades showed it."

Your goals this term likely will include these categories: academic work, employment, health and personal maintenance, family and home activities, membership and service participation, as well as recreation and leisure.

Self-Assessment: Assessing Term Goal Priorities ✔

Define your goals this term by filling in the appropriate blanks:

Academic Work
  Number of credit hours to complete: _____
  Desired grade–point average (GPA): _____

Employment
  Amount of money to earn: $_____ ÷ hourly rate ÷ weeks of term = _____
  Number of job hours each week: _____ weekly job hours

Health and Personal Maintenance
  Bathing, grooming, and dressing: _____ hours per day
  Meals: Hours per day to eat breakfast _____, lunch _____, dinner _____
  Sleep: _____ hours per night
  Physical exercise: _____ workout hours per week

Family and Home Activities Describe each one that applies to you.
  Time with family or being alone: _____
  Care giving (children, elderly, disabled or ill person):_____
  Cleaning, laundry, shopping, car service, and yard work: _____

Membership and Service Participation List each group with which you affiliate.

   Religious group and community service: _____

   College and community organizations:_____

Recreation and Leisure Describe each activity that applies to you.

   Movies, television, and telephone: _____

   Social events and parties: _____

Rank your goals of the term (by group category) according to their importance:

1 _____(first priority) 4 _____

2 _____ 5 _____

3 _____ 6 _____

On the Goals Worksheet in the Personal References section at the end of this text, transfer this list to Term Goals Ranked in Order of Priority.

■ Identify Activities and Time Requirements

To do a time management plan, list all categories of activities and the weekly hours needed for each category to meet your goals of the term. To earn at least a C average, you would devote 2 to 3 hours of study outside class for every hour in class. Some courses require more time than others; thus, the average of 2.5 hours is used Lynn's example in the accompanying figure. Nine years of research on first-year students (approximately 2,700 students a year) supports this formula.

Stay in focus for academic work, employment, health and personal maintenance, and recreation and leisure. If you want to complete 16 credit hours with at least a B/C average (for example, 2.50 GPA on a 4.0 scale), consider the following important guidelines:

Academic Work

As you can see from Lynn's example, carrying a 16-credit-hour load requires more time than a forty-hour-a-week, full-time job. If your grades are important, plan to:

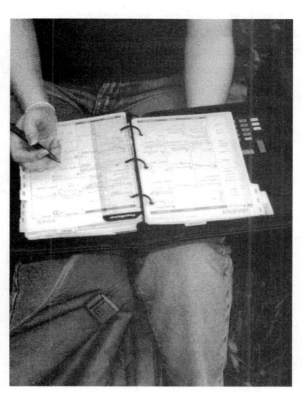

- Attend all classes. Never skip class.

- Study and do all homework. Devote two to three hours outside of class for every hour in class. Some subjects require less, but exams require extra studying time.

Employment

To succeed in both academic work and employment, the total hours of both categories should not exceed sixty-five hours per week. See Table 1 as a guide.

Figure 1—Lynn's Weekly Activities and Time Requirements

Lynn's Weekly Activities and Time Requirements

(16 cr hrs, 10 hrs at job)

	WEEKLY HOURS	TOTALS
ACADEMIC WORK		
Attend classes = number of credit hours this term	16	
Do homework/study for exams:		
term cr hrs 16 x 2.5 hrs each	40	
Commute to and from campus	3	
TOTAL ACADEMIC WORK HOURS		59
EMPLOYMENT		
Work at job	10	
Commute to and from job	0	
TOTAL EMPLOYMENT HOURS		10
HEALTH AND PERSONAL MAINTENANCE		
Bathe, groom, and dress: 1 hour(s)/day x 7 days	7	
Eat breakfast, lunch, and dinner: 3 hrs/day x 7 days	21	
Sleep: 7 hrs/night x 7 days	49	
Exercise: 4 hrs/week	4	
TOTAL HEALTH AND PERSONAL MAINTENANCE HOURS		81
FAMILY AND HOME ACTIVITIES		
Spend time with family or be alone for quiet time	3	
Perform care-giving responsibilities	0	
Clean, do laundry, shop, service car, and do yard work	3	
TOTAL FAMILY AND HOME ACTIVITY HOURS		6
MEMBERSHIP AND SERVICE PARTICIPATION		
Attend religious group; do community service	2	
Attend meetings and participate in activities	3	
TOTAL MEMBERSHIP AND SERVICE PARTICIPATION HOURS		5
RECREATION AND LEISURE		
Go to movies, watch television, and talk on the phone	3	
Attend social events and parties	2	
TOTAL RECREATION AND LEISURE HOURS		5
TOTAL HOURS IN A WEEK = 168.		
TOTAL WEEKLY HOURS TO MEET TERM GOALS =		166

Table 1   Guide to Weekly Hours of Academic Work and Employment

Weekly Hours of Academic Work Plus Employment			
Academic Hours			
In Class Hrs/Crs +	Study Hours*	Job Hrs	Total Hrs
6	15.0	40	61.0
9	22.5	30	61.5
12	30.0	20	62.0
15	37.5	10	62.5

Students should devote 2.5 hrs of study time for each 1 hr of in-class credit.

Health and Personal Maintenance

College students who excel in school, in service, and on a job maintain good health. The way you perform depends on how well you take care of yourself. Make an effort to:

- Eat three nutritious meals each day.
- Sleep seven or eight hours each night.
- Exercise for an hour each day at least four days each week.

Recreation and Leisure

Recreation and leisure, which are enjoyable and which help you develop social skills, offer well-roundedness and stress relief. Students who spend more time socializing than studying, however, have their priorities out of order. Focus on your goals as you prioritize activities.

Self-Assessment: Assessing Weekly Time Requirements

Referring to the Term Goal Priorities Self-Assessment, determine the weekly hours required for each activity. Total the hours for each category and then all categories. If your grand total is less than the 168 hours in a week, you have free time. If your total is more than 168, adjust your time allotments until they fit within the 168-hour week.

	WEEKLY HOURS	TOTALS
Academic Work		
Attend classes = number of credit hours this term	_____	
Do homework/study for exams—term cr hrs ___ x 2.5 hrs each	_____	
Commute to and from campus	_____	
Total academic work hours		_____
Employment		
Work at job	_____	
Commute to and from job	_____	
Total employment hours		_____
Health and Personal Maintenance		
Bathe, groom, and dress: ___ hour(s)/day x 7 days		
Eat breakfast, lunch, and dinner: ___ hrs/day x 7 days	_____	
Sleep: _____ hrs/night x 7 days	_____	
Exercise: _____ hrs/week	_____	
Total health and personal maintenance hours		_____

Family and Home Activities
Spend time with family or be alone for quiet time   _____
Perform care-giving responsibilities   _____
Clean, do laundry, shop, service car, and do yard work   _____
Total family and home activity hours   _____

Membership and Service Participation
Attend a religious group; do community service   _____
Attend meetings and participate in extracurricular activities   _____
Total membership and service participation hours   _____

Recreation and Leisure
Go to movies, watch television, and talk on the phone   _____
Attend social events and parties   _____
Total recreation and leisure hours   _____

Total hours in a week = 168. **Total weekly hours to meet term goals:**   _____

■ Establish a Calendar System and Organizer

An effective calendar system enables you to manage time well and to stay on schedule. Seeing the overall picture of a time period with important dates marked will help you meet deadlines, avoid cramming for tests, keep appointments, and plan for future events.

Term at a Glance

Begin with a calendar of the term to mark the dates of holidays, major projects, tests (including final exams), meetings, and personal events. Professors generally do not remind students about exam dates and assignment due dates, especially if the dates are printed in the course syllabus. Final exam times might be different from the regular class day and time. Plan to be on campus until you have taken the last exam.

What are the key dates of your courses?

Exercise 2 Scheduling the Term at a Glance

Photocopy the Term at a Glance form (Figure 2). Fill in the months and days of this term. Make enough photocopies of the calendar so you have one for each course as well as a master on which to write all major deadlines, exam dates, meetings, and personal events. (You also can find a copy in the Personal References section at the end of this text.)

1 **For each course.** From the course outline/syllabus, find the due dates of major papers, projects, and presentations as well as exam dates, including the final exam's date and time. Transfer the information to this term calendar; you might use a different color of ink for each category. Include assignments if there is room. *Place this calendar in the front of the course folder or notebook.*

2 **For a master calendar of the term.** From each course's Term at a Glance, transfer the dates of major papers, projects, presentations, and exams to the Calendar of the Term form in the Personal References section at the end of this text. Be sure to record all final exam dates and times. Include regular organization meetings and special personal events such as birthdays and weddings. Highlight or use one color of ink for courses, another color for meetings, and a third color for personal events. You might make copies to have this calendar near your desk (perhaps on your bulletin board), in your planner, and in your reference manual.

Figure 2—Term at a Glance

MONTH	MONDAY	TUESDAY	WEDNESDAY	THURSDAY	FRIDAY

Month or Week at a Glance

Desk calendars and appointment books are designed to be placed on your desk. They show a month or a week at a glance with enough space to write details and to add new appointments. You will refer to these calendars frequently for a weekly or monthly overview.

Planners (pocket organizers) come in a variety of styles and sizes. The calendar will picture either a month or a week at a glance. Some organizers have pockets for inserting a checkbook, credit cards, ID card, and driver's license. An address and phone number booklet as well as a note pad might be included. Choose the style and size that will work best for you. Write major dates and reminders in your planner, and carry it with you for each day.

■ Prepare a Weekly Schedule

One of the best tools of time management, a weekly schedule will help you stay focused on your immediate goals. After college you will use this tool to stay focused on your job. Preparing a weekly schedule is much like putting together a jigsaw puzzle. You start with the pieces you know where to place.

A college student whose first priority is to complete 16 credit hours and earn at least a 2.50 GPA would label these time blocks: attend class, work at a job (if applicable), eat, sleep, exercise, get ready, commute, attend meetings, study, do community service, have personal time, and attend social functions. In Figure 3, Lynn's Week at a Glance, all the pieces of the puzzle identified in Figure 1 fit within the week's frame.

Exercise 3 Scheduling a Week at a Glance

Make photocopies of the Week at a Glance form (Figure 4). So you will have a master to use later, do not write on the original form. From the Self-Assessment on determining Weekly Time Requirements, fill in your schedule for next week. Consider using a different color of highlighter or ink for each of the main categories.

Fill in the time blocks in this order:

(1) classes

(2) job hours if applicable

(3) eating

(4) sleeping

(5) meetings and extracurricular activities

(6) study periods

(7) exercise

(8) personal tasks—cleaning, doing laundry, shopping, running errands, servicing car

(9) being with family or alone

(10) recreation and leisure

Figure 3—Lynn's Week at a Glance

WEEK AT A GLANCE   WEEK OF _____

	SUNDAY	MONDAY	TUESDAY	WEDNESDAY	THURSDAY	FRIDAY	SATURDAY
6:00	Sleep	Get Ready	Get Ready	Get Ready	Get Ready	Get Ready	Sleep/Get Ready
7:00	Work Out	Breakfast To Campus	Breakfast To Campus	Breakfast To Campus	Breakfast To Campus	Breakfast To Campus	Breakfast
8:00	Breakfast Laundry	Algebra	Algebra	Algebra	Algebra	Study	Study
9:00	Laundry	English	Study	English	Study	English	↓
10:00	Get Ready	Study	University Life	Study	University Life	Study	↓
11:00	Church	↓	Phys Ed	↓	Phys Ed	↓	↓
12:00	Lunch	Biology	Lunch	Biology	Lunch	Biology	Lunch
1:00	Study	Lunch	Study	Lunch	Job	Lunch	Clean
2:00	↓	History	Biology Lab	History	↓	History	Errands/ Wash Car
3:00	↓	Job		Job	↓	Job	Study
4:00	With Family	↓	SGA Mtg	↓	↓	↓	↓
5:00	↓	Work Out	↓	Work Out	University Ambassador	Work Out	↓
6:00	Dinner	Dinner	Dinner	Dinner	Dinner	Dinner	↓
7:00	Study	Study	Study	Community Service	Study	Shop	Dinner
8:00	↓	↓	↓	Study	↓	Social Time	Social Time
9:00	↓	↓	↓	↓	↓	↓	↓
10:00	↓	↓	↓	↓	↓	↓	↓
11:00	Sleep	Sleep	Sleep	Sleep	Sleep	Sleep	↓
12:00	↓	↓	↓	↓	↓	↓	Sleep

Figure 4—Week at a Glance

WEEK AT A GLANCE   WEEK OF _____

	SUNDAY	MONDAY	TUESDAY	WEDNESDAY	THURSDAY	FRIDAY	SATURDAY
6:00							
7:00							
8:00							
9:00							
10:00							
11:00							
12:00							
1:00							
2:00							
3:00							
4:00							
5:00							
6:00							
7:00							
8:00							
9:00							
10:00							
11:00							
12:00							

■ Improve Time Management Skills

Managing time challenges most everyone. In college you have many activities and responsibilities. The pressure of deadlines, exams, job expectations, membership duties, and invitations to socialize can be overwhelming. Feeling pulled in many directions, you may become involved in more activities than you can handle.

Without good time management, you can easily be distracted and might procrastinate. You might be tempted to put off big projects until the day before they are due. You might underestimate the time to complete a project and miss the deadline. You might become mentally and physically exhausted, and you might not meet some of your goals.

Where can you go for help with time management?

You can improve your time management skills by developing efficient time scheduling, scheduling homework within study blocks effectively, managing large projects, and avoiding procrastination. When you can meet your goals, you will feel personal satisfaction and will enjoy college much more than if you allow yourself to lose control of time management.

Develop Efficient Time Scheduling

Good time managers accept responsibility for themselves and use time efficiently. Here are some guidelines:

- Schedule essentials first—including classes, sleep, meal time, and study periods.
- Cluster (in at least two-hour segments) study periods and job hours.
- Schedule no more than two classes to meet consecutively, and choose about the same number of MWF classes as TR classes. Spaced learning is more effective than concentrated learning, and you do not want three exams to occur on the same day.
- Use one-hour periods constructively—studying, eating a full meal, or doing personal business on campus.
- At a regular time each day—upon waking up in the morning or before going to bed—spend 5 to 10 minutes planning your day and reviewing the tasks at hand.
- Use waiting time constructively—review class notes and the list of tasks to do.

Schedule Homework Within **Study Blocks Effectively**

Doing homework, which includes studying lecture notes and the textbook, can be challenging. These suggestions can help you to schedule your homework within study blocks effectively:

- Knowing your best time of the day for learning, schedule the difficult subjects and tasks to do when you are most alert.

- Plan larger blocks of time for learning new material, especially difficult course material.

- Divide long reading assignments into chapters or pages–your concentration span.

- Schedule the subjects or assignments you like least before your favorite ones; an unpopular subject is a heavy burden when you are tired of studying.

- Do smaller assignments during one-hour segments or at the end of the day.

- Use short time periods (15 to 45 minutes) to review. For a class involving discussion, review notes just *before* the class. For a lecture class, review your notes immediately *after* class.

- During long study blocks, take a 15-minute break every two hours.

Manage Large Projects

Major projects generally cause some worry and stress. With a positive attitude and these tips you can manage large projects and meet deadlines:

- Observe deadlines. Post reminders at your desk or on your bulletin board, and write notes on your calendars.

- Before you begin, gather all the materials needed to accomplish the assignment.

- Break down the project into a series of small and more manageable parts (miniprojects).

- Overestimate how long it will take to complete the project.

- Set your deadline a day or two ahead to allow for last-minute problems (such as computer or printer malfunction).

- Upon finishing a long study period or big project, reward yourself with a walk, snack, or phone call.

Avoid Procrastination

The consequences of procrastination are unpleasant: getting behind schedule, being late with assignments, skipping class to study for an exam or finish another project, and having a bad attitude (which affects other people negatively). You can avoid putting off homework and cramming for tests by following these suggestions:

- Establish a routine (using your Week at a Glance schedule) and stick to it. Keeping on a time schedule cuts down on tensions, worries, and daydreams. Soon you will not have to decide what to do next; you will do it automatically.

- Set up reminders–sticky notes, "To Do" lists, and catchy slogans.

- Eliminate distractions. Notice what disturbs your concentration, and get rid of it or go to another place to study.

- Observe how you waste time and allow study time to be interrupted. Discipline yourself to focus and stay on target of deadlines.

- Hang a *Please do not disturb* sign on your door.

- Learn to say "No" when asked to do something or go somewhere: "I wish I could, but my research paper is due on Friday."

- Break down major goals, big projects, and long assignments into achievable steps.

- Do homework daily; do not let it pile up.

- Find a study partner with good study habits–a role model (support person).

- Once you start, keep going. Do not allow yourself to stop or to change your mind.

- Establish a goal-and-reward system. Set a goal to complete part of your homework by a certain time, and reward yourself with a treat when you meet the goal.

Exercise 4 Writing a Contract with Self

Type or write a *Contract with Self* using the accompanying form as a guide. Describe how you will meet your goals–including (but not limited to) the topics of this chapter on time management skills. Print a copy of your contract and review it every three to four weeks during the term. You might be asked to share your contract with a classmate so you can help each other be accountable.

Contract With Self

During this term I commit myself to the following goals:

- ✓ Scheduling Weekly Hours of Study Per Course
- ✓ Attending Classes
- ✓ Getting Along With Associates, Family, and Roommate
- ✓ Reading the Textbooks
- ✓ Taking Class Notes
- ✓ Studying for Exams
- ✓ Managing Time
- ✓ Socializing and Attending Parties
- ✓ Scheduling Employment Hours
- ✓ Eating
- ✓ Exercising
- ✓ Sleeping
- ✓ Managing Financial Obligations

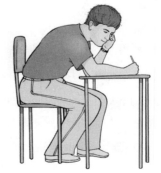

Signature _____ *Date* _____

Throughout college and in your career you will continue to work toward improving time management. Time is a resource; how we use it determines our productivity. Time is like money; how we invest it determines our profits–our rewards for meeting our goals.

Solve This Case—Getting Control of the College Routine

Now that her two children are in school full time, Marie, a single parent, has started college. She wants to become a physical therapist and has enrolled in 12 credit hours. She is a nurse's aide at the medical clinic and has reduced her work time to 30 hours a week. Approximately eight hours a week are devoted to supporting Paul's involvement on the soccer team and Sara's piano lessons. By the time Marie gets home from going to classes, working at the clinic, and escorting the children, she has only about two hours a night to study before going to bed.

Results from the first round of tests were disappointing–three C's and one D. Marie knows she must earn A's and B's to qualify for entrance into the physical therapy program. Paul and Sara have asked her to take them to an amusement park this Saturday; several of their friends are going. Marie feels overwhelmed.

1 If you were Marie, what three long-term goals would you have? Which would you rank first?
2 If you were in Marie's place, what would be your first priority this term?
3 What suggestions would you have for Marie in terms of:
   a Job hours?
   b Study hours?
   c Responding to Paul and Sara's request for the Saturday outing?

My Reflections Journal

Compose a one-paragraph response to each of the following questions. You may either print the page and turn it in on paper or e-mail the page to your instructor. Ask your instructor which method he or she prefers.

1 What is your life's mission? How do you plan to accomplish that mission?

2 What are the obstacles you must overcome to meet the goal of earning a bachelor's degree? How can you overcome these obstacles?

3 What are some of your best time management habits?

4 Do you have any habits that are not conducive to good time management? What are some of your major challenges as you attempt to develop better time management skills?

5 What are some changes you plan to make in improving time management and your efficiency?

6 Do you ever procrastinate? Which of the chapter suggestions do you plan to apply in order to minimize or eliminate any tendencies to procrastinate?

7 Is there any question you would like to ask your instructor?

Website Practice Test

On the website at http://www.casadyenterprises.com/collegeedgebook/practicetests.htm you can access a practice test to check on your understanding of the chapter concepts. You may print the results of this self-test to review before taking the respective in-class exam.

4 APPLYING YOUR LEARNING STYLE

Objectives

Upon completing this chapter, you should be able to:

- Be aware of what influences your learning style
- Identify your learning style
- Adjust to teaching styles
- Advance your thinking and learning skills

PERHAPS YOU HAVE wondered why some subjects are more difficult than others. Your brother or sister might excel in academic areas that are much different from yours. You might have questioned why you are more challenged than several classmates in a certain professor's class. In such a circumstance you might think you are dumb, but be assured you would not have been admitted to college if you were not intelligent enough to handle higher education courses.

A friend might have encouraged you to choose a certain professor's section because he or she found the course to be easy, but your experience turned out to be the opposite. At the other end of the spectrum you might have had no choice (because of scheduling) but to enroll in a professor's section against warnings that he or she was a tough teacher, and you were surprised to find the professor and the course to be a positive experience. Why?

Each student has unique characteristics related to thinking and learning. Both genes and environment are major influences on your learning style. By identifying your learning style and observing various teaching styles, you can make adjustments that enable you to achieve. By advancing your thinking and learning levels, you can maximize your success rate.

The marginal questions in this chapter will be answered in the Learning Style Worksheet of the Personal References section at the end of the text. You will compile information that will help you to identify your own learning style and to list all the learning techniques that will work best for you.

■ Be Aware of What Influences Your Learning Style

One popular explanation of why people think and act differently is provided by researchers of the brain. Skill performance and the thinking process are controlled by the brain, which is divided into two hemispheres—the *left brain* and the *right brain*. Each side is responsible for different skills and ways of thinking, but interaction between the two sides occurs in thinking and learning. To become aware of which hemisphere of your brain is dominant, do the Self-Assessment on Assessing Your Brain Dominance.

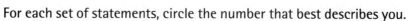

Self-Assessment—Assessing Your Brain Dominance

For each set of statements, circle the number that best describes you.

1 I like to "play it safe" rather than to guess or take risks.
2 I like the challenge of new ventures involving risks.

3 My thinking is based on looking at the facts.
4 My thinking is based on looking at the whole picture.

5 I solve problems by reading and by listening to professional experts.
6 I solve problems by imagining and seeing pictures.

7 I seldom am absent-minded.
8 I often am absent-minded.

9 I get satisfaction from improving something.
10 I get satisfaction from inventing or trying something new.

11 I am more effective in explaining by using words.
12 I am more effective in explaining by using actions and hand movements.

13 I prefer reading realistic or nonfiction stories.
14 I prefer reading fantasy or fiction stories.

15 I would rather be told how to do a new task.
16 I would rather be shown how to do a new task.

17 I like teachers who follow the syllabus and stay on schedule throughout the term.
18 I like teachers who are flexible and adjust the syllabus throughout the term.

19 I prefer multiple-choice or true/false tests.
20 I prefer essay tests.

Count the odd-numbered statements (1, 3, 5, . . .) that you circled. *Total* _____ *(L)*
Count the even-numbered statements (2, 4, 6, . . .) that you circled.   *Total* _____ *(R)*

If you circled more odd-numbered statements, your left hemisphere of the brain is dominant. If you circled more even-numbered statements, your right hemisphere of the brain is dominant. If you had a tie (5 Left and 5 Right) or totals within close range (4 to 6), you can use either side of your brain or both sides effectively.

Figure 1—Brain Mode Influences

Left Brain		**Right Brain**
Logical		Intuitive
Sequential		Random
Linear		Holistic
Rational		Emotional
Verbal		Nonverbal

Left Brain Influences

The left brain influences thinking and skills that are logical, sequential, linear, rational, and verbal (see Figure 1). People whose left brain dominates are highly organized, structured, and systematic. They think in terms of sequence (one thought directly following another, such as cause and effect, and one task at a time). Using reason and factual data to arrive at conclusions, they use words to describe and define things. They do well in reading, speaking, writing, finding facts, handling details, and interpreting symbols. Being analytic, they use reasons and facts (arranged in order) to arrive at conclusions. They keep track of time—thinking in terms of past, present, or future. They recognize and remember names quite easily.

Students with left brain dominance prefer objective tests (with right-or-wrong questions and answers) and questions that require listing points. Typically, they follow directions closely and are perfectionists. They do problem solving by looking at the parts. Tending to be extrinsically motivated, students with left brain dominance learn for personal achievement and need constant reinforcement. As good planners and time managers, they accomplish tasks efficiently.

Right Brain Influences

The right brain has an impact on thinking and skills that are intuitive, random, holistic, emotional, and nonverbal (see Figure 1). People whose right brain dominates are aware of feelings and emotions, creativity, and colors. Being able to visualize, they see whole things all at once and overall patterns with keen spatial awareness. They recognize and remember faces easier than names. Decisions often are made by following hunches or according to what feels or seems right. They respond to music, touch, and body language. With little awareness of time, they tend to procrastinate and allow tasks to pile up. They typically have several tasks in progress at once. Being creative, they are dreamers and improvisors as well as risk-takers who are prime candidates for becoming inventors. They like humor and having fun.

Tending to be intrinsically motivated, students with right brain dominance enjoy learning for personal awareness. With good long-term memory but weak short-term memory, they prefer taking subjective tests and solving a problem by looking at the whole picture. However, they may not pay attention in class and may not read directions carefully.

People tend to have characteristics of both hemispheres of brain dominance but often differ in the extent to which they show or express those characteristics. Thus issues about brain dominance also surface in the discussion of interpersonal relationships.

Are you left brain or right brain dominant?

How does this impact your learning preferences, strengths, and weaknesses?

Using Both Hemispheres

Both hemispheres (modes) of the brain interact and are used in most activities. When you read a novel, for example, the left hemisphere decodes the words while the right side interprets the emotion of those words. People who rely on both sides of the brain equally are balanced in nearly all aspects of their lives. Students in that category learn easily because they can call upon whichever learning mode is compatible with the teaching style.

To maintain good mental and physical health, people need to provide balance in their lives. People in left brain occupations such as business, education, and science need to include right brain activities such as viewing art exhibits and attending concerts. Artists and musicians (engaged in right brain professions), on the other hand, can benefit by attending activities of left brain dominance such as financial management seminars and health care lectures.

■ Identify Your Learning Style

The preferred way by which you learn new or difficult information and remember it is your learning style. Many professors teach in a manner that supports their own learning style. If theirs and yours match, you probably will get along well in the course. If the teaching methods support a learning style that is different from yours, however, you likely will encounter challenges. Your learning style might differ from one type of course to another. Before reviewing basic categories of learning styles, take the Self-Assessment on Assessing Your Learning Style.

Self-Assessment—Assessing Your Learning Style

To assess your learning style, imagine yourself as a student in three different history sections and then in three different computer sections. After each course's group of sections, you will choose the section in which learning would be easiest and most successful for you.

Part A—History Sections: Describing Major Wars

SECTION 1. The professor describes major wars by telling stories, reading excerpts from soldiers' letters, and playing tape recordings of news broadcasts. Students participate on panels and in small-group discussions to share experiences of relatives or friends who have served in the military during wartime. Each student has a chance to speak during most class periods.

SECTION 2. The professor describes war involvement by outlining the lecture on the board, showing videotapes, and displaying memorabilia. Students are assigned to read newspaper articles that were written during a war period and a book about our country's involvement. Writing assignments include reaction papers and book reports.

SECTION 3. The professor assigns the students to bring pictures, memorabilia, and newspaper articles of a major war in which a relative or friend has served. The class is divided into small groups, with each group representing a certain war. After sharing the pictures and other historic items, each group creates and performs a skit that role-plays our involvement in a major war.

In which history section would you find it easiest to learn about and remember the impact of major wars? _____

Part B—Computer Sections: To describe e-mail versus word processing

SECTION 1. The professor begins by listing on the board appropriate applications of e-mail versus word processing. Overhead transparencies illustrate the unique features of each software package as well as leading vendors. Sample printouts of e-mail messages and an envelope with a personalized letter from the professor are distributed to the students. Students are given a handout instructing them how to use word processing to prepare a reply letter in which they are to describe the software packages they know (including vendor)—due next class period.

SECTION 2. The professor asks the students to describe appropriate uses of e-mail and situations for which word processing should be the choice. Seated at computers, the students are guided in composing and sending an e-mail message to the professor. Upon receiving an envelope with a personalized letter from the professor, the students are then guided in composing and printing a response by using word processing software. To identify the software packages they know (including vendor), students are to stand under the respective posters on the wall.

SECTION 3. The professor has the students share with the class their experiences using e-mail. They are to identify appropriate situations for sending e-mail messages and give examples of its misuse. The professor cites personal experiences and describes the leading vendors. Then the topic switches to word processing, for which the students discuss in small groups the major types of documents they have prepared. The professor reads a letter of inquiry and tells the students to prepare a reply by using word processing software. All instructions are given orally.

In which computer section would you prefer to learn about and to prepare both e-mail messages and word processing documents? _____

In the key below circle the section of each course you chose. This will tell you your preferred learning style for each course. These learning styles are described in the next section, Comparing Learning Styles Informally.

Part A (History Class)
Section 1 Auditory
Section 2 Visual
Section 3 Kinesthetic

Part B (Computer Class)
Section 1 Visual
Section 2 Kinesthetic
Section 3 Auditory

Comparing Learning Styles Informally

Learning styles have been studied by a number of professional authorities. Among the well-known categories are: Visual Versus Auditory Versus Kinesthetic, Factual Versus Analytical, and Participative and Dependent Versus Competitive and Independent.

Visual Versus Auditory Versus Kinesthetic If you prefer to learn by watching the teacher outline the lecture, seeing illustrations in textbooks, and recopying your notes, you are a visual learner. If you learn best by listening to lectures and discussions, recording notes on tape, and reviewing your notes aloud, you are an auditory learner. If you learn best by doing, touching, or handling, you are a kinesthetic learner. See Figure 2 for more comparisons.

Do you tend to be an auditory, visual, or kinesthetic learner?

Factual Versus Analytical If you are better at making lists and memorizing facts, you might be more of a factual learner. If you like to analyze data, look for concepts, and consider basic implications, you likely are more of an analytical learner.

Do you tend to be factual or analytical?

Participative and Dependent Versus Competitive and Independent If you enjoy studying with others and taking part in class discussions, you are a participative and dependent learner. If you prefer listening to a lecture with no discussion, simply reading the textbook, and studying alone, you are a competitive and independent learner.

Figure 2—Comparing Learning Styles

VISUAL	AUDITORY	KINESTHETIC
Remembers what was seen	Remembers what was discussed	Remembers what was done
Recalls faces	Recalls names	Recalls meeting people
Takes notes; writes it down	Speaks aloud; records on tape	Practices application
Quiet—reads, writes	Noisy—listens, discusses	Active—fidgets, wriggles
Understands by seeing	Understands by hearing, talking	Understands by doing
Likes visual cues/order	Likes music, listening to stories	Likes action; points; gestures
Distracted by movement	Distracted by sounds	May seem distractible
Impatient if listening is long	Listens but cannot wait to talk	Does not listen well
Wants things well organized	Wants to hear self or others discuss	Wants to handle and examine

Each learning style has merit; no one style is better than another. Moreover, most students do not fit neatly into one category. You likely will use more than one style as you read your textbooks, take notes, and study for exams. As was revealed by your conclusion to the Self-Assessment on Assessing Your Learning Style, you might prefer one learning style for history and philosophy courses but a different style for computer and math courses.

Exercise 1 Analyzing Your Courses

For each of your courses, identify your preferred learning style. Rank the course rigor as *easy, average,* or *difficult.*

COURSE ID	COURSE NAME	YOUR LEARNING STYLE	COURSE RIGOR
_____	_____	_____	_____
_____	_____	_____	_____
_____	_____	_____	_____
_____	_____	_____	_____
_____	_____	_____	_____

Describe for each of the courses rated *difficult* the reason(s) why you feel the course is challenging. Is the professor's teaching style compatible with your learning style?

_____

_____

_____

_____

Considering Formal Assessments of Learning Styles

In addition to the informal approaches to analyzing learning styles, formal professional assessments have been developed. Among the most popular formal measures is the *Myers-Briggs Type Indicator®*, which is an assessment of one's personality preferences as they relate to learning. Based on Carl Jung's categories of personality preferences, this instrument uses four scales:

Where can you go to take assessment tests?

- *Extroversion Versus Introversion*—Do you prefer working with others (the outer world—extroversion) or working alone (the inner world—introversion)?

- *Sensing Versus Intuition*—Do you acquire information through careful analysis of facts (concrete and logical) or through intuition as you look at the overall picture (creative)?

- *Thinking Versus Feeling*—Do you make decisions by analyzing and weighing the factors of evidence (applying logic) or by your feelings (relying on emotions and personal values)?

- *Judging Versus Perceiving*—Do you relate to the outer world in a planned, orderly manner (setting goals and accomplishing them efficiently) or in a flexible, spontaneous manner (being open to various perspectives and hearing all sides of an issue)?

Your counseling and testing center or career services office can tell you which formal tests are offered on your campus. They can tell you where these tests are administered and whether a fee is charged for processing the test and interpreting the results.

Exercise 2—Discovering Assessment Testing Resources

Find out the testing services that are offered by the counseling and testing center and the career services office. After filling in this form, go to the Campus Resources form in the Personal References section at the end of the text and fill in the Notes sections of the respective offices. Also, complete the first four sections of the Learning Style Worksheet in the Personal References section.

Counseling and Testing Center
Where is it located (building and room)? _____

What is the phone number? _____

What is its website? _____

Who is the director? _____

List the assessment testing services available. Include the respective fees.

_____

_____

Career Services
Where is it located (building and room)? _____

What is the phone number? _____

What is its website? _____

Who is the director? _____

List the assessment testing services available. Include the respective fees.

_____

_____

■ Adjust to Teaching Styles

If the teaching style of a course is compatible with your learning style, you will have the easiest and most enjoyable learning experiences. When the information is not presented in your preferred style, you can learn to apply other styles. Use your most dominant learning style on difficult topics or courses. Your goal is to use the learning style that is best for the situation. If you need to adjust to the teacher's style, consider the following suggestions that can help you strengthen your less dominant learning styles.

Strengthening Visual Learning

You can strengthen visual learning—reading and seeing information (in print, on the board, from overheads, and from videos)—by doing the following:

How would you strengthen your visual learning?

▶ Read the textbook before hearing lectures in class.

▶ Preview chapters by reading the objectives, headings, subheadings, and vocabulary.

▶ Take notes on lecture information and announcements given orally.

▶ Draw a diagram to show relationships; make a chart; list or outline main ideas or points.

▶ Highlight or underline topic sentences, concepts, and key words.

▶ Glance away and recall the written information on your page.

Strengthening Auditory Learning

You can strengthen auditory learning—hearing information (from lectures, audiotapes, and your own voice)—by using these techniques:

How would you strengthen your auditory learning?

▶ Read aloud the textbook and lecture notes.

▶ Preview chapters by reading aloud the objectives, headings, subheadings, and vocabulary.

▶ Tape the difficult or key parts of the text and lecture notes; then listen to the playback.

▶ Pretend to teach other students the basic ideas or points; explain them out loud.

▶ Quiz yourself by orally asking questions from notes and the textbook.

▶ As you read a textbook or take notes, agree or disagree with the author.

Strengthening Kinesthetic Learning

You will benefit from applying information to activities (exercises, applications, projects) by considering these approaches:

How would you strengthen your kinesthetic learning?

▶ Find practical applications and do projects that involve using what you learn.

▶ Move your finger along text lines as you read and along class notes as you review.

▶ Take lecture notes, write main points in textbook margins, and write down information.

▶ For difficult material, draw a chart, diagram, or picture that helps you understand.

▶ Make special marks (underscore, highlight, label, number, use symbols) for key points.

▶ Using index cards, compose questions on the front; write the answer(s) on the back.

Using Several Learning Styles

In each course you likely will apply more than one learning style. In this course, for example, a student could have this combination of learning styles:

Analytical	Look for concepts and consider basic implications
Auditory	Learn by listening to lectures and discussions
Participative	Study with others and take part in class discussions

■ Advance Your Thinking and Learning Skills

Our minds engage in thinking most of our waking hours. We observe the world around us as we perform activities. Whether the activities are academic (studying, discussing a topic in class, writing a paper) or personal (running, mowing the lawn, washing the car, cleaning house, driving to school), we are thinking. Without any goals to direct the thought process, thinking is elementary and relaxed, or perhaps lazy. With a goal in mind, however, thinking becomes energetic and can be productive.

Beginning at a primary level in early education and progressing to a middle level in high school, thinking and learning skills should move to advanced levels in college. You are expected to be creative without the help of detailed instructions and to demonstrate critical thinking that involves applying, analyzing, and evaluating concepts or ideas. The development of critical thinking skills should enable you to make wise decisions and to solve challenging problems in class discussions and writing assignments as well as in life beyond college.

Thinking Creatively

The goal of creative thinking is to discover a new and better idea that will result in an achievement or accomplishment. Imagination goes to work in preparing to paint a picture or write a story, in brainstorming ideas for fund raising, in improving the efficiency of a task, in designing a letterhead, and in coming up with a clever introduction for a speech.

In the early stages of skill development, a professor will give detailed instructions and show precisely how a task is to be performed. An example would be how to design, format, and print a poster to promote student voting at the upcoming student government election. As the term progresses, the professor gives fewer instructions. Finally, he or she might assign a task without any instructions to challenge creative thinking: "Create a poster that will promote ticket sales for the international dinner. The best poster, as voted by the class, will get a prize."

Successful students and employees who are creative thinkers demonstrate imagination and show initiative without waiting for instructions or expecting a prize. Professors and employers both notice and appreciate creative thinkers.

Exercise 3 Designing a T-Shirt

In groups of three or four classmates, establish a name for your "company" and design a t-shirt that promotes one of the following at your college:

▶ The academic mission of your college

▶ A service project for your community

▶ Peer leadership or mentorship

Illustrate the shirt style, include graphic design, and designate the color scheme. Be prepared to present your creation to the entire class.

Thinking Critically

Critical thinking is applied when the goal is to face a challenge or to solve a problem. Educated people are expected to make sound decisions. Because the freshman year presents a variety of challenges for which intelligent decisions need to be made, critical thinking skills are important.

Dr John Caffee, a noted authority on the development of critical thinking skills, defines thinking critically as "carefully exploring the thinking process to clarify our understanding and make more intelligent decisions" (John Caffee, *Thinking Critically, 7th ed*, Houghton Mifflin Company, 2003, p 40). As we study issues, we explore situations by asking questions and view cases from different perspectives. Thinking actively involves reading, listening, and participating. We learn to support different perspectives with reasons and evidence and to discuss ideas with others in an organized and tactful manner.

Elevating Your Learning Level

The depth at which you learn information affects your retention of the material and your ability to think critically. The lower levels of learning assist your short-term memory, whereas higher levels of learning contribute to long-term memory. The more deeply you understand the material, the more recall you will have when you are taking a test.

Beginning with memorization (the first level) and advancing to evaluation (the highest level), here are suggestions for developing each level of learning.

Memorization You have applied memorization to spelling words correctly, naming the capitals of the states or provinces, reciting lists, and recognizing terms. Memorizing facts such as telephone numbers, manuscript style guidelines, and the multiplication tables can save you the time of looking up a reference or using a calculator. Memorized information helps form a solid foundation for higher levels of learning.

You can assist your memory by making flash cards, making associations, drawing a mind map, and using mnemonics. Flash cards could have a vocabulary term on one side and the definition on the other; or you could write a question on one side and the answer on the other side. Making associations can aid your spelling: The spelling of *stationery* ends with *ery* for pap*er*; the spelling is *stationary* (ends with *ary*) for *station a*t *r*ailroad *y*ard. A mind map has main topics connected by arrows or lines to supporting points in a logical pattern that serves as a one-page visual. Mnemonics are memory aids for recalling a list of items. A popular mnemonic is *HOMES* to remind you of the Great Lakes: Huron, Ontario, Michigan, Erie, and Superior. Remember "Good Dogs All Eat" as the strings on a violin—GDAE. The six S–guides for effective letter writing are shortness, simplicity, strength, sincerity, strategy, and structure. You can develop your own mnemonics as you review key points from class notes and the textbook.

What new memorization techniques might work for you?

To improve your memorization techniques, access the Internet for The Memory Page, http://www.thememorypage.net. This website aid is created and updated by Kevin Jay North as a free public service.

Comprehension To comprehend concepts and information that have been presented through lecture or textbook reading, you might translate, interpret, and summarize. In translating concepts and facts to your own words, be accurate and preserve the original meaning. "Endeavor to ascertain the individual who has been assigned to manage the project" could be written "Find out who is managing the project." "A marked discrepancy" simply means "a big difference." Accurate interpretation of a new concept can be verified by explaining it to someone. As teachers often say, "The best way to learn new material is to have to teach it," or "In teaching this new subject, I learned more than the students did." Another step toward comprehension is summarizing, which forces you to condense a lot of information to a few words—the main idea.

Application Case studies, simulation games, and scenarios are used to give students practice in applying course content to realistic situations. By applying what has been taught in class to your own life, you can master the concepts and skills as well as be satisfied with your accomplishments. For example, you can apply effective listening when you are introduced to someone, attend an orientation training for a new job, and receive instructions over the phone. You could share the message of a sermon with a homebound friend or the professor's lecture with a classmate who missed class because of illness. Money management principles can be applied to purchasing a car, choosing a credit card company, and obtaining a loan.

Analysis Contemplate or examine concepts, ideas, applications, and research findings. What were the strong points and weak points? Can ideas be sorted into categories? Under what circumstances does a method work? Compare or contrast one with another. Consider the pros and cons of choices or alternatives. Examples would be owning your own computer versus using the computer lab, living in a residence hall versus renting an apartment, and buying a new car versus a used car. You might analyze your time management skills. What are your strengths? What are your weaknesses? In which aspects of college life have your time management skills improved the most? How can they be improved?

Evaluation Appraise or assess the concept, application, or experience and determine its usefulness. Evaluation involves making a judgment and forming a conclusion, which depends on other thinking skills. Referees of athletic events and judges of talent shows evaluate performance according to rules and standards. Other examples of evaluation include critiquing a novel, judging a debate tournament, and ranking restaurants. Monitoring your academic progress involves evaluation. You might appraise your development of learning styles and study skills by comparing your grades (assignments and exams) in each of your courses from the beginning of the semester to the end. In which courses have you improved the most? Is any course so difficult that it could result in a low grade? After careful analysis and evaluation of your status this term, you are prepared to make appropriate decisions.

Making Sound Decisions

Some decisions are relatively easy and quick to make. *Should I take the long route of back roads with few traffic lights or the short route of major thoroughfares with more traffic lights?* During rush hours you probably can get to your destination quicker by taking the long route, but during hours of less traffic you would choose the short route.

   More challenging might be this dilemma: *Should I skip my 2 PM class on Friday to get an early start for the weekend?* The decision will depend on your values, your academic commitment (regarding class attendance, coverage of assignment and lecture notes, possibility of a quiz, and grade achievement), the course syllabus (whether an exam is scheduled), your grade average, whether you have a previous absence from the class, the consequences of not being in class, and the urgency of Friday evening's event. Factors such as personal illness and peer pressure to appease a commuter might complicate the decision.

Making sound decisions involves the use of high-level thinking skills, consideration of personal values, and knowledge of self. Good decisions contribute to happiness and success; poor decisions result in complications and problems.

Exercise 4 Making a Decision About Housing

Assume your roommate or neighbor at the residence hall plans on getting an apartment off campus next year and asks you to share apartment living. Explain how you would arrive at a sound decision. Apply higher-level thinking skills as you consider important factors before making the decision.

_____

_____

_____

_____

Under what conditions would you agree to sharing an apartment with someone?

_____

_____

_____

_____

Solving Problems

Problem-solving opportunities occur in many courses and present themselves throughout life in challenging ways. Many inventions and successful businesses have been the result of intelligent problem solving. Effective problem solvers maintain a positive attitude, admit what they do not know, and seek input from experts. They use a systematic approach and keep their emotions under control.

In solving problems the first step is to describe the problem accurately and completely. Then you consider the alternatives and objectively analyze the advantages and disadvantages of each. Finally, you reach a solution. The effectiveness of the solution is determined by follow-up evaluation. To solve a problem, you might take the following steps.

▶ *Identify the problem.* Recognize a problem exists and define it as specifically as possible. Can it be broken down into parts? Is the problem part of a larger problem? Are there related factors? Make careful observations. Avoid allowing assumptions and biases to distort the picture.

▶ *Gather relevant facts.* Obtain information and facts you need to consider various options. Research skills can help acquire accurate, timely, and relevant data. Ask questions and seek input from reliable sources. Employers often call the references of applicants to obtain additional or key facts that can aid them in the screening process. For example, they might ask about an applicant's dependability, ability to work with various personality types, and attention to details (following through and completing tasks).

▶ *Consider alternative solutions.* Usually, there is more than one way to solve a problem. Ignoring your personal biases and opinions, carefully consider each possible solution while attending to the major factors involved. In selecting a vendor, for example, the major factors to consider might be quality of merchandise and price. If a student does not have enough money to pay next term's tuition, he or she might consider taking out a loan, getting a better-paying job, enrolling as a part-time student, or adjusting living expenses (housing, transportation, and entertainment). Keeping the major goal(s) in mind, visualize the consequences of each alternative solution.

▶ *Develop a plan of action.* The next step is to develop a plan of action and initiate it. Stay focused and be persistent despite criticism or discouragement.

▶ *Evaluate the solution.* Measure the effectiveness or profitability of your solution. Does it work as well as you anticipated? If a solution turns out to be ineffective, you have learned what not to do in the future. Learning from a successful failure, you will have succeeded in eliminating one alternative solution. Then review the steps and modify or change your plan of action.

Exercise 5 Solving the Problem of Automobile Replacement

Assume you have a seven-year-old automobile (with 85,000 miles registered on the odometer) that is costing you frequent repair and service expenses. Because of its lack of reliability, you have missed classes and have been late to work several times. You need to get a different car but have only $4,000 in your savings account.

How would you solve this problem? Access the Internet to obtain information about buying and selling cars, which might include the retail and wholesale value of used cars as well as the repair and service record ratings of used cars. You might consider these Internet addresses:

http://autos.lycos.com/autos
http://autos.msn.com

http://autos.yahoo.com
http://www.autoweb.com

Describe your approach (on a separate sheet of paper):
- Identify the problem.
- Gather relevant facts.
- Consider alternative solutions.
- Develop a plan of action.
- Evaluate the solution.

By elevating your learning level, you improve your ability to make decisions and to solve problems intelligently. In college courses you are expected to incorporate higher thinking and learning skills than what you used in high school. Professors will evaluate your class discussion, papers, and exams accordingly. Lifelong learning involves continual development of one's thinking and learning levels.

Solve This Case—Parking on Campus

Javier is one of the many students who have had problems finding a parking place on campus. He commutes 15 miles to school and sometimes drives around the campus for half an hour to find a parking place near the classrooms and library. Choosing metered parking and reserved parking lots has resulted in several parking tickets, amassing $215 in fines.

When trying to register for the next term, Javier discovered a block—an encumbrance code for unpaid parking tickets that halted registration. A few courses that are required for Javier's major have only two seats open during the section times that Javier needs for a convenient schedule. Javier does not have the $215 on hand to pay the parking fines and feels desperate to get registered today.

1 If you were Javier, how would you solve the problems inherent to this situation?

- Identify the problem.
- Gather relevant facts.
- Consider alternative solutions.
- Develop a plan of action.
- Evaluate the solution.

2 What suggestions would you have for Javier to prevent experiencing these problems again?

3 Be prepared to share your responses with a small group of classmates.

My Reflections Journal

Choose one of the following questions for your journal composition, which should be approximately one page. Using your computer, you may either print the page and turn it in on paper or e-mail the page to your instructor. Ask your instructor what method he or she prefers.

1 For your most difficult course or one in which the teaching style is not compatible with your learning style, what are some steps you could take to facilitate learning?

2 Have you ever made a decision that you would have made differently by applying critical thinking skills? Describe how you could have made a better decision.

3 What is one of the most challenging decisions you need to make this term? What suggestions from this chapter do you plan to apply in solving it?

4 Among the methods teachers use to get students to think critically are to play devil's advocate, to ask why you have taken a certain stand on an issue, and to ask "What do you think about . . . ?" How do you react to these techniques?

5 What are your obstacles to being an effective problem solver?

Website Practice Test

On the website at http://www.casadyenterprises.com/collegeedgebook/practicetests.htm you can access a practice test to check on your understanding of the chapter concepts. You may print the results of this self-test to review before taking the respective in-class exam.

ENHANCING READING, LISTENING, AND NOTE TAKING

Objectives

Upon completing this chapter, you should be able to:

- Control your study environment
- Get the most from your textbook
- Become a better listener
- Take and review notes efficiently
- Prepare assignments for maximum learning

TO STUDY MOST EFFECTIVELY, you want to be able to concentrate and complete your homework accurately within the shortest time period. You can maximize your potential in studying and in getting good grades by following the basic suggestions of this chapter:

- Adjust or find an *environment* conducive to studying—with little noise, good lighting, and comfortable seating.

- In *reading your textbook,* mark in the book and/or write in a notebook the most important information. Develop a system of reviewing it to prepare for lectures, class discussions, and exams.

- During lectures, *listen* carefully and *take notes* efficiently so you can contribute intelligently to class discussions, retain the major concepts, and increase your critical thinking skills.

- *Prepare homework* in a professional manner to earn the highest possible grade.

■ Control Your Study Environment

The quality of your studying is affected by various environmental factors including noise, lighting, temperature, humidity, and furniture. Few adjustments are possible in a residence hall; an apartment or house offers more flexibility. In choosing or modifying your study area, review the following suggestions so you can enhance your study environment.

Choosing the Place

Where is the library? What are its hours?

For convenience, especially during late evening hours, you probably study in your room much of the time. But noise and interruptions lessen the ability to study efficiently. Many students go to the library, where it is quiet and where references are handy. A study room in the residence hall, your home, or a classroom building is another option. You want to avoid the distractions of visitors, telephones, radio, or television.

Reducing Noise

You might not like to study in silence. Soft, continuous music can be pleasing and may not interfere with your concentration. A moderate amount of background noise masks conversations and telephone rings. Yet research proves it takes at least 20 percent longer to study under distracting, noisy conditions than to do the same work under reasonably quiet conditions.

Intermittent sounds of people talking, visitors opening and closing the door, radio and television programs, as well as telephone rings and conversations are disruptive. Excessive noise causes people to become irritable and nervous, lengthens the time to do tasks, and increases the likelihood of making errors. More energy is required, and both concentration and decision-making ability are reduced in noisy environments. Therefore, it is important to reach an agreement about study conditions with your living partners.

Arranging for Proper Lighting

Be kind to your eyes; they cannot be replaced, and corrective lenses are costly. Discomfort from eye strain causes headaches and stress, which results in errors and lengthens the time to complete a task. To protect your eyes from abuse, arrange for proper lighting.

Proper lighting for studying should be evenly diffused as well as free from glare and shadows. The amount of light needed depends upon the type of homework you are doing. Viewing a computer screen requires less light than reading a textbook or proofreading a paper. Another consideration is age; persons over 40 years of age require more light than younger people do to perform identical tasks.

Factors that decrease the quality of light and increase eye strain are glare, shadows, and extreme contrasts in brightness. Glare and shadows occur when the light fixture is ahead of and directly above the desk. Light bounces up from papers and the work surface into your eyes, making it difficult to see parts of text. The surface of your desk or table should be a medium shade to provide enough contrast for papers to be distinguished.

Indirect lighting is better than direct lighting. Direct lighting casts most of the light downward from the light fixture (spreading light unevenly), which causes shadows, creates glare on paper, and makes annoying reflections on computer screens. Indirect lighting directs most of the light upward to the ceiling, from which the light is evenly reflected and diffused throughout the room; glare and shadows are reduced. If you purchase a floor lamp for your study area, consider purchasing an indirect lighting style fixture.

Natural light through windows can be adjusted by blinds or curtains to provide evenly diffused light without glare. Position your computer and desk so the window is perpendicular to your eyes. If you are right-handed, the light source should come from above the left shoulder to avoid a distracting shadow. If you are left-handed, light should come from the right shoulder. To avoid glare on the computer screen, do not face a window or have light come directly from behind.

Choosing Wall Color

If you can choose or change wall color, plan a supportive environment in which color and lighting complement each other. Color gives meaning to space. Pastel colors and light shades make small-sized rooms seem larger. If a window is on the south or west wall (emitting lots of light), you would choose a cool color—light blue or light green. On the other hand, if a window is on the north or east wall (bringing in less sunshine), you could enhance light by choosing a warm color—light mauve or light yellow.

Getting an Adjustable Chair

For many study hours you will be seated at your desk. In a poorly designed chair you can suffer back strain, neck strain, and headaches. Ideally, both the desk top and chair should be adjustable for various body heights. Because most desk tops are not adjustable, you need a comfortable chair with adjustments for back and seat heights as well as tilt control. Of course, being too comfortable in a leaned-back position might cause you to fall asleep.

Adjusting the Computer Screen and Keyboard

Adjust your computer screen and chair vertically until your eyes are just above the top of the screen. Tilt the screen slightly downward to eliminate or reduce glare. Choose a copy holder that positions the top edge of the source document even with the top edge of the screen and right next to it. If you key text from a source document on your desk or lap, your eyes have to jump up to the screen and down to your paper countless times. The results would be eye strain, neck and shoulder pain, and unnecessary errors from losing your place.

Setting Temperature and Humidity Controls

Extreme temperature and humidity levels adversely affect the way people and computers function. If your room is too hot, you will become sleepy; if you are cold, you will not be able to concentrate. Temperature ranging from 65 to 75° is acceptable; a stable 68° F is recommended. If the humidity rises above 60 percent, your disks and paper will absorb moisture. Should it drop below 40 percent, static electricity will build. Either situation causes computers and printers to malfunction, which could cause a crisis should your paper be due the next day. Humidity at a steady 50 percent is recommended.

Exercise 1 Evaluating Your Study Environment

Describe your study environment. Use these sentence starters as jumping-off points.

My best place to study is_____

Environmental problems of my place of living that hinder studying are

_____

To improve my study environment I plan to_____
_____
_____

■ Get the Most from Your Textbook

The ultimate goal of reading and studying a textbook is to learn information that can be applied to your life's goals. Your immediate goal is to learn information in preparation for taking lecture notes, doing assignments, discussing ideas in class, and passing exams.

Textbook prices increase as paper costs and labor costs continue to rise. Hardback books cost more than softback books to produce. The more color and illustrations, the more a book costs. Authors and publishers add color, graphics, and photographs to entice you to read the book as well as to help you identify major points.

To get your money's worth from your textbooks use all the helpful features. Develop a system of reading and marking the content for easy review. You probably have neither the desire nor the time to read all the text a second time.

Writing in Your Books

In high school you might not have been allowed to write in books, but in college you buy and have your own books. Use them in ways that help you to learn. Though you might get less money reselling a book that has marks and writing, the difference in sell-back prices is minor compared to that of your performance. Your grades will be higher if you have an effective system of marking your books as you read and review the text (see Figure 1).

Buying used books that already are marked might not be worth the difference in purchase price from that of a new book. The previous owner likely will have had a different teacher and a unique way of studying. Another student's marks can be confusing and misleading, attracting your attention to insignificant concepts.

Textbook authors and publishers often offer study aids that go along with their books. Common study aids are available on CD-ROMs, on websites, and in study guides. To find out what is offered with your books talk with the instructor of the respective course.

Where is the bookstore?

What are its hours?

Reading, Marking, and Reviewing Text

The system you develop will depend upon your learning style, the type of subject and its difficulty, the book's design, and how much the teacher uses the book. Develop ways that work for you, and modify your system according to these variables:

Figure 1—Reading, Marking, and Reviewing Text

the library, where it is quiet and where references are handy. A study room in the residence hall, your home, or a classroom building is another option. You want to avoid the **distractions of visitors, telephones, radio, or television.**

Reducing Noise

Okay Noise
  Soft
  Continuous
  Masks
Bad Noise
  Intermittent
  Excessive
Results of Bad Noise
  Disruptive
  Irritability
  Nervousnes
  Takes longer
  Takes more energy
  More errors
  Less concentration
  Less decision making

You might not like to study in silence. ^OK Soft, continuous music can be pleasing and may not interfere with your concentration. A moderate amount of background noise masks conversations and telephone rings. Yet research proves it takes at least 20 percent longer to study under distracting, noisy conditions than to do the same work under reasonably quiet conditions.

^Bad Intermittent sounds of people talking, visitors opening and closing the door, radio and television programs, as well as telephone rings and conversations are disruptive. Excessive noise causes people to become irritable and nervous, lengthens the time to do tasks, and increases the likelihood of making errors. More energy is required, and both concentration and decision-making ability are reduced in noisy environments. Therefore, it is important to reach an agreement about study conditions with your living partners.

Figure 2—Outlining and Composing Questions

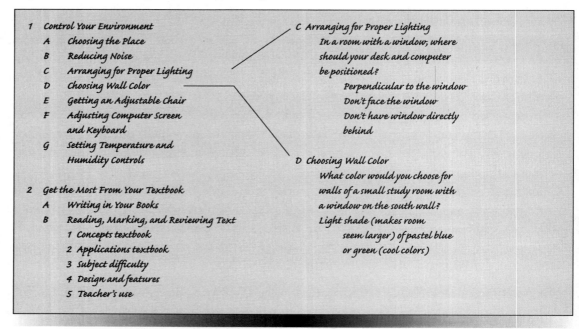

Concepts Textbook To effectively read a chapter of a textbook that presents concepts (history, political science, and psychology), follow these steps:

1 Read the introduction and the summary for an overview.

2 Make an outline of the first-level headings and their respective subheadings.

3 Read the text and either highlight or underline (with black or blue ink) what you consider important information.

4 Take a 10-minute break.

5 Guided by your outline, review the highlighted or underlined portions of text. Use bright red or green ink to mark parts most critical to remember. Write in the margins. If three points are given, number them 1, 2, and 3. If two ideas are contrasted, circle the key terms and connect them with "vs" (for *versus*). Use the asterisk (*) to mark main points. Cross out insignificant text and do not reread it. Instead of using a second color in the textbook, you might prefer to write a more detailed outline and transfer the important points to your notebook or folder.

6 Compose questions that could be asked on an exam. Write them in the margins of the textbook or on your outline next to the appropriate subheading. Place the chapter outline and proposed exam questions in the course's notebook or folder (see Figure 2).

Applications Textbook Algebra, statistics, computer applications, and accounting books have applications or problems with lists of instructional steps. The formulas and lists can be highlighted or circled so they stand out. Reminders can be written in the margins.

Subject Difficulty For complex courses, you will read and mark the text (or record on tape) more thoroughly than you do for easy courses. The more you know about a subject, the less you will mark in the book or record. Confusing and difficult content requires more processing than understandable and concise text.

Design and Features In reading, marking, and reviewing a book, you are processing the information and learning. If the textbook design has few side headings and illustrations, you will need to do more marking. On the other hand, textbooks with many side headings, illustrations, and definitions or notes in the margins assist your processing; less paragraph text has to be marked.

Teacher's Use The way you use a book depends on the teacher's style. How closely does the teacher's lecture relate to the textbook? How often does the teacher refer to and use the textbook in class? What proportion of test questions come from the book? The more often the teacher integrates the textbook into the course's activities, the more thoroughly you will read the book and process the information.

Study (read, mark, and review) your textbook before class. Then you will have the basis for understanding the lecture, preparing questions, and participating in class discussion. Your intelligence and preparedness will impress the teacher.

Exercise 2 Studying Your Textbook

1 Bring this textbook (or one used in another course) to show how you study a book by outlining, reading, and marking this chapter.

2 Describe your system of reviewing the chapter's main concepts or points.

_____

_____

3 For each major section of this chapter compose one exam question and its answer. Use one sheet of paper for all questions. Consider using a computer to generate your questions and answers.

■ Become a Better Listener

Successful students are good listeners and note takers. They pay attention to professors' lectures, classmates' presentations, and conversations. Effective listeners exert physical effort and mental alertness. Both energy and self-discipline are required to focus on a message. Skill in taking notes depends on listening well and knowing how to process the information efficiently.

Research on Listening

According to extensive research by Dr Ralph Nichols, a noted authority on listening, 98 percent of knowledge is learned through the eyes and ears. Of our daytime hours, 70 percent is devoted to communication—for which we spend our time as follows:

Writing	9 percent
Reading	16 percent
Speaking	30 percent
Listening	45 percent

Our earlier education included much formal training in reading, writing, and speaking. Though we spend more time listening than reading or writing or speaking, most of us have had little training in listening skills.

At the University of Minnesota, Dr Nichols conducted research to examine the listening ability of several thousand students as well as business and professional people. The people in the study were presented with short talks by faculty members and were tested for their grasp of the content. Substantiated by research conducted at other universities, the results of Dr Nichols' research included these findings:

- Immediately after having listened to a 10-minute talk, we remember only about 50 percent of what was heard.

- Two months after listening to a 10-minute talk, we remember only 25 percent of what was said.

Poor Listening

If you have serious problems listening, you might have hearing problems or a learning disability. Where would you go to check this out?

Ineffective listening is obvious. At social events poor listeners reveal themselves by asking a person's name soon after the introduction, talking only about themselves, not participating in conversation, abruptly changing the subject, or completing sentences or ideas for the speaker. At work poor listeners do not follow instructions, do not do what they are asked, or needlessly interrupt an associate or supervisor who is speaking.

At a lecture you reveal poor listening skill if you daydream, ask a question that already has been answered, or do something unrelated to the lecture. Your professor might assume you are not listening if during class you are looking at a distraction, writing something other than lecture notes, drawing images on your paper, slouching in your chair, fidgeting with your hands or an object, talking to a classmate, or reading.

Improving Your Listening Skills

Effective listening requires an open mind and attention to people's ideas, feelings, and needs. Seeking a wide range of viewpoints, we must be willing to hear and consider the opinions of others even when they conflict with our own. Good listening is an active process, using substantial energy to focus on the message. We can become better listeners by conscientious effort. You can increase your ability to understand and remember teachers' lectures as well as your classmates' presentations by practicing these principles.

Be open to the topic. The topic might not be interesting or might be too difficult to understand. Nevertheless, try to welcome new subject matter and stretch your mind to process challenging subjects.

Be an active listener. Sit alert, be attentive, and use good eye contact with the speaker. Use body language to show you are interested, you agree, or you question an idea. Should questions be invited from the class, have at least one question ready to ask. Take notes. Do not daydream or do anything unrelated to the talk.

Listen for major concepts and ideas rather than simple facts. Concentrate on the major concepts and ideas. Significant facts that support the main concepts or ideas are appropriate, but do not record merely facts. Look for the broad picture.

Correct or ignore distractions. If an open door or window allows noise to distract the presentation, get up and close it. If someone enters the room late and lets the door slam, ignore it. (When one enters a room after a talk has begun, it is courteous to be as quiet and unobtrusive as possible.) If the microphone squeaks, ignore it. If you cannot hear the speaker, raise your hand and politely ask if the speaker could talk louder or raise the microphone's volume level.

Take notes. As you listen for major ideas, take notes. The format and way you take notes will depend on the organization of the message as well as your background information, and the proposed use of the material.

Avoid being judgmental. If a speaker has unusual mannerisms or style, focus on the content rather than the delivery. Do not allow strong emotions to draw you off the subject. If you strongly disagree, be patient and withhold arguments until the speaker's ideas have been heard.

Concentrate. Keep your mind focused on the content. Think about how the message can apply to you. Be perceptive of the speaker's body language as well as spoken words.

Handle the speaking and listening rate differential. We can think faster than we can listen; we can listen faster than someone can speak; but we cannot write fast enough to keep up with the speaker.

Average thought rate	700 words a minute (WAM)
Average listening rate	400 WAM
Average speaking rate	150 WAM
Fastest writing rate	40 WAM

To handle this differential, you can anticipate the next thought, identify main points, and mentally review what the speaker has said. Read between the lines for what was meant rather than actually said. Reflect upon the message, and search for its meaning.

Exercise 3 Listening to the News

Listen to a half-hour national or local news broadcast on radio or television. Describe the day, the time, the channel selected, and the coverage (national or local news). Take notes. Be sure to concentrate on the key messages that are being reported. Turn in a printed copy of your information. In class this exercise will be discussed and further processed.

■ Take and Review Notes Efficiently

Your system of taking notes will depend upon the subject and the professor's style of presenting information. By reviewing these guides and applying the ones that improve your note-taking efficiency, you can increase your knowledge and get the best possible course grade.

Be present. No one can take notes for you as accurately and completely as you can. Announcements and information will be given that another person might neither record nor remember to share with you. Being present to take your own notes will give you an edge in processing them for review and exam study!

Sit up front. You can hear better if you sit up front rather than toward the back of the classroom. You will also have the best view of illustrations on the board and transparency overlays. Positioned where few distractions can misdirect your attention, you can concentrate better.

Listen for verbal clues. Verbal clues from the teacher indicate what is important:

A summary	*"To summarize . . ."*
Keywords	*"First, . . . Second, . . ."*
Reference to textbook	*"As the chart on page . . ."*

Watch for visual clues. Information the teacher writes on the board, displays on an overhead transparency, distributes as a handout, or discusses while walking out into the classroom is important. Be sure to study it, and expect to answer related questions on the next exam.

Use different colors of ink. Write your notes with blue or black ink. Highlight or use a pen with bright red or green ink to mark special points, reminders, and accompanying handouts.

Label and organize notes. Label and organize lecture notes in a pattern that parallels the respective course unit. The label should include the date and sequence number. Refer to the course syllabus so your notes coincide with that outline.

Adapt note-taking method to lecture style. Consider these methods of note taking, and adjust to the teacher's lecture style:

Figure 3—The Cornell Note-Taking System (Attributes of a Good Student)

Tuesday October 27	Dr Aripoli
	Attributes of a Good Student
Responsible	"I am responsible for me."
	Don't blame others or pass the buck
	Ultimate responsibility ——> yourself (adult)
Accountable	"I am accountable to others."
	We need to be good citizens
	Help improve campus, community, and society
Control	"Never give up control."
	Don't put yourself at risk such that you
	can't make decisions for yourself
	Ex. alcohol, drugs, assault
Irreversibility	"Some things cannot be change/reversed."
	As much as you are sorry and wish it had not happened, it did
	Ex. A "D" on an exam, a DWI on record, an accident and
	you are at fault, death of a parent, being fired, etc.

1 Outlining If the lecture leads from a general idea to specific points (the deductive approach) and the teacher is well organized, an outline works well. Outlining will be easy if the lecture parallels the textbook's chapter outline.

2 Annotating If the teacher's lecture coincides with a handout or the textbook, write notes in the margins of those pages. Highlight or underscore portions of the text that are emphasized. If much discussion occurs, you might not have room to write more than phrases. Keep related materials (textbook, lecture notes, and handouts) close together.

3 Summarizing As the lecture progresses, summarize the main thoughts in your own words. Separate opinions from facts, note relationships, and analyze them for practice in critical thinking.

An effective note-taking system that facilitates summarizing is the Cornell Note-Taking System (see Figure 3), developed by Walter Pauk at Cornell University:

Record–Write meaningful facts and ideas with legible writing.

Reduce–Reduce and summarize the notes for clarity and continuity soon after the lecture.

Recite–With main notes covered, state the facts and ideas in your own words. Uncover notes and verify what you have recited.

Reflect–Separate opinions and reflections from the notes. See relationships of personal thoughts and experiences to the lecture notes.

Review–Review your notes each week.

Figure 4—Listing Comparisons (The Seventh Myths of Marriage)

Thursday, November 5   *Dr Halverson*

Seven Myths of Marriage

Myth	*Truth*
1 *Marriage is an event.*	1 *Marriage is a journey and process. Wedding is the event.*
2 *My mate will change; I will change him/her.*	2 *If you can't marry the person as he/she is, don't do it. Accept his/her differences and respect your mate.*
3 *My mate will not change after the wedding.*	3 *We have to be adaptable and flexible—growing together in the different seasons of life.*
4 *Marriage is hard work.*	4 *Marriage is joyful as mates comfort, help, and support each other.*
5 *I know all there is to know about love, marriage, and my spouse.*	5 *Couples must continue learning and understanding each other throughout their lives.*
6 *Our mate should meet all our needs.*	6 *Marriage provides some but not all of our needs.*
7 *Love is all you need.*	7 *Love will not sustain a marriage unless it goes on to something deeper—agape love in the relationship.*

4   **Listing** Record main facts on one side of the paper and related principles on the other side. Another option would be to list comparisons on the left and right sides of the paper: pros versus cons, similarities versus differences, advantages versus disadvantages, or myths versus truths (see Figure 4).

5   **Mind mapping** Draw a visual design and cluster or link your notes to the illustration. Typical designs are circles, triangles, spokes of a wheel, corners of a square, and a tree trunk with branches. For example, you might draw a circle and make a pie chart divided into pieces with each piece representing a percentage breakdown (in proportionate size) of ethnic groups within your college. The combination of designs, shapes, and words forms a mind map that is easy to visualize and remember. Examples and facts can be connected to the design, as shown in Figure 5.

How can you contact a classmate of each course?

How can you contact your teachers?

Review notes soon after class. Go over your notes as soon as you can, perhaps during a break between classes. Rewrite them to cut what is irrelevant, to clarify disconnected thoughts, and to reorganize points. If you are confused about any notes or missed information, you might be able to fill in the missing links by recalling the lecture.

Consider swapping notes with one or two classmates to get another view of the lecture. You will see what others wrote that you might have missed, which will help clarify and complete your notes. If you still have gaps and are confused, see the teacher before the next class period.

Figure 5—Mind Mapping (Triple A's of a Successful College Student)

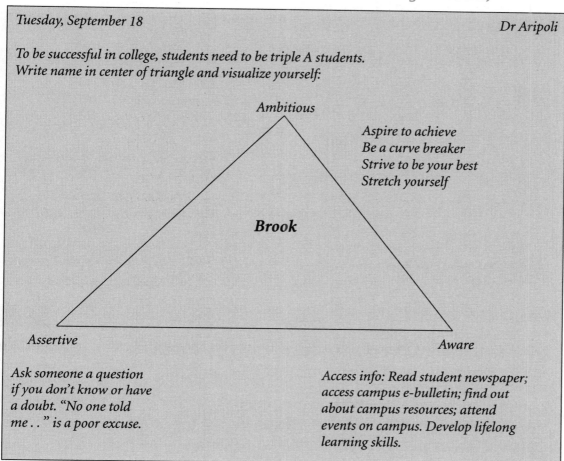

Tuesday, September 18   *Dr Aripoli*

To be successful in college, students need to be triple A students.
Write name in center of triangle and visualize yourself:

Ambitious

Aspire to achieve
Be a curve breaker
Strive to be your best
Stretch yourself

Brook

Assertive   *Aware*

Ask someone a question
if you don't know or have
a doubt. "No one told
me . ." is a poor excuse.

Access info: Read student newspaper;
access campus e-bulletin; find out
about campus resources; attend
events on campus. Develop lifelong
learning skills.

Visual learners typically rewrite notes. Auditory learners record on tape the main concepts and listen to the tape while commuting or cleaning. Try to understand in order to remember rather than to memorize what you do not understand.

Compose likely exam questions. Compose exam questions on one side of a page and the answers on the other side. Cover the answers as you review the questions. Then uncover the answers to give yourself feedback. The TRQ method (Take notes, Review, and Question), as illustrated in Figure 6, is an effective method of taking lecture notes and studying for exams.

Keep related materials together and arrange by topic. Keep lecture notes together with related handouts, the respective chapter outline, notes from textbook reading, and assignments. Arrange these materials by topic so you can conceptualize the information when you study. Do not put notes in one place, handouts in another, and assignments in yet another place. Disconnected segments throughout a notebook or folder do not merge in thought easily.

Efficient note taking will help you keep an open mind. You will be developing your ability to think critically and will be able to accept new concepts and ideas.

Figure 6—The TRQ Method of Taking Notes and Studying for Exams

STEP 3 QUESTION	STEP 2 REVIEW	STEP 1 TAKE NOTES IN CLASS
Compose possible text questions.	Summarize for clarity and continuity.	Listen for verbal clues.
		Watch for visual clues.
		Use different colors of ink.
	Is more information needed?	Label and organize notes.
		Adapt note-taking method to lecture style.
		Review notes soon after class.
	Place check mark if you understand.	Compose likely exam questions.
		Keep related materials together by topic.

Exercise 4 Taking and Reviewing Lecture Notes

Demonstrate effective listening and note taking by taking notes from a class lecture or guest speaker. Then do the following:

1 List the guides or methods presented in this chapter that you incorporated. Indicate the speaker's style of communication. Was it effective?

_____

_____

2 Compose an essay question that involves summarizing or analyzing a major concept.

_____

_____

3 Prepare an answer key to the essay question. Consider using your computer to type your answer.

_____

_____

Exercise 5 Sharing with Classmates

To facilitate your sharing information and exchanging notes with classmates, fill out the Classmates form in the Personal References section at the end of the text. For each of your courses, fill in the contact information of two classmates. Should you not be able to reach one, you will have an alternate. You can become support teams.

■ Prepare Assignments for Maximum Learning

The way you do assignments and submit them has an impact on how your work will be evaluated. In a job, rewards for excellent work are pay raises and promotions. In college, your rewards for excellent work are benefits from your learning (including good grades, references, and leadership positions).

Mature and responsible students anticipate the teacher's needs without waiting for specific instructions. To do a professional job in preparing assignments, follow these suggestions:

Label your papers. Your professors probably will tell you how to label assignments. If not, on each assignment include your name, the course identification, and due date.

> *Janet Hofer*
> *IDS 110, Sec 14*
> *September 18*

Type rather than handwrite your papers. Studies show that typed assignments are graded higher than handwritten papers with the identical words. Typed or printed material is easier to read and looks more professional. At many colleges, handwritten papers are not acceptable.

Use word processing software and a laser printer. Using word processing software, you can format attractive documents and make revisions without rekeying the text. A laser printer gives clear and crisp characters that have professional quality. Learn to use the equipment and software, back up your disk, and keep supplies on hand. Avoid having these excuses for a late paper: computer or printer failure, damaged disk, or no paper.

Where are the computer labs?

What are the hours?

Use a pen rather than a pencil. For in-class writing where keyboards are not available, use a pen rather than a pencil. Showing uneven and varying shades of darkness, pencil writing is difficult to read and is considered an unprofessional tool by many professors. Pen ink is clearer, sharper, darker, and more permanent. Two exceptions would be filling out bubble sheets for computer scoring (which require a #2 pencil) and doing accounting, math, and statistical problems that involve erasing and making changes.

Where can you go to make copies?

Make a copy. Especially for major papers, make a copy for your file. You might need it as a reference or proof that you did the assignment.

Staple together assignments of two or more pages. Unless you are instructed otherwise, assemble two or more pages of an assignment in proper order and staple them in the upper left corner. Staple at a diagonal for strength and ease of turning over the pages. Never submit multiple sheets loosely; a page could get separated from the rest and lost. Unless instructed otherwise, avoid paper clips; they catch onto other papers, which could result in your work getting lost. Do not turn back and tear an upper corner of the pages.

Cut off ragged edges. If you tear out a page from a spiral-bound notebook, cut off the ragged edges. They look tacky, catch onto other papers, and annoy teachers.

Complete assignments on time. Plan ahead with a goal of completing major papers at least a day before they are due. Mark term, monthly, and weekly calendars to remind you of due dates. Do not expect the teacher to remind you. Avoid procrastinating and completing your paper at the last minute. If your computer malfunctions or supplies run out, you have a dilemma.

Be on time for class. Some teachers have assignments due at the beginning of the class period. Important announcements might also be given at the start of class. Some professors lock the door when class begins so that late comers cannot enter.

By applying these suggestions, you will show you have learned how to prepare assignments properly. These professional practices will impress your professors (to get the best grades), employers, people with whom you do business, associates, and members of organizations you join.

Self-Assessment: Assessing Homework Preparation

Choose a homework assignment you have completed recently for any course. Referring to the suggestions given, assess the quality of your preparation and completion of the assignment by answering *Yes* or *No* to the questions. You might be sharing your assessment with classmates.

Identify the assignment: _____

1 Was it labeled according to the teacher's specification?   _____

2 Was the assignment keyed and printed?   _____

3 If handwritten, did you use a pen rather than a pencil?   _____

4 If it was torn out of a notebook, were the ragged edges cut off?   _____

5 If there were two or more pages, were they stapled together?   _____

6 Did you make a copy to keep?   _____

Attach the homework assignment (or its copy) to this self-assessment.

Employing these concepts of reading, listening, and note taking will help you maximize your potential. A good environment supports comfort and efficiency. You can excel in college by gleaning your textbooks for knowledge, becoming a better listener, and taking notes effectively. To compete in the academic world you want to prepare assignments in the professional manner that is expected in the employment world.

Solve This Case—How Can Derek Do Better?

Having just gotten back a book report from his English class and an exam from General Psychology, Derek is disappointed to have gotten D's on each. His grades were mostly B's in high school, where he did not have much homework and played on the basketball team. How could college be so different? Derek went to see Dr Allison, his Freshman Success course teacher, for a conference.

The opening conversation was about his roommate situation in the residence hall. Derek said he and his roommate get along well. They have several friends on the same floor who come to visit regularly. Phone calls from family and friends are appreciated, too.

Upon looking at Derek's textbooks and class notes for the two courses, Dr Allison saw that both textbooks were clean and hardly marked up. Derek said he would get more money back at the end of the term if he did not mark in them. Only two pages of class notes were written in his notebook. He said he spent many hours studying for the psychol-

ogy test and had read the assigned chapters a second time the night before the exam. When asked where and when he does most studying, Derek replied, "In my room during the evening."

Derek showed Dr Allison the handwritten two-page book report, which had been torn out of a spiral-bound notebook. He thought the grade was not fair, for only three spelling errors had been circled; but he could not find the second page to show the professor's comments.

1 Can you identify with Derek?
2 Does any aspect of this case relate to you as a student?
3 What action plan does Derek need to improve his study skills and homework preparation?
4 Be prepared to participate in role-playing either Derek or Dr Allison when you come to class.

My Reflections Journal

Reflect on your experiences as they relate to the topics of the chapter. From the five questions, choose three on which to write one paragraph each. Using your computer, you may either print the pages and turn them in on paper or e-mail the pages to your instructor. Ask your instructor which method he or she prefers.

1 After having read this chapter, what changes have you made in reading and studying your textbooks?

2 Describe a situation in which you felt someone was not listening to you. How did you feel? Has the experience had an effect on your desire to improve your listening skills?

3 What have been your challenges in taking notes from lectures? In what ways do you feel your note-taking skills can improve? Describe new techniques you are using.

4 Have you ever gotten homework returned with comments about your preparation or suggestions on what to do differently? What changes have you made in preparing homework assignments to be more professional?

5 How do you feel about college this week? What has been your happiest moment? What is one of your major concerns?

Website Practice Test

On the website at http://www.casadyenterprises.com/collegeedgebook/practicetests.htm you can access a practice test to check on your understanding of the chapter concepts. You may print the results of this self-test to review before taking the respective in-class exam.

6 TAKING TESTS

Objectives

*Upon completing this chapter,
you should be able to:*

- Prepare for college-level exams

- Apply effective techniques in
  taking tests

- React appropriately after a test

TO ACHIEVE GOOD GRADES in college, you want to do well on exams and major papers. In some courses the overall course grade is based heavily on the average exam grade or the overall points on exams. Taking exams is stressful. Midterms and final exams cover a large amount of material, and more than one exam may be scheduled on the same day. During an exam you might know the information, but your mind goes blank because of test anxiety. The desire to make good grades contributes to stress.

Taking a test can be stressful even when you have done all the right steps in preparation. However, you can minimize the challenges of test anxiety and maximize your performance by following helpful tips about test taking—preparing for college-level exams, applying effective techniques in taking tests, and reacting appropriately after an exam.

■ Prepare for College-Level Exams

How does your body react when you are taking a test? Does your mind go blank? Does your heart beat faster and your pulse speed up? Do you sweat more than normal, get a headache, or suffer from a stomachache? Do you have difficulty focusing? If so, you are among the many students who suffer from test anxiety.

Where could you go to get help studying for a test?

Some anxiety is normal and appropriate. In a challenging situation, you will do better if you are apprehensive and somewhat nervous than if you do not care how you perform and are too relaxed. But it still is important to prevent undue stress. Students who do their best academically attend classes regularly, prepare for exams, and maintain a positive attitude.

Attend Classes Regularly

Attend every class every day. Never skip class. No one can take notes for you as well as you can. If you are absent, you miss important instructions and announcements about how the exam will be composed and graded. In preparing for an exam, you would need extra hours to compensate for a lost lecture. So make class attendance a first priority. Keeping up with classes is easier than catching up.

What are the names and phone numbers of classmates you could ask to take notes for you in an emergency that causes you to miss the class?

If you do not do as well as you would like on an exam, you cannot fault yourself for not having been present to take notes. Most teachers are willing to help students improve if they have been attending regularly. They are less likely to devote effort and time for students who have been absent frequently or who have missed class a couple of weeks without a legitimate reason.

Prepare for Exams

If you are well prepared, your stress level is less than if you walk into an exam without having studied adequately. Keep up with your reading, note taking, and assignments each day.

- Read the text before the teacher's lecture on the topic.
- Go over your lecture notes soon after class.
- Use a bright-colored ink or highlighter to mark the major points.
- Review quizzes (with emphasis on questions you missed).
- Compose sample questions.

Review reading assignments and lecture notes once a week so you do not have to cram the night before a test. Try to *understand* the material rather than just memorize lists. Few short cuts can replace consistently diligent work.

The last major studying for an exam should begin three or four days before the test. Most three-hour courses require 8 to 10 hours of studying time the week before the test:

- Plan for two- or three-hour review blocks.
- Take a 10-minute break every one and a half hours or a 15-minute break every two and a half hours.
- Vary review activities—studying notes, handouts, and textbook—topic by topic.
- Find a quiet place to study where you can concentrate.

Ask your teacher to give an overview of the exam—the number of questions, the types of questions (true-false, multiple-choice, matching, listing, essay), the weight of the exam in the overall course grade, whether the test is to be open book or closed book, and whether the test covers new material or covers previous unit(s) as well as new material. Your teacher may provide review sheets. If so, study them carefully; some exam questions likely will come from review sheets.

If you want your brain to function well and your mind to stay focused throughout an exam:

- Eat nutritious meals in moderate amounts. Be sure to eat breakfast.
- Get at least seven hours of sleep each of the three nights before the test.
- Maintain a physical exercise schedule.
- Avoid using alcohol, caffeine, drugs, and nicotine.

Be overprepared for the exam. Study until you recall information without clues or cues. You will be able to finish the exam more quickly than if you have to hesitate in answering the questions. You will have less test anxiety and will remember the material longer if you have prepared well for the test.

You might also consider participating in a study group. In these groups you take turns composing questions to quiz each other. On difficult parts one person might be able to explain a concept to the group, or understanding might evolve from the general discussion process. For each study group in which you participate, fill out the Study Groups form in the Personal References section at the end of this text. This handy reference will facilitate your working together efficiently.

Are there classmates who might want to form study groups?

On the day of the test, bring the materials you might need to the classroom. Common supplies include pens, #2 pencils (sharpened), paper, bluebook, calendar, paper white-out or liquid cover-up, paper clips or small stapler, calculator. With permission from the teacher, you might also bring a pocket dictionary or spelling book. Have facial tissue handy.

Wear favorite clothes that are comfortable. Start early for class so you have time to collect your thoughts, adjust to the surroundings, and get your materials organized. Be in your seat at least 5 minutes before class is to begin. You will get the teacher's instructions completely; those who arrive late miss information.

Do not listen to panic talk of classmates before the test. They might not have prepared well for the test, and their panic could distract or distort your focus. If you are not as prepared as you wish, you cannot do anything about it at this late time. Focus on what you know and can do.

Use relaxation techniques (deep breathing, closing your eyes, and telling yourself to relax) to reduce stress. Visualize your notes, and tune out distractions (conversations, thoughts about another course, or concerns about a paper just returned). Focus on the test.

Handle Emergencies Properly

What if you have an emergency on the day of the exam and cannot make it to class? Contact the professor as soon as possible to explain your situation and to request an opportunity to take the exam later. Phone the professor's office or departmental secretary, or send an e-mail message. If you cannot speak with the professor, leave your phone number and times to be reached or your e-mail address. Most professors will allow students to make up an exam provided they are notified before the test hour and a make-up is arranged before the next class period.

Maintain a Positive Attitude

A positive attitude will help you perform at your best on a test. You might maintain this perspective: Exams let you know how you are doing in your courses. Each test is just one of several tests, and test scores are only one part of the overall course grade. If test taking is the most difficult part of the course, be thankful you can excel in other components of your grade to compensate.

One low test grade will not cause you to fail a course. If you fail a test, do not feel you are a failure in life. You can learn from the experience so you can do better on the next exams, which no doubt will carry more weight than the first exam of the term.

You also can keep in mind that other students are subjected to the same conditions. Some subjects are easier for you than others. *Never expect the impossible of yourself.* Keep the difficulty of the course in perspective. Remember, you have:

- Reasons for attending college
- Desire for learning the course material; you see its value
- Ambition for success

Establish a positive mindset. Cheer on your efforts with positive phrases like "I can do it!" or "I am thankful to be able to learn!" or "I have the ability to succeed!" Do not allow negative thoughts to enter your mind and control your actions. Tell yourself to relax, stay calm, and be in control. Visualize yourself being successful.

Finally, remember that exams are progress reports for teachers as well as students. If most scores are below average, the teacher probably does not feel any better about the situation than the students do.

Self-Assessment: Assessing Test-Taking Strategies

Assess your strategies in preparing to take a test. Label each of the descriptors with the number that best describes you:

    3—I regularly use this strategy.
    2—Sometimes I use this strategy.
    1—I seldom use this strategy and need to start applying it regularly.

____ Attend each class
____ Keep up with reading, note taking, and assignments on a daily basis
____ Review reading assignments and lecture notes once a week
____ Begin the last major studying for an exam three or four days before the test
____ Ask the teacher for an overview of the exam
____ Get at least seven hours of sleep each of the three nights before the test
____ Eat nutritious, moderate-sized meals, including breakfast
____ Arrive in class early on exam days
____ View exams as learning experiences rather than "winning or failing situations"
____ Maintain a positive attitude about taking tests

Total your points: _____

To assess your test-taking strategies:
26-30	Excellent
21-25	Good
16-20	Average
11-15	Below Average
10	Poor

■ Apply Effective Techniques in Taking Tests

Certain techniques apply to all types of exams, and certain techniques apply to only certain types of exams.

The two main categories of tests are objective and subjective. *Objective tests* have specific answers that are either right or wrong; they can be marked on a computer score sheet. Common types of objective test questions are true-false, multiple choice, and matching. *Subjective tests* ask questions for which each answer can earn up to a maximum number of points, depending on how the teacher evaluates the answers. Among common subjective tests are sentence completion (fill-in-the-blank), short–answer (includes listing), and essay questions.

Procedures for All Tests

Before you begin a test, do the following:

◗ Label your test. Write your name on the top of each answer sheet.

◗ Read the directions carefully and completely; be sure you know what they mean. If you do not understand them, ask the teacher.

◗ Ask if there is a penalty for guessing. If there is a penalty for incorrect answers, you lose those points. No penalty for guessing means you simply do not get any points for incorrect answers. If there is no penalty, make an educated guess (applying what you know) to eliminate wrong answers or to narrow your choices to possible correct answers. Then guess and write an answer.

⬩ Glance through the test to check on the number of pages, number of questions, and whether the test sheets are printed on both sides so you will not leave any part blank.

As you are taking a test, you likely will maximize your points by applying these tips:

⬩ Compare the number and type of questions to the class period's minutes.

⬩ Estimate the time you should devote to each part, planning more time for questions worth the most points.

⬩ Use your watch to help you budget time and stay on target. You might ask the teacher to announce time intervals.

⬩ On computer score sheets fill in each circle evenly dark so the computer will give you credit for your answer. Do not write notes on the score sheet.

⬩ Answer the questions you know first. Temporarily skip the ones about which you are not sure and for which you will need to use test-taking strategy. Other questions might bring recall. Do not stall on questions during the first pass.

⬩ If two responses come to mind, usually the first response is the better one.

⬩ Do not change an answer unless you are sure a better one should replace it.

⬩ If time remains at the end of the class period, use it to review your work: Was each question answered? Is each answer complete?

⬩ If a question appears tricky, qualify your answer: "True if . . .; False if . . ." or"(B) providing . . .; (D) providing . . ." The teacher might give you credit for demonstrating your knowledge and logic.

True-False Questions

Though each question typically is worth relatively few points, true-false questions can be tricky. Read them carefully; do not read words into a statement that are not there. True statements typically are longer than false statements. In a complex sentence every part must be true for the statement to be true. The following suggestions should help you:

• Circle the words *not* or *except* to help you read the statement carefully.

• Two negatives make a positive: *It is not unlike Ann to . . .* (which means, *It is like Ann to . . .*). Watch for negatives and negative prefixes: *dis-, il-, im-, in-, ir-, non-,* and *un-.*

• Test all qualifiers in a set (options followed by a semicolon or period): *all, most, some, none; always, usually, sometimes, never; more, equal, less; good, bad; is, is not; great, much, little, no.* If the statement of the question has the best qualifier, the answer is "True."

• Words that qualify a statement 100 percent are generally false: *no, never, none, every, always, all, only, entirely, invariably, best.*

• Qualifiers that generally are true: *seldom, sometimes, often, frequently, most, many, few, some, usually, generally, ordinarily.*

Multiple-Choice Questions

Before you begin answering multiple-choice questions, find out if each question is to have only one answer or if it can have more than one answer. Are you to mark all the correct answers? Read the lead part (stem) of the question *with each answer choice*; the right answer is the best match between the lead part and the answer. Cross out the options you eliminate to reduce distractions.

An easy multiple-choice question will have at least one silly answer as an option that quickly can be eliminated. The challenging questions have two or three options from which it is difficult to choose the right answer. The following guidelines should help you:

- Often the long and more inclusive answer is the correct one.

- Circle the words *not* or *except* to attract your attention to reading the statement carefully: Which of the following is *not* an objective type of test?

- When options cover a wide range of dates or values, generally the correct answer is a date or value near the middle.

- When *all of the above* or *none of the above* is the correct answer, the options will appear to be alike. Treat each answer choice as true (or as false) to see which choice is correct.

- Circle absolute words like *all, always, best, every, never, no, none,* and *worst.* Usually you can eliminate the choices with these absolute words.

- A general all-encompassing choice is more likely to be correct than specific statements, especially if exceptions to the specific statements are given.

Matching Test Questions

For matching test questions check the instructions to see if answers can be used more than once. Then glance down both columns to get an overview. Each column may have a different number of items. The following strategy would be efficient and conducive to scoring the most points:

- Start with the left column. Then read the right column. Consider *all choices* before marking your answer.

- Match the items you know first, eliminating choices for the rest of the items.

- Mark out answers with a pencil as you use them.

- If two choices appear correct for one item, circle both choices and draw lines to the one item. Then glance down the column of the circled choices to see if one choice would be the best match for another item.

- Do not guess until you have exhausted your recall of information.

Sentence Completion (Fill-in-the–Blank) and Short-Answer Questions

In writing answers for fill-in-the-blank and short-answer questions, you want to be concise and specific. The more specific your answers, the more points you likely will earn. Use keywords and facts from the textbook, lecture notes, and handouts. The following tips should help you:

- Check what the question is asking you to complete—date, name, country, definition, keyword, and so on. Think before you write.

- Check the length of a line and the number of lines provided for an answer; it might suggest the length of your response: a short blank, a word; a long blank, a phrase; a blank line, a sentence.

- Look for clues: singular versus plural, *a* versus *an* (suggests a word starting with a consonant versus a vowel), and grammar usage (*The goal is* _____ versus *The goals are* _____).

- If you do not understand a question, ask your teacher to clarify it. Should that not be an option, qualify your answer by including your reasoning.

- To guess, apply your common sense and reasoning abilities. Your answer might be given partial credit.

For the following short-answer question you will see why Student J's response earned only 1 out of 6 possible points and Student K's response earned the maximum points. *Question: How do the rate differences of speaking, listening, and writing affect note taking? (6 points)*

Student J's Answer: *Professors speak faster, and we can listen faster than we can write.* The answer lacks specific information on the rate differences and is incomplete (without mention of the effect on note taking). The answer earned 1 point.

Student K's Answer: On material that is easy to understand, we can listen at least 400 WAM. A professor speaks approximately 150 WAM, but a person can write only 40 WAM at best. Notes must be brief and contain only major lecture ideas or points; listening and note taking require mental and physical effort. The answer earned all 6 points because it was correct, specific, and complete; the answer revealed the student's understanding of the concept (rather than rote memory of facts).

Self-Assessment: Assessing the Taking of an Objective Test ✓

True-False Write *True* or *False* for the following statements in the blank provided.

1 A student who prepared well for an exam should not have test anxiety. _____

2 Skipping class will create you added test preparation effort and time. _____

Multiple-Choice Write the letter of the best answer in the blank provided.

3 In preparing for exams,
    a review highlighted textbook reading and lecture notes once a week.
    b ask the teacher what proportion of the test will be essay questions.
    c be aware that a three-hour course requires three to five hours of studying time the last week.
    d both a and b.
    e both b and c. _____

4 An appropriate attitude about test taking is
    a expect to fail, so any grade will be better than what you anticipated.
    b failure on the first test indicates you probably will fail the course.
    c think positively: "I can do it!"
    d both a and b.
    e both b and c. _____

Fill-in-the-Blank Write the best answer to complete the sentence in the blank provided.

5 In taking a test, answer the questions you _____ first.

6 If in reading a test question two responses come to mind, typically the _____ response is the better one.

Matching Write the best match of test type for each description. Each term can be used only once.

7 When options are a wide range of dates, generally the correct date is near the middle. _____ Essay

8 A subjective type of test. _____ Multiple-Choice

9 Each question is worth only a few points. _____ True-False

The answers to the sample objective test can be found at the end of this chapter.

Essay Questions

Each essay question is worth a maximum number of points. In responding, keep in mind that the quality of writing is more important than quantity. Professors usually are looking for specific concepts or points written in a concise manner. Some students write volumes of text in hopes of getting maximum points for the answer. Long responses that do not answer the question or that add more information than the question asks will earn few, if any, points.

Questions beginning with *What? How?* or *Why?* usually can be answered in a short paragraph.

Q: *What is the proper position of a computer in a room with one window?*

A: *To avoid glare on the screen, the computer should be positioned perpendicular to the window. If you are right-handed, you would want the window to your left; if you are left-handed, the window should be to your right.*

Advanced questions incorporate words such as *Analyze, Compare, Contrast, Describe, Evaluate, Explain, Interpret, Summarize,* and *Trace.* The answers require critical thinking and good paragraph organization skills.

Q: *Explain the speech and listening rate differential of a presentation on a familiar subject. How can a person stay "tuned in"? A: Whereas the speaker's rate is 150 WAM, your listening rate is about 400 WAM and your thought rate is 700 WAM. Your writing rate, however, is only 40 WAM. To handle this differential you can anticipate the next point, identify the basic points, review what has been said, and search for the meaning of the message.*

The following terms might be part of an essay question. Review them so you will know how to organize your answer.

Terms Used on Essay Exams

Analyze	Separate into parts to determine the nature of the whole; examine methodically.
Compare	Explain points of similarity and points of difference.
Contrast	Identify the differences when placed side by side.
Criticize/Critique	Analyze and judge; give evidence to approve or disapprove.
Describe	Tell about something with specific details (may be in narrative form).
Discuss	Examine and analyze something by giving the important details (including pros and cons) that are relevant to the issue.
Evaluate	Appraise something by citing advantages and disadvantages or strengths and weaknesses.
Explain	Clarify or interpret something by focusing on "how to do" or "why."
Illustrate	Make something clear by a diagram, example, map, or story.
Interpret	Explain the meaning or significance of something.
Justify	Give logical reasons to prove your point or support your argument.
Prove	Establish that a statement is true by citing convincing facts or logical reasons.
Review	Summarize and comment on the important aspects or statements of a subject, including a criticism or evaluation of it.
Summarize	Give the most important points in brief form.
Trace	Describe the progress or follow the course of events, showing the connection of one event to the next.

General Strategies

Your demonstration of reasoning ability, clarity, critical thinking, and good organization will earn points. To earn the maximum points on essay exams:

- Read the directions and all questions carefully. You might be asked to answer all questions or to choose a certain number (perhaps two out of three) to answer.

- Note how many points each question is worth, and budget your time accordingly.

- Begin answering the easiest questions first.

- If time is running out, outline the remaining parts; you might get partial credit.

- If you have time, review your composition and edit it. Do not leave early, for proofreading and additional editing could add more points to your grade.

Writing Your Essay

Read each question carefully; notice keywords from the textbook or the teacher's lecture. Then make an outline for your answer—organize your thoughts and main points.

- Be direct and specific; avoid meaningless text; use key notes.

- Start with the main (strongest) idea, and give facts to support it.

- Answer completely and number points of a list.

- Use directional words—*first, second; former, latter; compared to; versus.*

- Demonstrate understanding (logic) instead of rote memory (facts).

- Give facts rather than opinions; if your opinion is asked for, support it with facts.

- Make each paragraph support one idea.

- Be sincere and write naturally as if you were speaking to the teacher.

- Incorporate the teacher's often used ideas and phrases.

- Emphasize conclusions, recommendations, and results.

Appearance

Watch your presentation and your mechanics.

- Use an ink pen (perhaps an erasable ink pen), not a pencil.

- Write legibly so your script can be read easily.

- Leave space between questions and in the margins so you can add or edit.

- Apply the correct mechanics of our language: grammar, spelling, punctuation, capitalization, and word usage.

- Be neat in making corrections: draw a line through the text and write above.

Professors are experienced in detecting whether or not students know the answer. Essay exams take a long time to evaluate, so professors are looking for a direct rather than an indirect writing approach.

Take-Home Exam

Take-home exams generally require a more advanced or formal writing style than in-class essay exams. They take more time to prepare because you are expected to do a more professional job of writing—which includes perfect grammar, spelling, capitalization, punctuation, and word usage.

Carefully select material to support your answer. The directions might state a length limit to avoid long answers that talk around a point. The professor is looking for a direct, concise, and specific response upon which to attach points. Being limited to one paragraph or one page generally is more difficult than having to extend a discussion.

Open-Book Test

In open-book tests you are expected to respond to many questions within the short class period. Your success will depend on how quickly you can find the answers in your textbook and class notes.

The first step in preparing for such tests is marking with colored ink and highlighting pens the major facts and concepts in your textbook and class notes. Prepare reference sheets of definitions, important facts, formulas, and major concepts. Number and index your notes so you can find key points quickly. Use sticky notes cut in strips as tabs; attach them to the important pages; label the tabs.

Exercise 1 Writing an Essay Exam

Describe your experiences in writing essay exams. Include the courses, the method(s) of evaluation used by the teacher(s), and your preference—objective versus subjective exams. What were your difficulties or weaknesses in answering essay questions? Which suggestions given in this chapter will you apply to your next essay exam?

_____

_____

_____

_____

_____

_____

_____

_____

■ React Appropriately After a Test

Immediately after a test you need to relax and temporarily get your mind off the test. When the test is returned in class, you can analyze your performance and the strategies you applied. If you did well on the test, continue your good efforts. If your grade is lower than you expected or wanted to earn, face the challenge and seek help promptly. Consider these suggestions as you review your exam results:

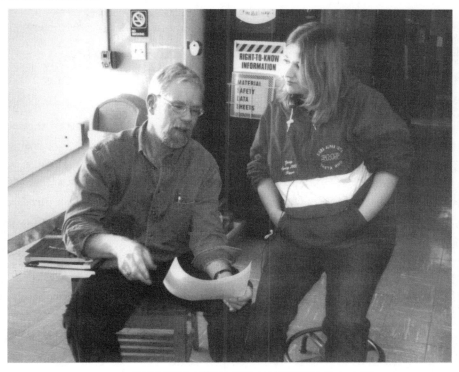

Go over the questions you answered incorrectly. Write the correct answers so you can review and study them for a comprehensive test. Analyze why you did not know the right answers so you can improve. If you feel your answer was correct or did not get enough credit, find that information in your textbook or lecture notes and ask the teacher to reevaluate the answer.

Learn from the experience how you can prepare for future tests. Consider the types of questions asked and the proportion of questions from the teacher's lecture versus the textbook. How similar were the questions to the ones you anticipated (and composed)? Was the information sought on the test broader or more specific than what you studied?

Exercise 2 Designating Teachers' Preference for Student Contact

Access the Teacher Information form in the Personal References section at the end of this text. For each instructor's entry, designate his or her preferred method of contact—by office telephone, e-mail address, or either. If a preference has not been given, ask so you can communicate with him or her in the most appropriate manner. On the form circle or highlight the preference.

Revise your exam preparation procedures. No doubt you will need to make adjustments in your time management schedule, your study skills, and your strategies for taking tests.

Make an appointment to see your teacher and seek help. The sooner you do, the easier it will be to overcome obstacles and the quicker you will be on the way to improving your exam performance. The following steps are recommended:

1   Take your textbook to show your reading and studying pattern.

2   Take your notes to show how you take notes and review them.

3   Begin the conference by saying something positive about the course; be sincere.

4   Explain that you did not do as well on the test as your ability would suggest.

5   Ask the teacher to go over the questions you missed on your test, to look at your textbook reading pattern, and to see your notes from lectures.

6   Explain to the teacher your time and method of studying each week as well as the three or four days before a test.

7   Ask the teacher for suggestions on how you can improve.

8   Confirm your plan of action.

9   Express appreciation for the teacher's time and suggestions for your improvement.

Your honesty and sincerity will be evident to the teacher. If you are willing to put forth effort to improve, you can and you will!

Exercise 3 Getting Help After a Test

For a course in which your test grade was below par, make an appointment to see the professor. Follow the suggestions given for communicating with your professor. Write reactions about the experience. Explain how you feel about your studying and test-taking techniques. What changes will you make the next time you study?

_____

_____

_____

_____

_____

_____

_____

By preparing for tests and applying effective strategies while taking exams, you can reduce test anxiety and maximize your performance. Throughout life you will undergo numerous types of tests—to get a driver's license in a new state (should you move), to be accepted into a graduate college, and to become employed (some companies require an employment test). With test-taking strategies well in mind, you can make the grade.

Solve This Case—How Could Sally Have Done Better?

When the tests were returned in biology class, Sally's heart sunk upon seeing that she had earned only 68 percent. When she left the class that day, Sally felt confident she had done well enough to earn at least a B. She answered the easy questions first and then went back to the beginning. She even finished the exam before about a third of the class.

Thoughts flashed back to the morning of the test. Having studied until 2 AM, she had gotten up at 7 AM to review notes for an hour. With barely enough time to get to class by 9 AM, she would reward herself by having coke and a donut afterwards.

As the professor went over the test results in class, Sally learned that she had not answered the questions on the back of the last page. Points had been taken off for misspelling some terms, which did not seem fair because this is not an English class. For the 20-point essay question, Sally had written a longer paragraph than Frank did. How could he have earned more points than she? The professor must not be fair.

1 What did Sally do right?

2 What are some mistakes Sally made before taking the test?

3 What are some mistakes Sally made while taking the test?

4 What suggestions would you give Sally so she can do better on the next test?

My Reflections Journal

For this journal writing you are invited to share your experiences in taking tests and in reacting to the results. Choose three of the five questions to address, writing one paragraph on each. Using your computer, you may either print the pages and turn them in on paper or e-mail the pages to your instructor. Ask your instructor which method he or she prefers.

1 Describe one of the most difficult exams you have ever taken. Why do you feel it was so difficult?

2 For which type of exam questions do you perform the best? Why?

3 How do you feel about your test preparation techniques for your most difficult course this term? What changes do you plan to make after having studied this chapter?

4 Have you ever observed or been aware of a classmate's cheating on an exam? How did you feel about it?

5 Have you had a conference with any of your instructors this term? If so, please share your thoughts about the experience.

Website Practice Test

On the website at http://www.casadyenterprises.com/collegeedgebook/practicetests.htm you can access a practice test to check on your understanding of the chapter concepts. You may print the results of this self-test to review before taking the respective in-class exam.

Answers to Self-Assessment—Taking an Objective Test: 1 False; 2 True; 3 d; 4 c; 5 know; 6 first; 7 Multiple-Choice; 8 Essay; 9 True-False

MAKING ACADEMIC DECISIONS

Objectives

Upon completing this chapter, you should be able to:

- Refer to the college catalog
- Meet with your advisor
- Decide on a major
- Plan next term's registration
- Maintain a sound academic record

AS A COLLEGE STUDENT, you have many decisions to make about courses, each term's schedule, and your major. The college catalog is both a reference about policies and procedures and an agreement between the institution and the students. It is important to know the rules that guide academic procedures and records, which are administered by the records office.

Professional guidance by your academic advisor can help you take the shortest and smoothest path to graduation. Though the responsibility for reading and following the college catalog is yours, an academic advisor can explain program requirements and answer questions about catalog information. The advisor can lead you toward self-discovery as you plan your future.

Your grades, which are listed term by term, reveal a lot about your personal characteristics and qualifications. For scholarship applications, job applications, and graduate school you will need to submit your academic record. Beginning with the first semester, work hard to maintain a sound academic record. One's grade-point average (GPA) can take a fast tumble, but it rebounds very slowly.

■ Refer to the College Catalog

What is the college catalog's website address?

A college catalog usually begins with an overview of the institution's profile, mission, role, and scope. It describes governance of the college and its basic policies, such as academic freedom, equal employment opportunity, educational accessibility, educational rights and privacy, and public availability of safety reports.

Self-Assessment: Your Understanding of the Catalog ✔

Use your college's catalog to answer each question True or False.

_____ 1 To learn German without fear of a low grade, you would audit the course.

_____ 2 In applying for a job, you would submit a copy of your degree audit.

_____ 3 A cumulative GPA refers to the GPA for all grading periods completed in college including transfer credit.

_____ 4 Should you decide to quit attending class, you should not assume the instructor will drop you from the course.

_____ 5 The highest scholastic honor of a college graduate is Magna Cum Laude.

_____ 6 If an emergency occurs that prevents you from completing the term, you should officially withdraw from college.

_____ 7 Most of the general education courses should be taken in the junior year.

_____ 8 Lower-division courses cannot be taken for credit by seniors.

_____ 9 A comprehensive major typically does not require a minor.

_____10 If you do not pay a library fine or parking ticket, you likely will get a block code or encumbrance code put on your academic record.

Check your answers with the key provided at the end of this chapter. If you answered nine questions correctly, you have a good understanding of your college's catalog.

What is the college's mailing address?

The academic calendar gives important dates of the fall, winter, spring, and summer terms. As you read the following sections, have your college catalog and admission papers handy so you can answer questions that pertain to your college and your academic work. The catalog likely is on your college website. Answers to the questions in the margins can be written on the College Catalog Information form in the Personal References section at the end of this text.

Admission

Your application for college was approved because you have the potential to succeed. The admissions office reviewed your ACT or SAT test scores as well as your high school rank and curriculum. If you did not graduate from high school, you were admitted upon having passed the General Education Development (GED) exam.

To transfer credits from another college, you must have a minimum cumulative grade-point average (GPA) for the courses that are accepted in the transfer. Most colleges will award credit for courses taken through other colleges that are accredited by a regional accrediting agency, but they might limit the number of credits that may be transferred.

Admission to a degree program might have higher requirements than admission to the college or university. Some programs have higher GPA and test score requirements than the minimum required for transfer admission. Examples would be teacher education, business administration, prelaw, and premed programs.

Costs

The costs of a term's enrollment will include the basic tuition fees and student services fees. For tuition, undergraduate students (freshmen, sophomores, juniors, and seniors) might be charged less than graduate students. In state-assisted colleges, the residents of a state generally are charged less than nonresidents.

Student services fees typically include fees for computer usage, health center visits, and student activities. Costs might vary according to the number of credit hours carried. Having paid those fees, you probably will use many of the respective services and will appreciate their availability. For most services, students get a better rate than what the general public would pay.

If you live in a residence hall, you have room and board costs. Because building features vary, each residence hall may have its own fee schedule. Additional costs might be involved in renting a refrigerator or microwave oven. Telephone installation and usage as well as parking lot usage could be added costs. Meal plans vary in cost when more than one option is offered.

Books and supplies will be substantial costs. Additional fees are assessed for certain courses to cover special supplies, equipment, or services that are in addition to regular instructional expenses.

Charges typically are assessed for late registration and replacement of an ID card. If you drop a course or withdraw from college, you will get a partial refund if you have paid all fees and have followed proper drop or withdrawal procedures. The amount of refund depends on the date of the action—day 1, days 2–10, and so forth.

What is the cost of your tuition per credit hour?

What student services fees do you pay?

What services do the fees cover?

Where do you go to pay tuition and fees?

Financial Assistance

Financial aid enables students to get money through scholarships, awards, loans, grants, work-study programs, and short-term loans. Both federal and state financial aid programs are available to public institutions. Most federal financial aid programs are based on need (the cost of attending college minus your contribution and that of your parents). Your financial aid office, which administers these programs, can explain the procedures to obtain financial support.

Student Rights and Responsibilities

Higher education aims to provide an environment in which you and others may develop as effective citizens and productive members of society. Freedom of expression and inquiry is essential. The college or university is responsible for providing quality instruction, developing high standards of achievement, and providing an atmosphere for self-expression and growth. You are expected to develop critical thinking skills and to engage in the independent search for truth.

Students are expected to be responsible members of the campus community. You are held accountable to the standards of conduct, academic integrity expectations, and college or university

rules printed in the catalog and accessed on the Internet (by campus web address). Carefully review the sections on students' rights and responsibilities as well as on academic dishonesty.

The college or university reserves the right to discipline or dismiss any student who fails to maintain its standards. Procedures are in place for handling class disruption, academic grievances, grade appeals, and academic dishonesty (such as cheating or plagiarism). The college or university judicial system ensures due process for faculty and students. You should take the initiative to study the rules and procedures of your campus. "No one told me" is not a valid excuse.

Academic Regulations

To maintain a sound academic record, you must know the following procedures and terminology of your college, which are described in the catalog:

Where can you get a transcript? Is a fee charged?

Academic Record (Transcript) A *transcript* is a record (permanently maintained by the college) that includes a list of courses in which you were enrolled as well as the credits and grades earned in those courses.

Academic Status Check your catalog to compare these academic status definitions:

- *Good Standing*–A student with a satisfactory cumulative grade-point average (GPA).

What is the minimum GPA required to be in good standing?

- *Probation*–Scholastic probation reminds students that their cumulative GPA is unsatisfactory. They might be required to reduce the number of credits carried, reduce their employment hours, and forego participation in certain activities.

What is the lowest GPA allowed before being suspended?

- *Suspension*–A freshman who fails to make a certain GPA or better in a term or session will be suspended (not allowed to enroll the next term), unless the college dean declares an exception based on the circumstances. At your school the policy might be the same for sophomores and juniors.

- *Reinstatement*–A student suspended for academic reasons for the first time is eligible to apply for reinstatement after remaining out of school for a minimum of one or two terms.

Auditing a Class Auditing a class allows you to attend and participate in a course but not receive credit for it.

Change of Schedule (Add/Drop) Check the academic calendar and procedures (where you go, what it costs, if money is refunded) to change your schedule:
- Prior to the beginning of classes
- During the change of schedule period at the beginning of the term
- After the change of schedule period

What is the last date to·drop a class without having to get the instructor's grade—the no-penalty drop date?

Classification You are classified according to the number of credit hours earned. For example, on a semester system at some colleges: freshmen, 0–29; sophomores, 30–59; juniors, 60–89; seniors, 90+ credit hours.

What is sophomore classification (number of credit hours to have earned) at your college?

Degree/Graduation Audit A degree/graduation audit is a report of some colleges that matches completed, in-progress, and registered courses with courses required on a specified degree program. The degree audit lists what is needed to complete the requirements.

Degree Program A degree program consists of a major and a minor or a comprehensive major (for which no minor is required) and the applicable requirements associated with the degree. You might need to be admitted to a degree program before completing a certain number of credit hours.

Encumbrances (Blocks) At some colleges an encumbrance or block code is placed on a student's record for reasons such as an unpaid bill or fine (for example, parking fines), failure to return books or equipment, and failure to be admitted into a degree program within the specified time limit. Encumbrances can prevent a student from registering for upcoming terms and might prevent the release of one's transcript.

Full-Time Student Knowing the minimum hours that qualify you as a full-time student is important. Dropping below that number can affect your financial aid and insurance premiums.

What is full-time status at your college during a regular term? during the summer?

Grade-Point Average (GPA) The term GPA refers to the GPA for any given grading period (term—semester, quarter, or trimester). A *cumulative GPA* refers to the GPA for all grading periods completed at the college or university; grades for transfer credits are not included in the calculation. A *combined GPA* includes transfer credits as well as those completed at the college or university.

Grade Reevaluation If you feel the instructor made an error in computing your grade, you should contact him or her within a time limit following the term in which the grade was assigned. Though the catalog might state a time limit, the earlier you make the appeal, the better; a suggestion would be within two weeks. Upon reviewing the grade computations, the instructor who sees an error can request a grade change; usually a short explanation is required. The responsibility for your grade remains with the faculty member. If your contact with the instructor does not result in your favor, you could appeal the decision. The chain of command after having met with the instructor is in this order: the department head, the dean, an appeals committee, and the vice president of academic affairs.

Grade Reports At the end of the term, grade reports are sent to your permanent address or are available online. Midterm grades usually are sent to students who are in their first term of enrollment, to those on scholastic probation, and perhaps to transfer students. Grade reports might be sent to academic advisors, coaches, and parents.

Who receives a midterm grade report at your college?

Grading and the Credit Point System Letter grades represent point values per credit hour. Grading scales vary among colleges. An A might be worth 12.0 points, 10.0 points, 7.0 points, or 4.0 points, depending on the college. Some schools use A+, A, A-, B+, B, B-, and so forth. In the accompanying illustration, an A is equal to 4.00 points.

A (4) =	Excellent work
B (3) =	Above average work
C (2) =	Average/satisfactory work
D (1) =	Below average/minimum passing work
F (0) =	Unacceptable work/failing/no credit
DP or N (0) =	Indicates course was dropped without penalty
P or S (0) =	Passing work; course was taken under the **pass/not pass** or **satisfactory/unsatisfactory** system
NP or US (0) =	Not passing; course was taken under the **pass/not pass** or **satisfactory/unsatisfactory** system
I (0) =	Incomplete; a small portion of the course has not been completed
A or V (0) =	Student was enrolled in and attended the course as an auditor

Instructor Drop In many colleges, if you do not attend a class by its second or third meeting and have not informed either the instructor or the departmental office, the instructor may drop you from the class. On the other hand, not attending the course later on does not automatically drop you from the course.

Overload Permission The maximum credit hour load is designated for each regular term and summer session. To enroll in more credit hours than the maximum allowed, you must get permission, typically from the dean's office.

Pass/Not Pass (Credit/No Credit or Satisfactory/Unsatisfactory) Regulations The purpose of having this option (identified many different ways) is to give you an opportunity to pursue outside interests without penalty or reduction of GPA.

Prerequisites You are responsible for having taken certain courses or having met certain conditions prior to enrollment in a course. If you have not fulfilled these prerequisites, the respective academic department may cancel your registration for the course before (or even after) classes begin.

Repeat Policy In some colleges you may repeat courses in which you earned a D or F grade to improve your GPA. Read the conditions in your catalog so you will know how the D or F grade would appear on your transcript and how your grades would be averaged. Repeating a course the second time in which an F was earned could result in an average of the three grades. For example: F, F, and B = 3÷3 = 1 or a D.

Scholastic Honors Your catalog specifies the minimum number of credit hours that must be completed at your college and how transfer credit hours are averaged. Students who earn high GPAs in completing the bachelor's degree are given special distinction. An example:

Graduating with Scholastic Honor

GPA	Scholastic Honor
3.90-4.00	Summa Cum Laude
3.75-3.89	Magna Cum Laude
3.40-3.74	Cum Laude

Other minimum requirements are the completion of 60 credit hours at the institution, a GPA of 3.40 or better at the institution, and a combined (institution and transfer) average of 3.40 or better.

Withdrawal Procedures If an emergency occurs that prevents you from completing the term, follow the withdrawal procedures (dropping *all* courses). Typically, a written request must be addressed to the records office. If a student who quits attending classes does not withdraw, all the courses will be graded an F at the end of the term. Withdrawal will affect grades, refunds, financial aid, residence hall contract, veterans benefits, parking permits, meal plan refund, and returning to the college or university.

What are the withdrawal procedures of your college?

What are the minimum credit hours required to earn a bachelor's degree?

What is the minimum overall GPA required?

Undergraduate Degrees and Requirements

The catalog identifies the academic structure–including colleges, schools, divisions, and departments–as well as the degrees (undergraduate and graduate) offered. To earn an undergraduate degree, you must meet certain requirements (see Figure 1). Refer to the catalog for graduation requirements—including minimum credit hours and overall GPA.

Figure 1—Graduation Requirements

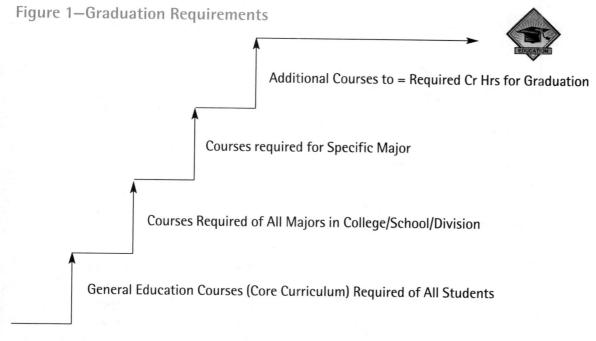

Additional Courses to = Required Cr Hrs for Graduation

Courses required for Specific Major

Courses Required of All Majors in College/School/Division

General Education Courses (Core Curriculum) Required of All Students

General Education (Core Curriculum)

At many colleges the foundation for advanced study is the general education (core curriculum) component, which is required of all degree-seeking students. The aim of general education is to develop decision making that leads to thoughtful, creative, and productive lives as well as to responsible citizenship. Most of the general education courses are to be completed during the first two years of college. Typically, the minimum cumulative GPA required is a C, and courses may not be taken on a pass/not pass or satisfactory/unsatisfactory basis.

General education courses usually include communications (public speaking or interpersonal communication), English, algebra, physical education, American history, natural sciences (biology, chemistry, geography, geology, physics, astronomy), social sciences (anthropology, economics, political science, psychology, sociology), and humanities (art, dance, modern and classical languages, history, literature, music, philosophy, religion, theater).

The college success course is a general education requirement on many campuses. According to research conducted in 2002 by Betsy Barefoot, Policy Center on the First Year of College, over 90 percent of the regionally accredited colleges and universities offer a special course for first-year students.

Description of Course Listings

Courses are numbered in a hierarchy beginning with developmental courses and moving up to lower-division, upper-division, and graduate courses. In the accompanying box, fill in your college's course numbering system.

COURSE NUMBERING SYSTEM

Numbers	Category Description
_____	Background/developmental
_____	Lower division—primarily for but not limited to freshmen
_____	Lower division—primarily for but not limited to sophomores
_____	Upper division—primarily for but not limited to juniors
_____	Upper division—primarily for but not limited to seniors
_____	Upper division—primarily for seniors and graduate students
_____	Graduate courses open only to graduate students

Each college, school, or division describes its major programs, minor programs, and course offerings. The office location, phone number, department head, and faculty are identified. Faculty are listed by rank order–beginning with the highest rank, professor. Next are associate professors, then assistant professors, and last the instructors. Retired professors who were awarded the distinction *emeritus professor* also are listed.

Courses might be identified by course prefix, course number, course title, credit hours (lecture versus lab), and course periodicity (terms offered). Figure 2 shows an example that represents some colleges.

Figure 2—Course Identification

MGT 286 Business Communication. 3(3-0) F,S. Prerequisites: ENG 110. Managerial business communication theory and practice that includes speaking to large groups, interacting within small groups, improving listening skills, composing messages, writing reports based on library research, making ethical decisions, and communicating with other cultures and nationalities.

MGT—*course prefix*
286—*course number*
Business Communication—*course title*
3—*credit hours*
(3-0)—*3 lecture hours; 0 lab hours*
F,S—*offered in the fall and spring terms*

Facts About Faculty and Administrators

To learn basic facts about your teachers, check the back of the catalog. For each ranked faculty member, you will find the year he or she came to your college, the teacher's rank, the institutions from which the teacher earned degrees, and the respective dates the degrees were conferred.

Exercise 1 Referring to Your College Catalog

Refer to your college catalog to answer the questions in the margins of this section of the chapter. Write your answers on the College Catalog Information form in the Personal References section at the end of this text.

■ Meet with Your Advisor

Your academic advisor, who is a member of the faculty or professional staff, works with you individually. Together you may discuss the benefits of higher education, your goals, and your responsibilities in pursuing a degree. Although some academic advisors only prescribe, ideally you and the academic advisor are partners. Responsibility is shared between the two of you with the advisor guiding you toward self-discovery while allowing you to do the planning of your education.

Who is your academic advisor?
How can you reach him or her?

If you have a declared major, you will receive advice from the respective department or a centralized advisement center for that specific area. Examples might be business, education, and psychology. If you are undecided about a major, your academic advisor will be assigned through the general academic advisement center.

Characteristics of a Good Advisor

A good academic advisor helps you learn about courses and programs of interest to you. He or she helps you identify options and weigh results when you are faced with difficult decisions. The advisor also tells you where to learn about policies and helps you see how they apply to you. With information on your grades and test scores, the advisor guides you in setting realistic goals and suggests steps you can take to decide on a major. Knowing your interests and abilities, the advisor helps you select courses. He or she reviews your academic progress through records on file and informs you about deadlines. Since the advisor realizes your personal and social life are integral to your academic life, he or she might inform you about respective workshops and seminars to consider.

Most students prefer to be partners in the advising process rather than recipients of advice. They want the freedom to make choices. When the advisor and you share responsibility for academic advisement, sessions likely will take longer than half an hour.

Responsibilities of Your Advisor

You can expect your advisor to be available during posted office hours. An atmosphere of openness and caring will facilitate meaningful communication, confidence, and trust. You will appreciate having help in defining realistic educational plans and career goals that are consistent with your abilities and interests.

Your academic advisor can be expected to monitor your progress and maintain a file to document that progress. You can also ask him or her to interpret policies, procedures, and requirements. All the academic transactions of freshmen (including course schedule and course changes–drops and adds) need to be approved and signed by your advisor, since he or she knows about departments' requirements and graduation requirements. Since the advisor also understands the school's bureaucracy, he or she can cut through days of red tape for you. Finally, an advisor will refer you to other professionals and special services for personal problems and remedial help.

Your Responsibilities as Advisee

To participate in the advising process, you should assess yourself, keep records of your progress, be prepared to meet with your advisor, and follow through with suggestions. You can establish and maintain effective communication as well as a good relationship with your academic advisor by following these tips:

Preparing to Meet with Advisor

- Make the appointment with your advisor–keep it and be on time.
- If unable to keep the appointment, call the advisor ahead of time.
- Be knowledgeable about the catalog and class schedule book or website.
- Bring the catalog, class schedule book, and your academic records to the appointment.
- Be prepared to ask intelligent questions about your degree program.
- Make a list of questions to ask your advisor.

Participating During the Appointment

- Discuss your long-range goals.
- Discuss your choice of major.
- Make final decisions about academic choices.
- Clarify your values, abilities, interests, and goals.

Following Through After the Appointment

- Keep the advisor informed of changes in schedules or change of major.
- Follow through on actions discussed at the advising session.
- Accept responsibility for your academic choices and decisions.

Plan to visit with your academic advisor more often than just one visit per term to prepare for registration. You and your advisor can function better as a team if you keep him or her aware of your academic progress and challenges.

Advisor Dilemmas

You want an academic advisor with whom you feel comfortable and confident. If you have difficulty talking with your advisor, try to take some initiatives during the conversation; he or she might be undergoing undo stress that is not related to your visit. If after several appointments and attempts to improve the relationship you still are dissatisfied, you can initiate a change of advisors. You simply go to the department secretary of the respective advisement center and ask, "Would it be possible for me to get a new advisor?" You do not need to give reasons.

For a few majors there might not be a choice of academic advisors, because only one is available. In that event if your situation is serious, see the department head.

Exercise 2 Meeting with Your Academic Advisor

On the Academic Advisor sheet in the Personal References section at the end of this text, review the following information about your academic advisor: *name, professional title, department, office location, office hours, phone number, e-mail address.*

Meeting with your academic advisor is an opportunity to practice your communication skills. *Prepare a list of topics or questions,* and consider e-mailing the list to your advisor prior to your meeting.

Record the dates of appointments, and briefly describe the discussion and resulting action after each of your meetings. File this sheet in your Degree Progress file folder.

■ Decide on a Major

Deciding on a major involves studying career options that are compatible with your abilities, values, interests, and personality. You will participate in that process soon. Meanwhile, consider these ideas before you register for the next term:

▶ To explore "What Can I Do with a Major in. . .?, access this web site: http://www.uncwil.edu/stuaff/career/Majors

▶ Take classes that will expose you to a number of majors. A variety of courses are offered to fulfill the general education requirements; be selective in your choice.

▶ Acquaint yourself with resources and services on campus to learn more about yourself and about career options.

▶ Begin to recognize areas that are of special interest to you, the courses you like best, and the courses in which you get the best grades.

▶ Identify your abilities and begin to narrow your choices.

If you have not declared a major, try to do so in your sophomore year. By then you will have had a variety of courses and may have had a career paper or unit in a course. As a sophomore, you will be completing most of the general education requirements and will be ready to begin more advanced and specific courses.

Exercise 3 Deciding on a Major

At a campus majors fair or by individual office visits, obtain information from two or three different departments. Take this opportunity to ask questions and communicate with professors about possible majors. Included in your questions might be the following:

1 What majors do you offer? Is each a comprehensive or a regular major? Which minors are recommended for a regular major?

2 What are the GPA requirements of each?

3 Which general education courses are required for each major?

4 Which core courses have to be completed before admission to the program?

5 What are examples of career opportunities? Salary range?

6 Is a master's degree necessary to be competitive in this field?

7 How can students enhance their marketability with this major?

8 How do employment opportunities in this region compare with those in other parts of the nation?

■ Plan Next Term's Registration

As soon as next term's class schedule is available, start planning your schedule and make an appointment with your advisor. Then he or she will have ample time to work with you, and you will avoid the problem of classes closing and the last-minute rush of students waiting in line for help.

Where do you go to register for classes?

Getting Ready for Advising Appointment

Be prepared and well organized. The following tips might help:

1   If you have transfer credits from another college or university, check with the records office to see if they have been evaluated. Get a copy of your academic summary (computer printout of courses completed and in progress) from the records office or by accessing your information on the college website.

2   Review and bring your catalog, class schedule book, and academic records.

3   Make a list of questions to ask and items of concern to discuss with your advisor.

4   Before seeing your advisor make two tentative (a) lists of class choices and (b) schedules of classes for next term. Check the prerequisites.

5   Check the college website to see whether your chosen classes are still open.

6   Order a degree audit.

7   Check to see if you have any encumbrances.

8   Check on your designated registration date and time.

9   Make a tentative list of potential courses for the next three terms. Considering time management, outline a realistic and well-balanced course load.

Planning an Efficient Schedule

If you register toward the end of the registration period, you probably will not have many choices of courses and section times. Assuming you have choices, consider these suggestions for drawing up an efficient schedule:

▶   Avoid blocking more than two courses back to back. Three consecutive classes can be very stressful, particularly if their tests fall on the same day.

▶   Avoid scheduling too many intermittent one-hour breaks—class, hour break, class, hour break, class. A few one-hour breaks throughout the day can give you time to review notes, run errands, and eat. But too many one-hour breaks are disruptive to efficient time management.

▶   Balance your schedule with a variety of course types—perhaps math, music, physical education, English, and history—so you do not have too heavy reading, too heavy science, or too heavy writing to accomplish.

▶   Schedule some classes for Monday, Wednesday, and Friday (MWF) and some classes for Tuesday and Thursday (TR). If all courses meet on MWF or on TR, you would have extra stress and test anxiety from the imbalance.

▶   Consider the courses in which you might need special help. You might need extra time for studying and tutorial assistance.

Selecting General Education Courses

In fulfilling your general education requirements, you probably have a variety of subject areas as well as courses within an area from which to choose. In selecting general education courses, you might look for a course that:

- Is in a subject you have studied before and know you will like
- You know nothing about and would like to explore
- Helps you develop one of your strengths
- Helps you improve one of your weaknesses
- Teaches you about our culture—history, literature, art, music, theater, geography
- Teaches you about social problems—economics, interdisciplinary studies, sociology
- Is an introductory course for a major you are considering
- Helps you understand yourself—philosophy, psychology, religious studies, sociology
- Helps you understand the physical world—geology, biology, chemistry, physics
- Helps you lead a healthier life—biomedical sciences, physical education, psychology
- Examines major institutions of our society—agriculture, economics, political science
- Improves your communication skills—English, communication, modern and classical languages

Exercise 4 Preparing for Future Terms

1 On a sheet of paper, list the courses you will have completed by the end of this term. Photocopy the form Planning for Future Terms that follows (Figure 3), and make a tentative list of potential courses for the next three terms (and summers); include credit hours.

2 Using the forms supplied by your college website, make two tentative class schedules for next term.

3 Take these sheets to your academic advisor at the next appointment. File them in your Degree Progress folder.

Figure 3—Planning Future Terms

Term _____   Year_____

COURSE CODE	NAME OF COURSE	CREDITS
_____	_____	_____
_____	_____	_____
_____	_____	_____
_____	_____	_____
_____	_____	_____
_____	_____	_____

Term _____   Year_____

COURSE CODE	NAME OF COURSE	CREDITS
_____	_____	_____
_____	_____	_____
_____	_____	_____
_____	_____	_____
_____	_____	_____
_____	_____	_____

Term _____   Year_____

COURSE CODE	NAME OF COURSE	CREDITS
_____	_____	_____
_____	_____	_____
_____	_____	_____
_____	_____	_____
_____	_____	_____
_____	_____	_____

Your academic advisor is important in guiding you toward self-discovery in determining and reaching your goals. Advisors devote time and interest in helping their advisees. In the desire to maintain positive communication with your academic advisor, be sure to express appreciation.

Exercise 5 Expressing Appreciation to Your Academic Advisor

Write a thank-you letter to your academic advisor. Be specific in describing how he or she has helped you, and express appreciation for what it means to have professional guidance in achieving your academic goals. Remember to sign your letter before mailing it.

■ Maintain a Sound Academic Record

Your academic record, permanently filed at the records office, will be required various times throughout your life. Which of the following examples would you want on file?

In the *Academic Summary* (Figure 4) you see a good student whose course work has been consistent—with an overall B average. The student never dropped a course and never skipped a regular college term.

In the copy of a *Transcript* (Figure 5) the student's performance has been inconsistent. Having earned a cumulative GPA of 3.00 and 3.34 the first two semesters, the student has ability to do at least B work. The N's sprinkled throughout the record indicate the student could have missed classes, done poorly on assignments and exams, and then dropped the course to avoid a low grade. Few employers would risk hiring this student.

How to Figure GPA

A term's GPA is figured as shown in this example, for which the grading scale is A = 4.0:

Credits	x	Grade	=	Points
3		A=4		12
3		C=2		6
3		B=3		9
3		C=2		6
1		A=4		4
13				37

37 points ÷ 13 credits = 2.85 GPA

Midterm grades help you the face reality of your performance. If your grades could be better, you still have a chance to bring up your average by the end of the term. If you have any D's or F's on your midterm grade sheet, see the instructor promptly. Upon finding out what is required to bring up your grade, decide if you can do so. If not, see if you can drop the course. If you drop the course after the deadline, the instructor must record a grade—probably a D or F.

Figure 4—Academic Summary

```
PRINTED                      STATE UNIVERSITY                              PAGE 1
03/12/04              RECORDS AND REGISTRATION                    CAMPUS USE ONLY
                      STUDENT ACADEMIC SUMMARY


NAME: ███████████████████    SOC SEC NO: ████████████    REC STATUS:  E


FORMERLY: ██████████████████████        DATE OF BIRTH: ██████████████


CLASS:  SOPHOMORE    ADVISOR CODE:  K144        SEMESTER/YEAR OF APPLICATION:  FA 02

EXAM ID: A    EXAM YEAR: 01        SCORES:  22  19  19  21  20     HIGH SCHOOL RANK:  64

DEPT 1 MAJ: MKRM2       DEPT 2 MAJ:     MINOR:        DEG PROG:  D      GRAD SR:

SCH ACT:        ENCUMBR:         ATH CODE:         VA CODE:      FA CODE:  RES:  096

SMS TOT HRS: 45     SMS ATT HRS: 45      SMS GR PTS: 138    SMS GPS: 3.07     PTS DEF: 0
 TR TOT HRS:  0      TR ATT HRS:  0       TR GR PTS:   0     TR GPA: 0.00     PTS DEF: 0
CMB TOT HRS: 45     CMB ATT HRS: 45      CMB GR PTS: 138    CMB GPA: 3.07     PTS DEF: 0
HRS P/NP:  0
```

SEM/YEAR	CR CD	CRS NUM	TITLE	CR	GR	CM	LOC
FA 02	COM	115	FUND/PUBLIC SPEAKG	3	B		
	DAN	180	INTRO TO THE DANCE	3	B		
	ENG	111	COMPOSITION	3	B		
	IDS	110	INTRO TO UNIV LIFE	1	B		
	MTH	135	COLLEGE ALGEBRA	3	B		
	PSY	121	INTRO PSYCHOLOGY	3	B		
			SEM CREDIT	16			
			CUM TOT: 16 16 16 48 3.00				
SP 03	AST	115	BASIC ASTRONOMY	5	B		
	ENG	120	COMPOSITION	3	A		
	GRY	100	WORLD REG GEOGRAPHY	3	A		
	PLS	101	AM GOV 1/ORG/FUNC	3	B		
	PLS	001	SENATE BILL #4 MET	0			
			SEM CREDIT	14			
			CUM TOT: 30 30 30 96 3.20				
FA 03	CIS	121	INFO COMP INFO SY	3	B		
	ECO	155	PRIN MACROECONOMIC	3	C		
	FGB	135	INTRO TO BUSINESS	3	C		
	MUS	241	INTRO TO MUSIC	3	A		
	RIL	231	LEGAL ENV/BUSINESS	3	B		
			SEM CREDIT	15			
			CUM TOT: 45 45 45 138 3.07				
SP 04	ACC	201	INT FINANCIAL ACCT	3	IP		
	CHM	107	CHEM FOR CITIZEN	4	IP		
	IDS	280	STUDENT/LIFE LEAD	1	IP		
	MGT	286	BUS COMMUNICATIONS	3	IP		
	PED	100	FITNESS FOR LIVING	2	IP		
			SEM CREDIT	13			

```
* * * CONTINUED ON NEXT PAGE -----        DO NOT RELEASE TO THIRD PARTY * * *
```

Figure 5—Transcript

STATE UNIVERSITY

NAME: ▮▮▮▮▮▮▮▮▮▮   STUDENT NO: ▮▮▮▮▮▮▮▮▮▮ 1 OF 1

DATE OF BIRTH: ▮▮▮▮▮▮   FORMER NAME: ▮▮▮▮▮▮

L	COURSE CODE	COURSE NO.	COURSE TITLE	CR	GR
TR	01		SAINT LOUIS UNIVERSITY MO		
			SEM HRS: 3		
TR	01		SAINT LOUIS UNIVERSITY MO		
			SEM HRS: 3		
FA	01				
	GRY	140	ELEMENT/EARTH SCIG	2	B
	AOS	109	INTRO TO THE DANCE	3	B
	IDS	110	COMPOSITION	1	P
	ENG	111	INTRO TO UNIV LIFE	3	B
	BIO	102	COLLEGE ALGEBRA	4	B
	MTH	3	INTRO PSYCHOLOGY	3	B
TOT HRS: 22			SEM HRS: 16 CUM GPA: 3.00		
TR	01		ST LOUIS COMM COLL-MERAMEC		
			SEM HRS: 3		
SP	02				
	MTH	145	CONTEMPORARY MATH	3	B
	AOS	190	INTRO/MICRO APPLIC	3	A
	ENG	120	COMPOSITION	3	A
	PED	100	FITNESS FOR LIVING	2	A
	COM	115	FUND/PUBLIC SPEAKING	3	A
	PLS	101	AM GOV I/ORG/FUNC	3	B
	PLS	001	SENATE BILL #4 MET	0	
TOT HRS: 42			SEM HRS: 17 CUM GPA: 3.34		
FA	02				
	ART	100	TWO DIMENS DESIGN	3	A
	GRY	100	WORLD REG GEOGRAPHY	3	B
	HST	122	HIST OF US 1877-PR	3	N
	MUS	241	INTRO TO MUSIC	3	A
	PSY	121	INTRO PSYCHOLOGY	3	A
TOT HRS: 54			SEM HRS: 12 CUM GPA: 3.45		
SP	03				
	ART	101	THREE DIMEN DESIGN	3	D R
	ART	115	DRAWING 1	3	C
	HST	122	HIST OF US 1877-PR	3	F R
	PHI	110	INTRO TO PHILOSOPHY	3	N
	PED	147	BEGINNING JUDO	1	B
TOT HRS: 61			SEM HRS: 7 CUM GPA: 3.04		
			* * CONTINUED **		

L	COURSE CODE	COURSE NO.	COURSE TITLE	CR	GR
FA	03				
	ART	215	DRAWING II	3	C
	ART	235	SCULPTURE I	3	B
	ART	255	PHOTOGRAPHY I	3	A
	ART	212	CERAMICS I	3	A
TOT HRS: 73			SEM HRS: 12 CUM GPA: 3.08		
SP	04				
	ART	101	THREE DIMEN DESIGN	3	B RD
	ART	223	METALS/JEWELRY I	3	B
	ART	355	PHOTOGRAPHY II	3	B
	ART	357	PHOTOSHOP	3	C
TOT HRS: 82			SEM HRS: 12 CUM GPA: 3.11		
FA	04				
	ART	354	PHOTO METH/MATRLS	3	A
	ART	371	HST/WESTERN ART I	3	N
	HST	122	HIST US SINCE 1877	3	C RF
	ENG	351	SURVY OF AM LIT II	3	N
TOT HRS: 88			SEM HRS: 6 CUM GPA: 3.22		
			* * END OF RECORD * *		

DATE ISSUED: 12/28/2004
TRANSCRIPT PREPARED FOR:

COLUMBIA COLLEGE
ADMISSIONS
600 S MICHIGAN AVE
CHICAGO   IL   60605

State University
Official Record
RAISED SEAL NOT REQUIRED

Director of Records and Registration

The name of the university is printed in maroon across the face
of the transcript. The word copy appears when photocopied.
Copies and transcripts issued to the student should not be
accepted as an official institutional document.

DO NOT RELEASE TO A THIRD PARTY WITHOUT WRITTEN CONSENT OF THE STUDENT

Exercise 6 Deciding About Dropping a Course

Assume you are having difficulty in college algebra, one of your general education requirements. College Algebra is a prerequisite to courses in sequence in the basic core of your major that you need to take next year—one in the fall and one in the spring. Include in your response the answers to the following questions:

1 Under what conditions would you decide not to drop the course?

2 What conditions would cause you to drop the course?

3 If you drop the course, what could you do to get back on track for next year's schedule?

_____

_____

_____

_____

College success is enhanced by an understanding of the college catalog and by a positive relationship with an academic advisor who is a partner in educational discovery. Responsible students welcome opportunities to research departmental offerings as they decide on a major. They carefully plan ahead for each term's registration and diligently work to maintain a sound academic record.

Solve This Case—David's Academic Advisement Dilemma

David had registered for five courses during the registration period but had not paid the minimum amount to hold his registration. The day before classes were to begin, David went to his advisor and explained that he had been dropped from his classes when he didn't pay. Upon paying the registration fees, he discovered many of the classes he wanted were closed. He asked the advisor to get him registered into the same five courses.

The academic advisor helped David get registered for five courses, but two courses (though they applied to general education requirements) were not his choice. No more than two courses were back to back; several one-hour breaks were part of the Tuesday/Thursday schedule. The advisor explained that was the best schedule possible at such a late date.

At the end of the term David earned a D in one of the two courses and an F in the other; his term GPA was 1.65. David went to his academic advisor and complained, "The reason I did poorly is because I took those two courses you recommended but I did not want. You have my ACT and placement test scores. Why did you make me take those two courses?"

1 What is David's main shortcoming?

2 Describe three ways by which David demonstrated irresponsible behavior.

3 Does the dislike of a course give a valid excuse for poor performance?

My Reflections Journal

In expressing your thoughts about academic life, choose three of the following five questions and write one paragraph about each. Using your computer, you may either print the pages and turn them in on paper or e-mail the pages to your instructor. Ask your instructor which method he or she prefers.

1 How do you feel about your academic work? Which courses do you enjoy the most? Which courses are most challenging?

2 Have you made any changes in deciding about a major? What led to your making this change?

3 Have you met with your academic advisor recently? How would you describe your relationship with your academic advisor?

4 How does your family feel about your college work and the choices you have made?

5 What is the best academic experience you have had this week? Why?

Website Practice Test

On the website at http://www.casadyenterprises.com/collegeedgebook/practicetests.htm you can access a practice test to check on your understanding of the chapter concepts. You may print the results of this self-test to review before taking the respective in-class exam.

Key to Assessing Your Understanding of the Catalog: 1 True, 2 False, 3 False, 4 True, 5 False, 6 True, 7 False, 8 False, 9 True, 10 True

Causes of Stress in College

Death of spouse (1st position)	*Loss of financial support for college*
Female in unwed pregnancy	*Failure of important or required course*
Death of parent	*Sexual difficulties*
Male in unwed pregnancy	*Serious argument with significant other*
Divorce	*Academic probation*
Death of close family member	*Change of major*
Death of close friend	*New love interest or relationship*
Divorce between parents	*Increased workload in college*
Jail term	*Outstanding personal achievement*
Major personal injury or illness	*First term in college*
Flunking out of college	*Serious conflict with teacher*
Marriage	*Lower grades than expected*
Being fired from job	*(25th position)*

The causes of stress in your life might be among those commonly experienced by college students, or they might be unique. Regardless, you want to measure your vulnerability to stress. Then you can modify conditions to reduce the likelihood of stress. An exam is not stressful in itself; the way you approach the exam determines how much stress you will experience.

Self-Assessment: Assessing Vulnerability to Stress ✔

In this exercise you will increase awareness of the factors that contribute to your stress. Rate each item according to how much of the time each statement applies to you:

     1 (never)   2 (seldom)   3 (sometimes)   4 (usually)   5 (always)

____   1   I meet deadlines without undue pressure and worry.

____   2   I get at least seven hours of sleep a night.

____   3   I receive affection, encouragement, and help from my family.

____   4   I do not worry about meeting unrealistic and high expectations of my academic performance by my family or a scholarship (requiring a high minimal GPA).

____   5   I exercise 20-60 minutes three to five times a week.

____   6   I refrain from smoking daily. (If you have never smoked, write 5.)

____   7   I refrain from consuming one alcoholic beverage a day. (If you do not drink, write 5.)

____   8   My personal relationships are positive without difficult challenges.

____   9   Financial resources adequately meet my basic expenses.

____ 10   I get strength from my religious beliefs and spiritual experiences.

____ 11   I attend and participate in a campus activity or student organization each week.

____ 12   I eat three balanced and nutritious meals a day.

_____ 13 I have one or more friends with whom to share successes and discuss problems.

_____ 14 My physical health is good—free of headaches, backache, acne, mouth sores, nervousness, indigestion, ulcers, colds, or flu.

_____ 15 My housing and living mate(s) are pleasant and supportive of my college life.

_____ 16 I speak openly with my living mate(s) when domestic issues or problems occur.

_____ 17 I do something for fun at least once a week.

_____ 18 I manage time effectively without procrastinating and cramming.

_____ 19 I refrain from drinking caffeine beverages (coffee, tea, sodas) daily.

_____ 20 I have some quiet time and personal space for myself each day.

Total the figures, and see where your score falls within the Vulnerability to Stress scale:

90+	_Slight Vulnerability (Excellent)_	40-55	_Profound Vulnerability_
75-89	_Low Vulnerability_	Under 40	_Extreme Vulnerability_
56-74	_Moderate Vulnerability_		

Exercising

Where can you go on campus or off campus to participate in aerobic exercise?

Where and when do yoga classes meet on campus or off campus?

The effects of mental stress can be reduced by the physical stress of daily exercise. Begin by stretching your body; then advance to aerobics. Aerobic exercise helps you control anxiety by improving the capacity of your lungs, heart, and vascular system. Exercising until you work up a sweat facilitates the body's waste-removal process and helps the body return to a more relaxed state.

Aerobic exercise can improve studying efficiency. As the heart rate increases and more oxygen enters the blood stream, clarity of thought and creativity improve. Positive personality and mood changes occur as fitness levels increase. Self-esteem and self-image improve while anxiety, depression, and tension decrease.

Relaxing

Relaxation techniques can decrease the heart rate, slow down breathing, and calm emotions. Relaxation requires a quiet environment, a passive attitude (releasing burdens and distractions from the mind), and a comfortable position. Progressive relaxation, developed by Edmund Jacobson, MD, has been used to treat headaches as well as other stress-related physical problems. By deliberately relaxing all of the muscles, group by group, you can shed accumulated tension from your body. Types of relaxation techniques you might consider are a massage, warm bath, yoga, or deep breathing.

- A massage (manipulation of muscles, tendons, joints, skin, and fat tissues) can relieve muscle contractions and thereby induce relaxation.

- A warm bath—soaking for 20 minutes—just before going to bed will help you to sleep well.

- _Yoga_, a system of exercises practiced to promote control of the body and mind, enhances spiritual insight and tranquility.

- Slow, deep breathing can reduce stress quickly: Inhale for 7 seconds and exhale for 8 seconds; do this four times per minute for 2 minutes.

Finally, socializing with others, meditation, laughing, and engaging in recreational activities can help you relax as well.

Eating Nutritious Food and Taking Supplements

Proper diet is extremely important. Disorders that arise from stress often result from nutrient deficiencies. Our bodies do not handle nutrients well when tense and nervous. Stress depletes the body of vitamins and minerals needed to build up the body's immune system.

If stress is not controlled, serious illnesses can develop. Research has proven that among the disorders and diseases enhanced by stress are acne, arthritis, back or neck pain, cancer, cold sores and canker sores, depression, hair problems (color, quality, and thickness), hay fever and allergies, headaches, heart disease, insomnia, and ulcers.

Foods with high levels of caffeine, saturated fat, refined flour, or refined sugar should be avoided: colas, fried foods, junk foods, sugar, white flour products, potato chips, and dairy products. Instead, we should eat plenty of fresh fruits and vegetables—at least half of our diet.

Vitamin B complex, important for proper functioning of the nervous system, aids in improving brain function and in reducing anxiety. Also important are calcium, magnesium, amino acids, and vitamin C.

Where can you go to buy vitamin supplements?

Coping in Other Ways

The intensity of stress depends on how a person perceives the situation. Stress is enhanced by lack of social support from friends and family, negative comments from associates, anger, guilt, resistance to change, and focusing on bad experiences. Other ways to cope with stress include the following:

Where can you learn about intramural sports and other recreational opportunities?

- Give and receive affection regularly.

- Practice your spiritual beliefs.

- Participate in recreation and social activities.

- Have friends with whom you can confide and discuss problems.

- Be honest and open about your feelings.

- Do something for fun once or twice a week.

- Avoid procrastination by scheduling time according to priorities.

- Set aside quiet time to meditate, reflect, and imagine pleasant happenings.

- Learn to say "No" when asked to do more than you can manage.

- Laugh (it relaxes the muscles).

- Maintain a positive attitude.

- Try to be more flexible.

Does your counseling center offer depression screenings and/or stress relief workshops?

- Accept what you cannot change.

- Focus on the present and the future; recall only positive aspects of the past.

- Get counseling—individually or in a group session—by a professional.

Exercise 1 Coping with Stress

Using a clock with a second hand, practice deep breathing:
1 Inhale slowly and continuously for 7 seconds.
2 Exhale slowly and continuously for 8 seconds.
3 Repeat steps 1 and 2 at the rate of four per minute—for 2 minutes.

From the lists of symptoms and causes of stress given in this chapter, describe:

a Symptoms of your reaction to stress

_____

b Major causes of stress within the last six months

_____

c Successful ways you have found to reduce stress

_____

■ Plan a Healthy Diet

Because no one food (or food group) can meet all your nutritional needs, the key to healthy eating is choosing a variety of foods in amounts that are right for you. Each day your body needs fiber, protein, carbohydrates, vitamins, minerals, fats, and water to function efficiently. Planning a diet that contains all the basic elements might seem impossible, but a few fundamental steps can improve your eating habits almost immediately.

Following the Food Guide Pyramid

An excellent aid to planning a healthy diet is the Food Guide Pyramid (Figure 1), published by the United States Departments of Agriculture and Health and Human Services. The Food Guide Pyramid gives recommended daily servings for each of the six food groups. Foods at the base levels of the pyramid (breads, cereals, grains, pastas, fruits, and vegetables) should form the foundation of our diet. The major sources of fiber and carbohydrates, they are low in fat and contain many vitamins and minerals. Carbohydrates are the body's principal source of energy. Fiber is important in our diet to add bulk, to lower cholesterol, and to help prevent certain diseases.

In an upper level of the pyramid are the dairy foods as well as the meat, fish, and poultry group. They provide important nutrients, including protein, but should make up a smaller portion of your diet. Protein is essential for growth and plays a role in all body functions.

The foods at the top of the pyramid (fats, oils, and sugars) should make up only a small part of a healthy diet, but they are essential for health. Fats help maintain healthy skin and hair, transport certain vitamins, and regulate blood cholesterol levels.

Figure 1—Food Guide Pyramid

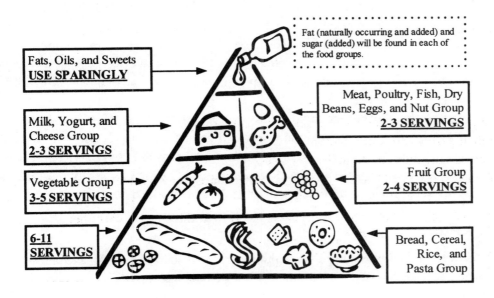

Exercise 2 Keeping a Food Journal or Diary

For the next three days, make a list of everything you eat and drink as well as the approximate time you eat it. Be as accurate as possible. Then answer these questions:

1 How do your eating habits compare to the Food Guide Pyramid?

2 At what time of day are you eating the largest quantities of food?

3 What changes (if any) should you make in your diet to eat in a healthier manner?

Considering a Vegetarian Diet

Should you consider staying off meat, include a variety of foods in your diet: fruits, vegetables, whole-grain breads and cereals, legumes (such as soybeans, lima beans, chickpeas), nuts, seeds, and soy products. Adding an occasional egg and low-fat dairy product made from low-fat or skim milk can help you get all the nutrients you need. Most diets designated as "heart healthy" are semi-vegetarian diets.

Making Changes the Healthy Way

Does your health and wellness center offer health screenings to check blood pressure, cholesterol count, body fat, and so forth?

Current research has shown that the quantity we eat, the time we eat, and what we eat are all important for weight management. These topics are discussed in the following sections. Before making major changes to your diet, assess where you are and identify problem areas or concerns. Then you can begin to make appropriate choices and modifications. Experts recommend that we keep our daily total fat intake at or below 30 percent of our total calories, because fat is a concentrated source of calories (providing 9 calories per gram) and can lead to cholesterol buildup and atherosclerosis.

The amount of fat you eat per day depends on your caloric level. Most healthy adults need 1,800 to 2,200 calories per day to maintain weight. If you participate in collegiate athletics, have chronic health conditions, are pregnant or are breast-feeding, follow your physician's recommendations. If you are trying to lose weight, no more than 20 percent of your total calories should come from fat. Never go below 20 percent fat unless you are under a doctor's care.

Eating Disorders

Eating disorders are emotional problems that often are related to body image and self-esteem. People who become obsessed with thinness allow their weight and dieting efforts to determine their self-esteem. They judge themselves on how well they control what they eat. Convinced that eating is the cause of their problems, they become trapped in rigid patterns that focus on food. They dwell on counting calories, weighing themselves, and placing themselves on several restricted diets.

Anorexia Nervosa This condition is characterized by self-starvation, fear of getting fat, severe weight loss (less than 85 percent of normal expected weight), and a distorted image of the body. Symptoms of severe weight loss include cold hands and feet, dry skin and hair, constipation, digestive problems, insomnia, fainting spells, depression, and (for women) the loss of menstrual periods.

Bulimia Bulimia is binge-eating followed by purging (vomiting or abusing laxatives) and/or exercising excessively. Symptoms include constipation, digestive disorders, dehydration, dental problems, mood swings, sore throat, muscle weakness, and rapid weight gains and losses.

Compulsive Overeating This may cause the person to progress from being overweight to becoming obese. Symptoms include shortness of breath, high blood pressure, and joint problems.

Eating disorders lead to diseases. If you recognize any of the symptoms, seek help from a professional at the counseling center or health center.

How Much You Eat

To maintain weight, a person needs 30 calories per kilogram of body weight. Assuming you have a moderate activity level, determine your caloric intake in the following way:

1   Divide weight in pounds by 2.2 (1 kilogram = 2.2 pounds) = weight in kilograms.

2   Multiply weight in kilograms by 30 (number of calories needed to maintain weight) = the number of calories you should consume per day to maintain your weight.

To give an example: A person weighing 150 pounds would need 2,040 calories a day (150 ÷ 2.2 = 68 kilograms; 68 x 30 = 2,040 calories). Exceptions to the formula are athletes and women who are pregnant or are breast-feeding.

When You Eat

If you consume most of your calories in the evening before bedtime, they are more likely to be stored as fat than calories consumed earlier in the day. You might eat three regular meals or four to five smaller meals. Many experts recommend spreading your caloric intake more evenly over the day and taking a larger percentage of calories at breakfast.

What You Eat

Cleo Casady, a world-class runner, conducted extensive efforts in his efforts to get his cancer in remission. Casady, who set several national records and two world records for his age group in running ultramarathons, put his cancer in remission and extended his life six years by exercising regularly, eating nutritious meals, taking vitamin/mineral/herb supplements, and meditating. He developed a list of recommendations for not only preventing cancer and heart disease but also for staying healthy (as shown in the next table).

Cleo Casady's Recommendations

Avoid These Foods	*Choose These Foods*	*Partake in Moderation*
Cheese, ice cream	Oatmeal, raisins	All animal fats
Sugar (white or brown)	Chicken, turkey (white)	Coffee or tea
Salt, pepper	Fish, seafood	Red meats
Candy, chocolate	Potatoes	Syrups
White flour, white bread	Fresh, raw fruits	Eggs
Colas, soft drinks	Fresh, raw vegetables	Honey
Potato chips, French fries	Whole grain breads	Milk
Donuts, sweet rolls	Whole grain cereals	Cottage cheese
Fried foods, bacon, burgers	Dried beans, brown rice	Salad dressings
Processed meats	Fresh fruit juices	Butter
Processed cereals with sugar	Olive oil, canola oil	Low-fat yogurt

If you are not eating properly, you might consider taking vitamin and mineral supplements, which work with other nutrients in food. Vitamins are organic substances that help regulate cell functions in your body. Minerals maintain healthy nerve functions, regulate muscle tone, and help form blood and bone tissues. Because the body cannot produce them, they must be obtained through the foods you eat and possibly supplements.

Snacks

Contrary to popular belief, snacking can be good if you make healthy choices. If you have concerns, see a registered dietitian. Healthy choices for most adults include:

- Dry cereal—add raisins or other dried fruit
- Raw vegetables and vegetable juices
- Fruit and fruit juices
- Nuts and seeds
- Popcorn (plain)
- Yogurt
- Pretzels
- Low-fat crackers

Eating Away from Home

When we eat away from home, our menu choices might be limited or might tempt us with many unhealthy options. Fast-food restaurants particularly challenge us. These tips for eating at a restaurant or cafeteria can help:

▶ Ask for nutrition information to help you make wise choices.

▶ Choose items that are baked, broiled, or steamed.

▶ Avoid foods that are fried, breaded, sautéed, or covered with sauce or gravy.

▶ Select red sauces (instead of white or creamy sauces) with pasta.

▶ Ask for sauces, gravies, and dressings on the side so you can control the amount.

Planning Meals

By preparing your own meals and eating at home, you can eat better and more economically than by going out to eat. Planning menus and shopping for groceries require careful thought. To save time and money while increasing nutrients in your diet:

- Plan weekly menus.

- Schedule time for grocery shopping.

- Prepare foods on weekends and freeze them for quick reheating later in the week.

- Add frozen vegetables or cut-up carrots, celery, or peppers to meals.

- Bake a potato as a main course. Use its baking time to study, relax, or work out.

■ Enhance Your Physical Well–Being

Maintaining good health requires regular exercise. The amount and quality of physical activity you get contribute to your overall level of health. Students who exercise regularly have lower risk for heart disease, osteoporosis, diabetes, and high blood pressure. They are less likely to be anxious or depressed. Even moderate exercise can provide substantial health benefits.

If you have difficulty starting an exercise program or working it into a busy schedule, consider some increase in physical activity. For example, you might park farther from class and walk an extra block, take the stairs instead of the elevator, or ride your bike instead of drive.

Aerobic exercise programs increase cardiovascular fitness by the frequency, intensity, and duration of the workouts. According to Dr Kenneth Cooper's research, the top five activities to provide the best aerobic conditioning potential are cross-country skiing, swimming, jogging or running, outdoor cycling, and walking. Others include roller skating, aerobic dancing, handball, racquetball, squash, basketball, tennis, minitrampoline, and horseback riding. Most experts recommend workout periods of moderate intensity—20 to 60 minutes in length, three to five times a week. If you have been inactive and have gotten approval from your physician, start out slowly with light intensity and gradually build up to the optimum level.

If you want to get involved in a formal exercise program, you might consider these tips:

- Choose something you enjoy. Try several forms of exercise to find the one you like.

- Work out with a partner. Exercising with another person is more fun, provides you with incentive, and is safer.

- Convenience is important. Having to drive 30 minutes to a gym or to buy expensive equipment can lessen one's desire to continue the program.

- Make it fit your daily routine. A program for which you have to alter your schedule drastically or get up an hour earlier probably will not last long.

- If you have not been active, are 35 years of age or older, have chronic health problems, or are pregnant, get a check-up with a physician before you start any program.

Where on campus would you choose to participate in regular exercise?

The amount and type of exercise you choose will depend on your individual fitness goals. Exercise programs can be designed to improve flexibility, increase muscle mass and strength, promote weight loss, enhance cardiovascular endurance, or train for a specific event. Each of these goals would require a different training program.

Exercise 3 Setting Personal Exercise Goals

List three ways you could incorporate physical activity into your daily schedule.

1 _____
2 _____
3 _____

Rank your top three choices of physical exercise.

1 _____
2 _____
3 _____

What is your specific goal for a formal or structured exercise program?

■ Improve Your Sleep

Proper sleep amounts and patterns help you to feel better, to perform optimally, and to maintain your health and wellness. Often you take sleep for granted until you are deprived of it. Sleep deprivation is a serious problem among college students. Research on over 13,000 freshmen within the last six years reveals that students who average 7 to 8 hours of sleep a night earn the highest GPAs; those who average five or fewer hours a night have the lowest GPAs.

Identifying Sleep Problems

One-third of U.S. adults experience sleep problems due to medical, psychological, and sleep environment causes. These challenges include difficulties with the duration or quality of sleep, problems falling or staying asleep, physical problems, psychological problems, behavioral abnormalities during sleep (sleepwalking, bedwetting, or sleeptalking), and daytime sleepiness. Sleep disturbances can relate to disruption of your daily internal clock pattern (rest and activity cycle). College students with late night activities often shift their lifestyle away from their natural clock pattern and as a result have sleep problems. Other major factors that affect sleep include foods, drugs, medication, alcohol, caffeine, and tobacco.

Improving Sleep Preparation

Prepare for sleep and go to sleep at a regular time. Avoid heavy snacks or exercise before bedtime. Use stress management. Eliminate caffeine and nicotine. Try a warm nonalcoholic drink at bedtime. Exercise moderately each day and avoid naps. Keep your bedroom dark and quiet. "Cool down" from studying with some quiet music or light reading before bedtime. If serious sleep problems continue, consult your physician.

Exercise 4 Identifying Sleep Patterns

What is your sleep pattern? Answer the questions and be prepared to share your responses in class.

1 What time do you go to bed each night?_____

2 How long does it take to fall asleep?_____

3 Do you awaken during the night? If so, how often and for how long? _____
_____

4 What is the duration of your sleep each night?_____

5 Are you tired during the daytime?_____

6 Do you fall asleep during the day? _____

7 What could you change or improve about your sleep?_____
_____

■ Grow in Health and Wellness

The educated person who embraces wellness will commit to a lifelong process involving balanced growth of a healthy mind, body, and spirit. Being well is much more than mere physical fitness or a lack of illness or absence of disease. Modern concepts of wellness encourage people to achieve a balance in at least the following areas of their life: intellectual, emotional, social, occupational, physical, and spiritual.

The Wheel of Wellness

Dr Bill Hettler developed the wellness wheel concept in 1976, which is shown in Figure 2. Since that time, individuals and institutions have modified the wellness wheel according to their beliefs. Many models now include environmental, cultural, and diversity spokes in the wheel. The principle of the wellness wheel is to illustrate in a graphic form the concept of balanced growth in the various important sectors of our lives. Without this balance our wheel would roll unevenly.

The wellness wheel philosophy calls for lifelong growth. If we grow intellectually but stop growing occupationally, we will become frustrated. Physical growth without associated emotional and social growth creates another imbalance. A person in a wheelchair could be a better example of balance than an Olympic athlete if he or she does his or her best physically and develops in the other facets of wellness—in the emotional, spiritual, intellectual, social, and occupational dimensions.

Figure 2—The Wheel of Wellness

Reprinted by permission of
the author, Bill Hettler.

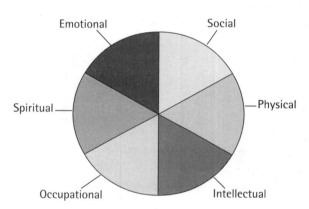

Definitions and Applications of Wellness Components

To further your understanding of the wellness concept, review these definitions and ways to strengthen each "spoke of the wheel."

Social Wellness Social wellness is the result of an interest in the organizations and peoples of society as well as a willingness to engage constructively with these groups. One achieves it by forming friendships, volunteering one's services, and being politically active.

Physical Wellness Physical wellness is achieved through scientifically sound exercise, nutrition, and medical participation; avoidance of alcohol and drugs; and responsible sexual activity. Read about health, exercise regularly, eat nutritious meals, and get periodic exams by a physician.

Intellectual Wellness Intellectual wellness involves an attitude of openness and curiosity, love for learning in many areas, and respect for knowledge, learning, and analysis. It is achieved by reading books, discussing concepts, attending lectures and concerts, developing new hobbies, and accepting challenges.

Where would you go to find out about campus programs that might enhance your intellectual wellness?

Occupational Wellness Occupational wellness is achieved through a willingness to seek work that fulfills you and gives purpose to your life. Visit your career services office. Study the information found there, do library research, take a vocational interest and aptitude test, and talk with people in your proposed occupation.

Spiritual Wellness Spiritual wellness is searching for greater meaning and purpose in life and exploring personal values and beliefs. Study an established religion, read about other beliefs, and take philosophy courses.

Where do you go to nourish your spiritual wellness?

Emotional Wellness Emotional wellness is an awareness of your needs and feelings as well as those of other people, and acceptance of your limitations. Emotionally well people know how to reduce stress and obtain help when they need it. They can form meaningful relationships with others and are assertive without being aggressive. Take an interest in others, discuss your thoughts and feelings with friends, and manage stress.

If you are interested in personal growth, consider taking a wellness survey test at your campus health and wellness center. Some campuses provide wellness residence hall opportunities for further experiential learning. Communities that affirm wellness support educational efforts to promote balanced wellness.

Does your health and wellness center offer a wellness survey test?

Exercise 5 Personal Growth and Development

1 On a scale of 1 (low) to 10 (high), rate yourself on each sector or spoke of the wellness wheel:

Social ____   *Intellectual* ____   *Spiritual* ____
Physical ____   *Occupational* ____   *Emotional* ____

2 Which sectors do you plan to further develop this year so that your wellness wheel will be balanced? For each, describe how you plan to do so.

_____   _____
_____   _____
_____   _____
_____   _____
_____   _____
_____   _____

Maintaining health and wellness enables you to do your best in school, at work, at home, and with friends. Personal growth and development are among the important goals you will try to perfect throughout your life.

Solve This Case—What Could Yung Do to Enhance Wellness?

When the company for which he had been employed for twelve years downsized, Yung lost his job but was given the opportunity to attend college. Though his wife has a job as a secretary at a law firm, their financial situation is tight. Yung works twenty hours a week at a part-time job to help with the expenses. Work, college, and family keep him too busy to help at church or to bike with friends anymore.

Averaging five to six hours of sleep a night, he gets up just in time to shower and to review class notes for 30 minutes before leaving for campus. En route he drives by a local fast-food restaurant to get a croissant and a cup of coffee. Between classes he gets a coke and chips to tide him over to dinner time, when the family typically will go out to eat at a pizza or Mexican food restaurant.

Four weeks into his first term in college, Yung has suffered frequent headaches and a common cold. He and his wife seem to argue more frequently over minor issues. In classes he finds it difficult to concentrate and often has to force himself to stay awake. When he goes to bed, however, he cannot get to sleep. What a dilemma!

After the first round of exams, Yung considers withdrawing from college and getting a full-time job. Perhaps college is not the answer to his dream of becoming a computer analyst.

1 What are Yung's major health and wellness problems?

2 In what ways is Yung's wellness wheel out of balance?

3 How could Yung improve his health and wellness so he can meet his goals of getting a college degree and being a good father and husband—all within a tight budget?

My Reflections Journal

Take time to reflect on three of the questions. Then write your thoughts in one short paragraph each. Using your computer, you may either print the page and turn it in on paper or e-mail the page to your instructor. Ask your instructor which method he or she prefers.

1 On a scale of 1 to 10 (with 10 being high), rate your stress level this week. What ways are you finding to cap or to reduce unhealthy stress?

2 On a scale of 1 to 10 (with 10 being high), rate your diet and eating habits. After studying this chapter, do you intend to make any changes? What are they?

3 On a scale of 1 to 10 (with 10 being high), rate your physical well-being. What are your plans to maintain or improve your physical fitness?

4 How do you feel about your health and wellness?

5 How is college going for you this week?

Website Practice Test

On the website at http://www.casadyenterprises.com/collegeedgebook/practicetests.htm you can access a practice test to check on your understanding of the chapter concepts. You may print the results of this self-test to review before taking the respective in-class exam.

9 BEING RESPONSIBLE

Objectives

Upon completing this chapter, you should be able to:

- Identify the effects of alcohol abuse
- Know the effects of tobacco use
- Recognize the dangers of illicit drugs
- Reduce the risk of sexually transmitted diseases
- Reduce the risk of sexual assault
- Clarify your values

AS A NEW COLLEGE STUDENT, you have the freedom to make many choices. You choose your courses, class schedule, study time, friends, and social activities. Being an adult, you know that freedom's partner is responsibility. You must accept responsibility for your actions and realize there might be risks associated with your behavior for both yourself and others.

Many risks are involved in some of the important decisions you will have to make. An error in judgment could keep you from reaching a goal. Once done, some actions cannot be changed. By staying in control of your life and practicing personal safety, you can maximize the college experience.

Personal safety is important. Consider the Center for Disease Control and Prevention's National Center for Health Statistics 2000 report on people of all races and both sexes:[1]

✖ The five leading causes of death in the United States (listed in order of rank) are heart disease (first), cancer, stroke, chronic lower respiratory disease, and accidents (fifth).

✖ For young people aged 15 to 24, three out of four deaths are injury-related—either from unintentional injuries (ranks #1), homicide (ranks #2), or suicide (ranks #3).

On many college campuses, the most common crimes are drug and alcohol offenses, sexual assaults and offenses, as well as burglaries, thefts, and robberies. Many vehicular, sexual, and assault offenses are associated with alcohol binge drinking.

Educated people are expected to be accountable to others—from family and friends to society at large. Your actions affect not only your well-being but also that of others.

Self-Assessment: Assessing Personal Risk

For each of the following actions or activities rate the extent and frequency of your participation each week:

4 = Daily (Six or seven times a week)
3 = Often (Four or five times a week)
2 = Sometimes (Two or three times a week)
1= Seldom (Perhaps once a week or every two weeks)
0 = Never

	ACTIVITY	0	1	2	3	4
1	I attend parties at which alcohol is served.					
2	I drink alcoholic beverages at parties.					
3	At a party I leave my soda glass on a table when getting more food.					
4	I drink alcohol when I am alone.					
5	I drive while under the influence of alcohol.					
6	I smoke.					
7	I am around others who smoke.					
8	I use marijuana and/or other illicit drugs.					
9	I engage in sexual intercourse without use of a condom.					
10	I date more than one partner.					
11	My partner has repeatedly criticized me, insulted my beliefs, lied to me, and/or embarrassed me in public.					
12	I walk alone to class, to the library, and/or to my car after dusk.					

Total your score. If your score is 3 or below, congratulations on practicing safe behavior and having minimal risk in your personal life!

Score of 0–3   Minimal Risk Zone
Score of 4–6   Caution Zone
Score of 7–9   High Risk Zone
Score of 10+   Danger Zone

Upon completing this chapter, you will know how to reduce or even eliminate risk from your life while practicing responsible behaviors.

Identify the Effects of Alcohol Abuse

Of all substances used on college campuses, alcohol causes the most problems. A review of the medical and societal effects of alcohol abuse might help you make personal choices as well as help others. A MADD (Mothers Against Drunk Driving) newsletter revealed these statistics: From the Revolutionary War in 1775 through Desert Storm in 1990, American battle deaths totaled 1,186,800. From 1900 to 1990 alcohol-related vehicular accidents killed 1,315,000 Americans. One report cites alcohol involvement in 67 percent of college student suicides, in 90 percent of campus rapes, and in 95 percent of violent campus crime.[2] Alcohol can cause chronic and acute medical problems for the user. Societal problems result for both nonusers and users, as reported by the National Institute on Alcohol Abuse and Alcoholism.[3]

Medical Effects

Alcohol is a central nervous system depressant. At low levels it disinhibits some elements of brain control and lowers alertness. These effects can occur within one or two drinks, depending on the person's age, weight, gender, rate of consumption, nutrition, dehydration, drinking experience, general medical health, prescribed medications, and other factors.

As the number of drinks increases, reaction time, coordination, and judgment further diminish. Change in emotions, fatigue, and further impairment ensue until eventually the drinker can lapse into unconsciousness and even death from arrest of breathing or heartbeat.

Heavy drinking can impair sexual relations, shrink testicular and ovarian size, and damage the liver. Other medical problems observed in abusers of alcohol include blackouts, seizures, pancreas inflammation, high blood pressure, ulcers, muscle wasting, nerve damage, as well as heart irregularities and weakening.

An alcoholic has a cancer risk ten times greater than that of nonalcoholics. Furthermore, alcohol can cause poor-quality sleep, depression, hallucinations, paranoia, and other psychiatric and neurologic problems. Alcoholic mothers can have babies with multiple abnormalities (such as fetal alcohol syndrome).

Twenty years of research by the American Medical Association on how alcohol affects the brains of alcohol abusers revealed that alcohol inhibits brain development and size in people of ages 14 to 21. The most serious consequence of alcohol abuse is death. Over 1,400 college students die each year from alcohol-related injuries.[4]

Societal Effects

The Harvard School of Public Health has published the results of surveys conducted from 1994–2001 of college students at over 140 U.S. four-year colleges.[5] For this study the authors defined *binge drinking* as five or more drinks in one sitting for men and four or more drinks in one sitting for women. When drinking, binge drinkers were more likely than nonbinge drinkers to drive, have unplanned sex, damage property, and assault others. Students who drank at the binge level three or more times within two weeks were classified as *frequent binge drinkers*. Results of this survey included the following:

- Of all the college students, 43 percent were binge drinkers and 20 percent were frequent binge drinkers.

- Of the frequent binge drinkers, 62 percent of the men and 49 percent of the women drove after drinking.

- Of the frequent binge drinkers, the following percentages applied:

Did something they regretted	63 percent
Missed a class	61 percent
Forgot where they were or what they did	54 percent
Got behind in school work	46 percent
Argued with friends	42 percent
Engaged in unplanned sexual activity	41 percent
Got hurt or injured	23 percent
Damaged property	22 percent
Did not use protection when having sex	22 percent

- Of the frequent binge drinkers, 47 percent had five or more alcohol-related problems since the school year began. All rates in the report were significantly greater among binge drinkers than among nonbinge drinkers.

- Students who do not drink or who drink legally and moderately report having encountered the following problems with binge drinkers:

Had study or sleep interrupted	61 percent
Had to take care of a drunken student	54 percent
Had been insulted or humiliated	29 percent
Experienced an unwanted sexual advancement	20 percent
Had a serious argument or quarrel	19 percent
Had property damaged	14 percent

Presley et al[6] surveyed over 45,000 students at eighty-seven colleges in 1990-1992. Their study showed that males tended to binge-drink more than females. The heaviest-drinking students (those who averaged 9.3 drinks per week) received the lowest grades (D or F grade average). Adverse consequences were more pronounced in students under the legal drinking age.

Individual Choices

If you choose to not drink at all, are there campus organizations you can join for like-minded people?

If you fit any of the following categories, you place yourself at a high risk regarding alcohol consumption: underage persons, pregnant women, persons with medical problems or medications, vehicle drivers, or persons engaged in a dangerous activity (such as sky diving).

If you choose to drink, your average alcohol use should not exceed one drink per day. Within twenty-four hours you should not consume more than two drinks. A standard-sized *drink* is described as one 12-ounce can of beer, one 5-ounce glass of wine, or 1 ounce of 80-proof liquor. No more than one drink should be consumed in one hour.

Factors that affect the rate alcohol is absorbed into the body (blood alcohol content—BAC) should be noted:

▶ *Eating.* Food in the stomach slows the absorption of alcohol and intoxication.

▶ *Alcohol Content.* The higher alcohol content of a drink, the more quickly a person will get intoxicated.

▶ *Carbonation.* Carbonated beverages are accepted by the blood stream and are metabolized more quickly than noncarbonated drinks.

▶ *Cold drinks.* Compared with warm drinks, cold drinks are absorbed more rapidly into the blood stream.

▶ *Speed of drinking.* The faster a person drinks, the more drastic are the consequences.

▶ *Emptying time of stomach.* On the average, a person metabolizes alcohol at the rate of about one drink per hour.

▶ *Medication.* Some prescription drugs and over-the-counter drugs negatively interact with alcohol.

▶ *General state of health.* Stress, anger, fear, and illness affect the body's ability to metabolize alcohol.

If anyone in your family has a history of alcohol or drug abuse, do not drink. Close relatives of alcoholics have four times an increased risk of becoming alcoholics also. Alcoholism is a disorder involving genetic factors, social factors, and biologic factors. Alcohol is the most abused drug in America.[7]

Help to an Intoxicated Friend

What if one of your friends is suffering from acute alcohol intoxication? The signs and symptoms are irregular or infrequent breathing (an adult's normal rate of breathing is 8 to 12 breaths per minute); cessation of breathing or convulsions; clammy, pale, or bluish skin; as well as decreased alertness and decreased response to questions. As a friend, you should:

▶ Call 911.

▶ Place the person on his or her side. In the event of vomiting, the vomit will drain out of the mouth, reducing the risk of the person choking on the vomit.

▶ Stay with the person until the paramedics arrive.

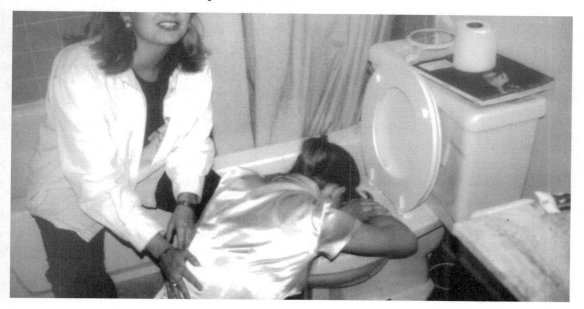

A frequent drinker needs to understand that there is a problem to be resolved. Typically denial and rationalization occur. Friends, family, physicians, and counselors all play a role in helping the person recognize and treat the problem. Alcoholics Anonymous, a self-help group, operates in most communities and meets on many college campuses. The health and wellness center can tell you where and when the group meets.

Exercise 1 Finding Solutions

Describe your solutions to these questions:

1 What can you do for yourself and your friends to change dangerous alcohol practices?

2 What would you do to reduce alcohol problems if you were the college president?

■ Know the Effects of Tobacco Use

Tobacco use affects everyone in our society, including nonusers who suffer health problems in reaction to secondhand smoke. Whether by smoking, chewing, or dipping, tobacco use is highly addictive. Over 90 percent of adults who smoke cigarettes start smoking before age 19.[8] Most American smokers would like to quit. In fact, 80 percent have attempted to stop smoking during their lifetime. Less than 5 percent of smokers reach the ex-smoker status without experiencing relapses.[9] People who choose to use tobacco put themselves and others at medical risk.

Cigarette smoke produces over 4,000 chemicals that have a variety of physical, toxic, and cancer-causing effects. Nicotine (released by smoking, chewing, or holding the tobacco against the gums) markedly stimulates the central nervous system. The peripheral nervous system is at first stimulated and then depressed.

Blood and heart rates usually are increased. An increase in the blood concentration of beta endorphin (a pain-alleviating and pleasure-promoting nervous system chemical) occurs. Smokers will inhale increased amounts of carbon monoxide, which impedes normal oxygen transport and leads to headaches and lightheadedness. Blockage of the arteries (atherosclerosis) is increased throughout the body, and chances of having a heart attack or a stroke are increased.

Sinus infections, bronchitis, and pneumonia are increased in smokers. Impairment of lung function, eventual emphysema, and obstructive lung diseases are increased. Abnormal breathing occurs even in teenage smokers.

Cigarette smoking accounts for 30 percent of all United States cancers. In addition to lung cancer, smokers have increased rates of cancers of the mouth, larynx, esophagus, bladder, kidney, pancreas, stomach, and some types of leukemia.

Ulcers are more common among smokers, and skin wrinkling is accelerated. Smoking while pregnant increases the risk of having smaller babies, miscarriages, retardation, and sudden infant death syndrome. Withdrawal syndrome can manifest with irritability, tobacco craving, and restlessness.

In nonsmokers the exposure to smoke increases rates of allergic reactions, lung cancer, heart attacks, lung infections, and other diseases. Smokeless tobacco increases atherosclerosis and the risk of mouth cancer.

■ Recognize the Dangers of Illicit Drugs

The use of illicit drugs causes a high level of suffering. Associated illnesses include hepatitis and sexually transmitted diseases. Drugs also lead to crime, motor vehicle accidents, and lost academic potential. A review of the most common illicit drugs on campuses might help you reduce risks and confirm your values.

Marijuana and Hashish

Marijuana (also called pot, grass, reefer, or joint) is the most commonly used illicit drug among college students. Marijuana is made from the dried leaf of the Cannabis sativa plant; hashish and hash oil come from the plant resin. Use of marijuana can increase the heart rate, weaken heart muscle, and cause reddening of the eyes. Often a subjective perception of relaxation and mild euphoria is induced, along with some impairment in thinking, concentrating, and remembering. Marijuana throws off the sleep cycle. Other dangers are feelings of panic, impairment of coordination, paranoia, and psychosis. Chronic users may lose interest in goals and may experience withdrawal signs and symptoms.

Stimulants

Cocaine and amphetamines or methamphetamines (also called meth, crank, crystal, speed, and chalk) are the next most commonly used illicit drugs among college students.[10] Both stimulants are primarily inhaled nasally, but they can be injected or smoked. Freebase and crack are the smokable forms of cocaine. Ice is the smokable form of methamphetamine. Lasting longer than cocaine, meths are very dangerous (fumes are explosive) and have a high danger of addiction.

Cocaine affects the concentration of brain neurotransmitter chemicals, giving a brief stimulation of mood and a feeling of increased well-being. The blood pressure, heart rate, and temperature usually increase. Addiction and withdrawal are common among users, and a depressed feeling can occur when cocaine abruptly wears off.

Both cocaine and amphetamines can produce agitation, severe anxiety, confusion, depression, paranoia, increased risk of heart attack, hallucinations, convulsions, and death.

Hallucinogens

LSD (*d*-lysergic acid diethylamide), mescaline, psilocybin, and MDMA (methylenedioxy methamphetamine—slang street name Ecstasy) are examples of hallucinogens. Distorting the user's perceptions, these drugs can induce panic, rapid mood swings, blurred vision, tremors, flashbacks, and lack of coordination. Dangers include brain damage, unconsciousness, coma, psychoses, unpredictable behavior, and suicide.

Depressants

Among the variety of drug types in the category of depressants are the narcotics, barbiturates, and tranquilizers. Derived from the opium poppy, the narcotics include heroin, morphine, and Demerol. Common tranquilizers are Valium and Xanax. In addition to experiencing depression, some users have sensations of drunkenness or euphoria. Highly habit-forming, depressants cause withdrawal reactions from those addicted. These drugs can cause convulsions, low blood pressure, respiratory arrest, and death.

Date-Rape Drugs

Used at club and rave scenes, date-rape drugs cause the victim to pass out so rape can be accomplished. Among the dangerous date-rape drugs to avoid are Rohypnol, GHB, and Ketamine.

Rohypnol An illicit drug that dissolves readily in liquid, Rohypnol typically is dropped into a beverage. The tiny white tablet (with Roche and a ① or ② on one side and a scored white cross on the other) is colorless, tasteless, and odorless. Rohypnol is ten times more powerful than Valium. Often mistakenly called Rufinol, this drug also is called Roachies, La Rocha, Mind Erasers, Rope, Ropies, Rib Roche, Roofies, R-2, Ralph, Mexican Valium, Ruffies, Rophies, and Roach-2.

Within 15 to 20 minutes of intake, Rohypnol produces drowsiness; the strongest effects occur in one or two hours after ingestion. Many victims experience a blackout period. The sedation lasts six to eight hours; memory loss extends to twenty-four hours. Seizures can occur within a week. Other side effects include amnesia, impaired motor skills, impaired judgment, lack of inhibitions, dizziness, and confusion. An overdose can cause mental confusion, lethargy, poor coordination, reduced reflexes, low blood pressure, coma, and death.

GHB (Gamma Hydroxybutyrate) Often administered as a clear liquid, GHB has a salty taste. Bad effects occur within 15 minutes. GHB can cause intoxication followed by deep sedation that can last up to eight hours. The victim might experience reduced inhibitions, nausea, convulsions, amnesia, and loss of consciousness. Mixed with alcohol, GHB can cause the central nervous system to shut down, resulting in respiratory distress, coma, or death. Street names include Liquid G, Liquid X, Cherry Meth, G, Gamma 10, and Easy Lay.

Ketamine This is a tranquilizer used by veterinarians for small animals before surgery. The effects last from four to six hours up to forty-eight hours. The victim can have convulsions even two

weeks later. Other names include Special K, Vitamin K (though not an authentic vitamin), KitKat, Ket, Cat Valium, Super C, Purple, and Keller.

Cautions at Social Functions

To reduce the risk of substance-related rape, attend social functions with a friend, and watch out for each other throughout the event. Watch what you drink:

✓   Do not accept beverages from someone you do not know well and trust.
✓   Do not accept open container drinks from anyone you do not know extremely well.
✓   Open your own drink; do not let anyone else open your can or bottle.
✓   Do not leave beverages unattended.

Other Drugs

Drug users usually will abuse multiple classes of drugs separately and together. Alcohol commonly is used along with illicit drugs, which compounds the medical and social risks.

Does your campus offer a drug prevention program?

Inhalation of gasses, glue aromas, paint, and other substances for stimulant effects has multiple medical risks, including toxic reaction and respiratory arrest. Men more than women use steroids to build muscles. Steroids can cause acne, balding, testicular shrinkage, male breast development, unfavorable cholesterol concentrations, liver bleeding, liver cancer, and psychiatric changes.

Caffeine in beverages and in over-the-counter, non-prescribed medications frequently is used to stay awake. Caffeine can induce irregular heartbeats and withdrawal headaches and can also disrupt normal sleep.

Exercise 2 Researching on the Web

Access your favorite website and search for three articles on one of the following topics.

- Binge Drinking on College Campuses
- Health Effects of Alcohol
- Health Effects of Smoking
- Date-Rape Drugs (or select one—Rohypnol, GHB, or Ketamine)

From a review of the three articles, write five major facts or points of interest you learned. Using your computer, e-mail or print your review for your professor. Be sure to include a bibliography.

■ Reduce the Risk of Sexually Transmitted Diseases

Sexual behavior is the greatest risk factor in contracting sexually transmitted diseases (STDs). Persons who engage in unprotected intercourse (oral, anal, or vaginal) with infected persons increase their risk of acquiring a sexually transmitted disease. Over twenty different types of STDs are known today. The most common STDs are described in the next section and further detailed in Table 1.

Table 1 Common STDs

BACTERIAL	VIRAL	PARASITIC
CHLAMYDIA • "The Clam" or "Gooey Stuff" • Most common bacterial STD and most often present without symptoms. • Symptoms may include a clear to cloudy discharge or drip from the vagina or penis, burning when you urinate, or pain in abdomen. • Treated with antibiotics; if not treated can cause serious health problems such as pelvic inflammatory disease and sterility. *GONORRHEA* • "Dose" or "Clap" or "Drip" • Most common in ages 15–30. • Symptoms may include a yellow–greenish discharge from the vagina, penis, or anus; painful urination or defecation; or low abdominal pain. • Treated with antibiotics. *SYPHILIS* • "Syph" or "Bad Blood" • Primarily transmitted sexually but can be spread through skin contact (by penetrating broken skin) with someone in the infectious stages or from mother to child at birth. • Symptoms may include a painless sore at the site of infection which goes unnoticed, followed by a rash on palms and soles of feet. Swollen lymph glands and painless sores in the mouth also may occur. • Treated with antibiotics. *CHANCROID* • More common in men than women. • Symptoms may include painful, open lesions; sometimes accompanied by swollen, tender lymph nodes in the groin; painful urination or defecation; and painful intercourse. • Treated with antibiotics. Co-infection with other STDs is common.	*GENITAL WARTS* • "HPV" or "Human Papillomavirus" • More than 20 types can infect the genital area. Individuals may have more than one type. Infection rate highest among women younger than 25. Leading cause of cervical cancer in young women. • Symptoms may include painless, fleshy, cauliflower-like warts on and inside the genitals, anus, or throat. • There is no cure. External treatments include removal by laser, acid application, freezing, and burning. *GENITAL/ORAL HERPES* • "Herpes" or "The Gift That Keeps on Giving" • Recurrence of herpes is very common, occurring in 75 percent of cases. • Symptoms may include small painful blisters on the sex organ or mouth (cold sores) lasting one to three weeks. Itching and burning occur before the blisters appear. • No known cure. There are medications to relieve symptoms and help prevent future outbreaks. *HIV/AIDS* • "Human Immunodeficiency Virus" causes progressive damage to the immune system, resulting in "Acquired Immune Deficiency Syndrome." • Symptoms may not be present for several years or may easily be mistaken as cold or flu. A rash may develop shortly after being infected. Others can include fever, weight loss, nausea, sleeplessness, thrush, fatigue, swollen glands, and/or diarrhea. • No known cure. Some treatments can delay the development of AIDS. *HEPATITIS B* • One of six major types of hepatitis. • Spread through sexual contact or contact with genital fluids and feces or from mother to fetus. • Symptoms may include muscle aches, fever, fatigue, and loss of appetite. • Most infections clear up within four to six weeks. A preventative vaccine is available.	*CRABS* • "Pubic Lice" • Spread through sexual contact with someone who has lice or by lice-infected clothing, bedding, or towels. • Lice live on and bite the skin, causing intense genital itching and sometimes a rash or bluish spots. • Treatment includes prescribed shampoo or cream rinse. All clothing, bedding, and towels should be washed with hot water and bleach or dry cleaned. *SCABIES* • "Mites" • Highly contagious, scabies is spread by sexual and skin contact as well as by direct contact with infected clothing, bedding, or towels. • This jellyfish-like bug zig-zags beneath the skin and feeds on blood, causing itching and skin infections. • Treatment includes prescribed shampoo and cream rinse. All clothing and bedding must be washed in hot water, dried at hot temperatures, or dry cleaned. *TRICHOMONIASIS* • "Trich" • Transmitted through intercourse to 10 percent of sexually active men and 15 percent of sexually active women. Moist objects, damp towels, and toilet seats also can spread the infection. A mother may infect her child at birth. • Symptoms may not be detected or could include vaginal discharge, discomfort during intercourse, and painful urination. • Treatment is available from a doctor.

Types of STDs

Most sexually transmitted diseases can be divided into three groups: bacterial, viral, and parasitic.

Bacterial STDs These include chlamydia, gonorrhea, syphilis, and chancroid. These infections are caused by bacteria that are passed through unprotected sexual intercourse with an infected person. Bacterial infections often are treated with antibiotics and usually can be cured. If undetected, these STDs can cause severe complications (such as pelvic inflammatory disease, which may lead to ectopic pregnancy and infertility).

Viral STDs These include genital warts (human papilloma virus—HPV), genital herpes (herpes simplex virus—HSV), HIV/AIDS (human immunodeficiency virus/acquired immune deficiency syndrome), and hepatitis B (hepatitis B virus—HBV). Although each of these viruses is unique, they have one characteristic in common—no cure. Only the symptoms can be treated. Genital warts and genital herpes are spread through sexual contact with an infected person. Genital herpes also may be acquired through skin-to-skin contact if lesions are present. HIV and hepatitis B are contracted through blood-to-blood (sharing needles for drugs or body piercing) or unprotected sexual contact with an infected person. An immunization is available for hepatitis B that can prevent infection.

Acquired immune deficiency syndrome (AIDS) is caused by HIV, a virus found in blood and sexual body fluids that impairs and eventually destroys the body's immune system. Thus people with HIV/AIDS are extremely vulnerable to diseases and infections. From the time of HIV exposure to one's detection of the virus, there is a window of two to six months when the virus can be detected only by a medical test. During the incubation period, ranging from five to ten years, the person appears healthy but begins to lose weight and to lose t-cell count. A healthy person has 800 to 1,200 t-cells. When an HIV infected person's t-cell count drops to 200, he or she is considered to have full-blown AIDS. Challenged by numerous health problems, the client has to take expensive prescription drugs (at the right time and in proper sequence with food) to stay alive. Death is likely to occur within three to five years. The typical age of death ranges from 25 to 44 years.

Parasitic STD These include crabs (pubic lice), scabies (mites), and trichomoniasis (trich). Though the treatment for each of these infections varies, parasitic STDs can be cured. Antibiotics usually are prescribed for trichomoniasis, and special creams or shampoos are used for crabs and scabies. If a person is diagnosed with crabs or scabies (which may be transmitted through contact with infected cloth), his or her bedding and clothing should be disinfected too.

Signs and Symptoms

Sexually transmitted diseases have a variety of signs and symptoms, including:

- Abnormal discharge (change in color, odor, or consistency)
- Pain or burning sensation with urination
- Redness, sores, blister, bumps, or rash in genital area
- Pain in the pelvic area
- Vaginal bleeding when it is not time for the monthly period
- Rectal itching, pain, or discharge
- Painful intercourse
- Itching in the genital area

Many people who have a sexually transmitted disease, however, have no signs or symptoms. During the window stage (person has been infected but does not have symptoms yet), these persons are infectious and may transmit the disease to their partners. People who have had unprotected intercourse, multiple partners, partners who have had other partners, or intercourse with a person known to be infected should see a health care provider to be tested.

Risk Reduction

Abstinence from sexual activities involving exchange of body fluids is the only sure way to prevent the transmission of sexually transmitted diseases. Persons who choose to be sexually active, however, can choose behaviors that are less risky. Some low-risk activities include touching, massaging, kissing, and sharing fantasies. Activities that are more risky include intercourse (oral or vaginal) with a condom or other barrier. Highest-risk activities include unprotected anal or vaginal intercourse.

Decisions about Sexual Behavior

Among the important decisions college students have to make are those about sexual behavior. Will you choose to be sexually active? Will you have one partner or multiple partners? Students usually are encouraged to be sexually active by such influences as peer pressure, hormones, and a close relationship. Thoughts of being sexually active often are dampened by concern for your reputation, fear of pregnancy or STDs, feelings of being used, and religious beliefs.

Ideally, decisions on sexual behavior should be carefully thought out based on personal values and beliefs. In real life, however, critical decisions often are made spontaneously and emotionally and under the influence of alcohol or other drugs. By knowing your values and planning how you will act in risky situations, you can reduce the chance of making a wrong decision that could stop you from reaching the goals you have set.

Choosing a method of contraception (birth control) is a very personal decision. Some of the factors that affect decision making include personal values and beliefs, religious beliefs, medical history, and lifestyle. Being aware of possible risks and benefits for each contraceptive method enables you to make an informed decision. If you have questions or need help in making a decision, consult a health care provider, counselor, or religious or spiritual advisor.

Oral Contraceptives (Birth Control Pills) Oral contraceptives are the most widely used and one of the most effective forms of contraception—about 97 to 99 percent effective when used correctly and consistently. The pills prevent pregnancy by preventing ovulation or by causing changes in the cervical mucus. Although some women experience side effects, oral contraceptives generally are extremely safe and easy to use. They do not require the cooperation of a partner and do not interfere with spontaneity. Birth control pills, however, do not prevent sexually transmitted diseases.

Can you get oral contraceptives at your health center? If not, where is the nearest Planned Parenthood?

Barrier Methods of Birth Control Barrier methods include condoms, diaphragms, cervical caps, and spermicide. When used correctly and consistently, the effectiveness of these methods ranges from 70 to about 90 percent. Some people feel that these methods interfere with spontaneity, and most require the cooperation of a partner.

Both male and female condoms offer some protection from STDs, including HIV, if they are used consistently and correctly. Many different brands are available on the market today, including those made of lambskin, latex, and polyurethane. Lambskin condoms are not recommended, because the pore size is large enough to allow viruses and bacteria to pass through the condom. Latex condoms with water-based lubricant are recommended as the best choice in preventing STDs. If either partner has a latex allergy, however, another option would have to be considered.

Other Methods of Contraception Other methods include hormonal implants or injections, abstinence, periodic abstinence based on ovulation timing (natural family planning), and surgical sterilization. Implants and injections work like birth control pills and are as effective but do not require remembering to take a pill daily. Sterilization is 99 percent effective but usually is irreversible. None of these methods prevents STDs.

Abstinence, defined as refraining from sexual intercourse (oral, anal, or vaginal), is the only 100 percent effective method of preventing pregnancy or transmission of STDs.

Communication with Partner

Effective communication between you and your partner can prevent problems and build trust. The decision to become sexually active should not be made in haste or when under the influence of alcohol or other drugs. Communicate clearly with your partner about what is acceptable to you and what is not, about whether you will be mutually monogamous, about birth control and who will be responsible for using it, and about your sexual history (including any STDs). Open communication, honesty, and tactfulness are important ingredients of positive relationships.

Does the counseling center offer workshops on partner relationships?

Exercise 3 Communicating Effectively

Chris and Pat are college freshmen who have been dating for three months. Chris wants to be sexually active, but Pat is unsure.

1 What are some of the issues that Chris and Pat need to discuss?
2 When would be a good time for them to discuss this topic?
3 What are some ways they can present their feelings in a non threatening manner?

Using a computer, write your responses to these questions. In groups of two or three classmates, discuss your responses.

◼ Reduce the Risk of Sexual Assault

Many people associate sexual assault and rape with being physically attacked in a dark place by some unknown person. Studies show, however, that in 80 percent of the cases the perpetrator is someone the victim knows. Typically, sexual assault results from an abusive relationship.

You can detect an abusive relationship by asking yourself if your partner has repeatedly criticized you, ignored your feelings, insulted your beliefs, been jealous or accused you of imagined affairs, insisted that you dress a certain way, insulted your friends or family, manipulated you with lies and contradictions, or embarrassed you in public. The relationship becomes even more abusive when the partner throws objects at you, hits or punches you, threatens to commit suicide if you leave, or forces you into sexual acts.

Sexual assault is an act of sexual aggression and violence expressed through force, anger, and intimidation in which a person is made to engage in sexual activity without consent. One out of three or four women and one in nine men are victims of sexual assault.[11]   *Rape* is sexual intercourse that occurs without a person's consent through the use of force or coercion. Whereas only one out of ten rapes may be reported in the general population, on the college campus rapes by dates and acquaintances may be reported only one out of one hundred times. The legal definition of rape is not well recognized by many college students.

Nonrape sexual assaults are more likely to occur between strangers on a weekday, whereas acquaintance rape is more likely to occur to a freshman or sophomore female on a weekend. The victim often cannot consent because of incapacitating alcohol or drug use.[12]

Steps to Take After an Assault

If you are a victim of sexual assault or rape, follow these important steps:

- Go to a safe place (friend's house—someone you trust) where you can get help.

- Seek medical help—emergency room of a hospital. Do not bathe, douche, shower, or change clothes; but take a clean set to change into afterwards. They can test for date-rape drugs if usage is suspected. A hospital examination (including the collection of forensic evidence) is important should you decide to prosecute the perpetrator.

- Within three weeks go back and be tested for STDs and pregnancy.

- Report the assault. If on campus, call the safety, security, or transportation department to dispatch the police and/or an ambulance. If off campus, call 911. Reporting a sexual assault does not commit you to filing charges against the perpetrator. Reporting the assault may help you feel safe, may prevent the person from committing another assault, and may help law enforcement officers build a case against the perpetrator.

- Seek counseling to help you deal with the emotional and practical issues.

If you are helping a survivor of sexual assault, you can see that the above steps are taken. In addition, believe the person, do not blame him or her, be a good listener, and show respect. Your help and emotional support are needed.

Do you have a rape crisis or victim center on campus or off campus? What phone number should be called by the victim of an assault or date rape?

Safety Opportunities

Peer pressure and risk-taking behavior threaten the safety of students, for which safety precautions can be undertaken collectively and individually. Wellness residence halls, health education, college success courses, the counseling center, religious groups, and the safety or security department offer programs to strengthen campus safety.

Where is the safety, security, or transportation department?

The Federal Crime Awareness and Campus Security Act and the Student Right to Know Act require the annual publication of campus crime statistics by colleges and universities that receive federal money. Campus security departments typically offer assistance, including transport shuttles, escorts at night, enhanced lighting, security advice pamphlets, and self-defense classes.

Which office would you call to request a walking escort?

You can practice safety precautions to prevent or protect yourself against sexual assault. Keep your doors locked, and wear seat belts. Carry a noise maker. Walk in well-lighted places and with someone. Call for a walking escort. Label possessions.

By embracing safety-oriented changes on campus, you can help to make the campus a better community in which to live. Demonstrating responsible citizenship, you can help initiate programs and participate in activities that promote safety and well being.

Exercise 4 Identifying Personal Safety Concerns

List three unsafe activities you have noted yourself or others engaging in this past week:

1 _____

2 _____

3 _____

What can you do to avoid risky behavior and to improve safety for yourself?

_____

_____

_____

Clarify Your Values

When you were younger, your parents probably taught you about traits such as honesty, respect, loyalty, and friendship. As an adult, you have the opportunity to reexamine and reflect upon those teachings as well as to modify or strengthen them based upon your own experiences. You will be comfortable with yourself if you are comfortable with your beliefs and values.

Are you honest in representing yourself to others? Do you respect other people's rights to have opinions different from yours? Are you loyal to your friends? Do you consider the feelings and needs of others? In establishing goals, you reflect personal values. If you value integrity, you conduct yourself in a manner that earns respect and trust from others. Your actions speak louder than words. People with integrity live according to their principles and values; they act in a manner that exemplifies those values.

Learning to know yourself and to like yourself can help you avoid many of the problems discussed in this chapter. High levels of self-esteem and self-respect make it easier to say *No* to drugs and alcohol, or to know your limits. If you respect yourself, you will be more likely to choose friends and partners who will be your equals and who will respect your feelings and desires. If you value longevity and happiness, you will take good care of your body by choosing the healthier behaviors.

Exercise 5 Identifying Healthy and Safe Activities

As alternatives to parties that expose students to alcohol and drugs, identify three healthy and safe activities that are open to all students. For each activity, give the date and place of the next event as well as the sponsoring group. Be prepared to promote these options in class.

ACTIVITY OR EVENT	DATE AND TIME	PLACE SPONSORING	GROUP

Notes

1. National Center for Health Statistics. (2002). *Final 2000 Mortality Statistics Now Available*, vol. 50, no. 15. Hyattsville, MD: National Center for Health Statistics. http://www.cdc.gov/nchs/releases/02facts/final2000.htm

2. CASA Commission on Substance Abuse at Colleges and Universities. (June 1994). *Rethinking rites of passage: Substance abuse on America's campuses*. New York, NY: Columbia University.

3. National Institute on Alcohol Abuse and Alcoholism, National Advisory Council. (2002). *How to Reduce High-Risk College Drinking*. Bethesda, MD.

4. Hingson,R., Heeren, T., Zakocs, R., Kopstein, A., and Wechsler, H. (2002). Magnitude of alcohol-related morbidity, mortality, and alcohol dependence among U.S. college students age 18-24. *Journal of Studies on Alcohol, 63*(2), 136-144.

5. Wechsler, H., Lee, J.E., Kuo, M., Seibring, M., Nelson, T.F., and Lee, H. (2002). Trends in college binge drinking during a period of increased prevention efforts: Findings from 4 Harvard School of Public Health College Alcohol Study Surveys: 1993-2001. *Journal of American College Health, 50*(5), 203-217.

6   Presley, C., Meilman, P., and Lyerla. (January 1995). *Alcohol and drugs on American college campuses,* volume II: 1990-1992 (pp. 43-51). The Core Institute, Southern Illinois University.

7   Johnson, E. (1992). *Principles and practices of student health,* vol. I, *Foundations* (pp. 711-756). Oakland, CA: Third Party Publishing Co.

8   D'Onofrio, C. (1992). *Principles and practices of student health,* vol. I, *Foundations* (pp. 168-184). Oakland, CA: Third Party Publishing Co.

9   Holbrook, J. (1994). *Harrison's principles of internal medicine,* 13th ed. (p. 2436). New York: McGraw-Hill.

10 Evans, J. (1992). *Principles and practices of student health,* vol. III, *College health* (pp. 613-620). Oakland, CA: Third Party Publishing Co.

11 Wallace, H., Patrick, K., Parcel, G., and Igoe, J. (1992). *Principles and practices of student health,* vol. III, *College health* (pp. 727-742). Oakland, CA: Third Party Publishing Co.

12 A comprehensive sexual assault prevention program. (January 1996). *Journal of American College Health Association,* 44(4).

Solve This Case—Deciding Who Is Responsible

Jane, a college freshman, was glad to be away from home and the strict guidelines established by her parents. Because she lived in a small town where everyone knew everyone else's business, she felt she never was able to get away with anything.

One weekend at college she had a date with a handsome and interesting guy named Greg. They went to a big party, where Jane met many new acquaintances. Two were Jordan, a 23-year-old college senior, who had supplied all the alcoholic beverages for the party, and Crystal.

During the evening, Jane drank more than she usually did. When the party was over, Greg and Jane went to his house and had unprotected sex. After Greg took Jane back to her room, she sobered up and realized the potential dangers of her evening's activities. Her main concern was pregnancy. She called Crystal to ask for a "morning after" pill—an "after-the-fact" birth control device. Crystal had told her about secretly taking a supply from her mother (a nurse). Crystal assured Jane the pills were absolutely safe and effective—not to worry.

Within hours of taking the pill, Jane began to suffer extreme nausea and severe cramping. She was rushed by ambulance to a hospital. After medical treatment and two days in the intensive care unit, Jane survived the traumatic experience and recovered.

1   Who was responsible for Jane's traumatic experience? The six characters are listed in order of their appearance in the story. Rank the characters (from **a** to **f**, with **a** being the most responsible) in the order of their responsibility for Jane's traumatic experience.

____ Jane   ____ Jordan
____ Jane's parents   ____ Crystal
____ Greg   ____ Crystal's mother

2   Work with the other members of your group to decide a group rank order for the six characters. Report your group's decision and rationale to the entire class.

a _____ (most responsible)
b _____
c _____
d _____
e _____
f _____

My Reflections Journal

This journal entry invites you to clarify your values. Write a one-paragraph response to each of the following questions. Using your computer, you may either print the pages and turn them in on paper or e-mail the pages to your instructor. Ask your instructor which method he or she prefers.

1 What beliefs and ideas do you most value?

2 Why are these important to you?

3 How do these values influence your decisions about alcohol, other drugs, and sexuality?

4 Who has been the most responsible for shaping your personal value system? How did this person influence you?

5 Have your values changed since you began college? If so, how? If not, why?

Website Practice Test

On the website at http://www.casadyenterprises.com/collegeedgebook/practicetests.htm you can access a practice test to check on your understanding of the chapter concepts. You may print the results of this self-test to review before taking the respective in-class exam.

10 USING COMPUTERS

COMPUTERS ARE POWERFUL tools with which we can prepare professional-quality documents, perform extensive research, and communicate throughout the world. Though most students have been introduced to computers in high school, at home, or through employment, they will use computers in new ways in college. Technology keeps advancing, and new software emerges on the market daily. Keeping up to date is a constant challenge for administrators, faculty, and students.

Once you know where to access computer facilities, you will need to know the hours and operating procedures for those sites. In addition, you will want to know which applications and specific software can be accessed at each site.

Knowing about basic application software tools will help you in doing many types of assignments. To gain specific concepts and skills as well as advanced applications, however, you would want to enroll in computer information systems or computer science courses.

Using the Internet, you can access the World Wide Web and search for information to include in reports and research projects. As you do so, you should be aware of ethical and legal issues so you can practice responsible behavior.

Self-Assessment: Assessing Your Understanding of Computer Usage

For each of the computer usage concepts or applications, rate your understanding and proficiency by placing a check mark in the appropriate column. Use this scale:

1 =   I know hardly anything about it.
2 =   Below Average: It has been introduced and demonstrated, but I have not used it.
3 =   Average: I have some understanding and experience but have not used it recently.
4 =   Above Average: I have used some basic features recently but am not proficient.
5 =   Excellent: I use it frequently and am proficient in most of the advanced features.

	COMPUTER USAGE CONCEPT OR APPLICATION	1	2	3	4	5
1	Computer lab facilities on campus					
2	Computer programming language					
3	E-mail					
4	Facsimile (FAX)					
5	Word processing software					
6	Graphics software					
7	Spreadsheet software					
8	Database software					
9	Presentation software					
10	Internet searches					

Your self-assessment will help your instructor to become aware of your capabilities as the chapter activities are being planned.

■ Access Computer Facilities

Where is an open computer lab that is convenient for you?

What are its days and hours of operation?

To use computer facilities on your campus, you need to know where the computer labs are located and the type(s) of computers, printers, and software programs available. Some labs are open to all students; others might be restricted to a special group (for example, business majors, math students, foreign language students, upper-division science majors, graduate students).

Each computer lab location probably has a handout that describes procedures for becoming an authorized user, privileges, costs, and hours of operation. Your campus might have a general computer lab fee for all students or a fee for users only. Lab fees help cover the cost of computer equipment, services from lab assistants, software (including site licenses), supplies (paper, disks, blank CDs, printer cartridges, and toner), and repair service.

Having your own equipment is convenient, since you do not have to drive or walk to a computer lab facility and can work on your computer any hour of the day or night. However, the cost is higher, for you must pay for the hardware, software, supplies, and repair service. If you wish to access outside resources (such as the library, World Wide Web, or e-mail), you need a modem that enables your computer to send or receive information over telephone lines.

For many of your courses, you will have assignments requiring the use of computers. It is important to develop a system of naming computer files so you can retrieve them quickly. In the following example, each document or file name begins with the respective course ID. Delete documents that are no longer needed.

Document/File Name	*Description*
ENG-Essay-Ethics	Essay on Ethics, ENG 120
ENG-Journal-1	Journal #1, ENG 120
HST-Outline-WWI	Outline of WWI Events, HST 107
IDS-Tchr-Intrvw	Interview of Teacher, IDS 110
PSY-Autobiog	Autobiography, PSY 121

Computer labs generally supply paper for the printers—a convenience for students. You might have a special document, such as an application letter or résumé, for which you need special paper. Check with the lab supervisor before purchasing paper to be sure that the paper is compatible with the printer type.

Have you asked the lab supervisor about the kind of paper to purchase for special documents?

Exercise 1 Listing Computer Facilities

Go to the Personal References section at the end of this text and fill out the Computer Facilities form to describe three campus computer facilities you might use this term. For each facility you will have the building and room as well as the following information:

Computers	Phone Number
Printers	Type of Users Served
Software/Programs	Kind of Special Paper to Buy
Days and Hours of Operation	

■ Describe Basic Types of Software and Networks

Advancements in software development and network capabilities continue to open doors for computer users. The following overview might help you in describing your computer experience.

Software (Programs)

Software provides instructions (a program) that direct the computer to perform various functions. The following are basic categories of software.

Operating System Software This software commands the hardware components to carry out the instructions of the application software (described below). Examples for a word processing application include reading keystrokes, translating them to digitized form, and bringing them to the screen; storing keystrokes on disk and enabling them to be recalled; and sending a document to print. Widely used operating systems (platforms) include Mac OS®, MS-DOS®, UNIX®, and Windows^{XP}.

Where can you go off campus to get the most inexpensive software of your choice?

Application Software This software directs the computer to perform a basic function. The popular commercial packages sold by software vendors are shown below:

Application	Software
Word Processing	Microsoft (MS) Word, Corel WordPerfect
Database	IBM DB2, MS Access, Oracle, Paradox
Spreadsheet	MS Excel, Quattro Pro
Graphics	MS Publisher, Pagemaker, Photoshop, QuarkXpress
E-Mail	Outlook Express, Web-Based E-Mail
Presentation	Corel Presentations, MS PowerPoint

Customized Software Prepared for a specific industry or profession, customized software fits the unique needs of similar types of users. An example for students is career guidance software that helps you assess your work-related values, interests, and activities as well as explore occupations. Customized software is used extensively in corporations and in professions. Attorneys, for instance, might use customized software to maintain client ledgers, prepare invoices, monitor unpaid expenses when a case is settled, maintain a calendar or docket, and do accounting tasks.

Windowing Software Designed for integrating applications, windowing software enables you to switch to another software application without leaving the first one. For instance, you could access your e-mail or prepare a graphic chart without leaving the spreadsheet program. With a layered pattern, the screen of one application appears on top or in front of another application. The windowing feature can split the display screen into smaller portions so you can see two or more applications at once. Also, each window could show different parts of the same file, so you could integrate parts of several sources into one document.

Programming Languages These are the basis of software development. Each feature of an application package is made possible by a series of instructions. The more features of a software package, the more memory is required on the disk to house all the instructions. Vendors upgrade software packages to provide new and better features as well as to correct flaws in the previous version or level. Sample programming languages include C++, COBOL, Java, and Microsoft Visual Basic.

Networks (Connections to Other Computers)

Networks enable computers to exchange, share, and process information. A local area network (LAN) serves users within a building or campus of buildings. A wide area (global) network (WAN) links users throughout the world.

Local Area Networks A local area network (LAN) links various components of a computer system (workstations, file servers, and printers)—even different brands and models—within a small geographic area. On campus, information can be shared and exchanged among users in computer labs, the library, administrative offices, faculty offices, and resident hall rooms. If you live off campus, you can access the computer system from your residence by getting a modem. The modem converts digital impulses (computer data) to analog impulses (those carried by telephone lines).

Wide Area (Global) Networks Wide area (global) networks (WANs) are telecommunication networks that make use of telephone lines, microwave radio links, fiber optics, and satellites to send and receive information worldwide. Connecting to the Internet (the world's largest open computer network) enables you to tap into the World Wide Web, which opens doors to huge libraries of information at the click of your mouse.

■ Identify Application Software Tools

Applications you probably will use in college are communication (e-mail and FAX), word processing, graphics, spreadsheet, database, and presentation software.

Communication (E-Mail and FAX)

Within seconds your urgent messages and important documents can be sent from one machine to another by electronic means. In addition to the telephone, two popular communication systems college students use are electronic mail (e-mail) and facsimile (FAX).

E-Mail E-mail involves sending keyboarded messages from one computer workstation to another or to a group of people whose computers are located in various places. You could send an e-mail letter to all family members who have an e-mail address. Should an emergency require that you leave campus, you could notify all your professors by e-mail. The day or time is irrelevant, because the message will be ready for them to read when they arrive at their offices and turn on their computers.

Sending e-mail is easy and quick. You merely access your e-mail software, click on the instruction for sending mail, key the e-mail address of the recipient (examples: **sundell@wuacc.edu** and **janhill@juno.com**), key the message, and click on the *Send* instruction. You could include one or more attachments (for example, a word processing document or a spreadsheet document).

If you are sending a strictly confidential message, be aware that e-mail is not the best choice. Your e-mail can be accessed by users within the college computer system as well as by Internet users. Thus, whatever you send by e-mail should be safe for any person to read.

Exercise 2 Sending an E-Mail Message

If you do not have an e-mail address, go to a computer lab to get your campus user ID. You probably will need your student ID card with personal picture. A temporary password will be given to you, which you will change later. A password is a security guard to protect your files from being accessed by anyone else.

Your User ID _____ Your E-Mail Address _____

Password Restrictions: Maximum # of characters _____; minimum # of characters _____; special characters not allowed _____.

*Required Characteristics of a Password:*_____

_____

Have your User ID and Password with you in a secure place until they are memorized.

Send an e-mail message to your teacher that describes the high points of this week, the most difficult course(s) this term, and what you like best about this class. The closing lines should be: your name, course ID and section number, and e-mail address.

FAX Short for facsimile (meaning exact copy), FAX transmission involves sending a copy of a page from one FAX machine to another over telephone lines. With the capability of copying any image on paper, a FAX device can transmit graphics as well as text. You can send filled-in forms, charts, drawings, longhand, and pictures.

Where can you go to send a FAX?

FAX is chosen over first-class mail when speed is important but crisp, dark print is not critical. For example, a transfer student might need to have his or her academic record sent for evaluation before registering. A deadline for an assignment (handwritten or printed) could be met in the event of illness that prevents your attending class. For group projects, a draft of the paper could be exchanged among team members for review and revisions—assuming each team member can access a FAX machine.

Word Processing

The application software most widely used by students, faculty, and administrators is word processing. You can translate your thoughts and ideas from your brain, through your fingertips, onto the screen, and into print. Revision and editing enable you to produce professional-looking documents, including letters, newsletters, reports, and resumes.

Many features are available to help you input and revise documents. With *Insert* and *Delete* you can correct errors as you key and further revise the document later. Should revision cut out an entire paragraph on page 3 of a 9-page report, you would not have to rekey the document. If you were notifying seven businesses and eight friends about your new address and phone number, you would key the letter once and the names and addresses once; then the *Merge* feature would produce all fifteen letters within a few minutes.

You might review the list of time-saving features of word processing software in the Table 1 and mark the ones you use frequently as well as those you would like to learn.

Table 1 Word Processing Features and Respective Uses

WORD PROCESSING FEATURE	EXAMPLE OF FEATURE'S USE
Decimal Tab	Aligns dollars and cents in a column
Full Justification	Aligns text evenly at left and right margins
Global Search and Replace	Changes *KS* to *Kansas* at each occurrence
Repagination	Adjusts page endings during revision
Thesaurus	Offers a substitute word for clarity
Widow/Orphan Protection	Checks for single line at top or bottom of page
Mail Merge	Combines a form letter with sets of variables
Spell Check (Speller)	Checks for words not in dictionary
Numbering	Prints page numbers in sequence
Sorting	Puts lists in alphabetical or numeric order
All Caps (Caps Lock)	Capitalizes letters but leaves numbers
Indent	Aligns a six-line quote five spaces from left margin
Macro (Stored Keystrokes)	Inputs a name and address block with two keystrokes
Move (Cut & Paste)	Repositions a block of text within a document

For a professional-looking document, select a laser printer. Printed assignments in an attractive, easy-to-read format likely will earn a higher grade than handwritten work.

Graphics

Graphics software is used to add illustrations to research papers and to make visual aids (slides or transparencies as well as handouts) for presentations. When columns of numbers from a database or spreadsheet are converted to a chart or graph, the information is easier to understand and more persuasive. Graphics can be printed on paper, added to presentation software, or prepared as an overhead transparency. Pie charts, line graphs, and bar charts are most effective when produced in color by ink jet printers and laser printers.

Graphics software requires a large amount of memory. To store a page of graphics at 300 dpi (dots per inch) could require 1.5 MB (megabytes) of memory. A computer requires about three times more memory for color displays than for monochrome.

If you are not experienced in using graphics programs or the graphics features of your word processing software, you could use a substitute method. Design your own artwork on a separate sheet of paper or find an image in a clip art book. Apply the enlarge or reduce feature of a photocopier to size it; then cut it out and paste it onto the appropriate page of your report. Recopy the page with its cut-and-pasted illustration for a final product. If line marks are visible, cover them with a liquid cover-up product.

Exercise 3 Designing Personal Letterhead

Using word processing and graphics, design personal letterhead that includes your name, mailing address, telephone number, and e-mail address. Include a graphic image representative of yourself.

Spreadsheets

Spreadsheets enable you to perform calculating functions and to make decisions. By using formulas that give the results of what-if assumptions, you can project outcomes of different assumptions or economic conditions. For example, you could determine what your overall term grade-point average would be if your grade in a 3-credit-hour course is a B versus a C.

Business and economics courses have case studies for which spreadsheets are used to project growth, net income, and profit margins. Teachers enter students' scores from assignments, projects, and exams onto a spreadsheet that calculates the final grades.

Spreadsheet software organizes information in rows and columns so it can be calculated. Rows are read across the screen or page and are identified by numbers—1, 2, 3, etc. Columns are read down the page and are identified by letters A, B, C, etc. Each intersection is a *cell*. The C6 cell address is located at the intersection of column C and row 6. Cells may contain labels (words), values (numbers), or mathematical formulas and functions. The results of spreadsheet calculations can be converted to illustrations by graphics software.

Databases

Database software enables information to be stored electronically in an organized form so it can be manipulated and retrieved easily for different purposes. Colleges set up separate databases for students, faculty, administrators, staff, alumni and development gifts, budgets, classroom facilities, and so forth to manage the different blocks of information.

The student database includes the following information fields: name, local address, local phone, permanent address, permanent phone, birth date, social security number, sex, guardian, classification, ACT or SAT scores, credit hours completed, credit hours of current enrollment, credit hours transferred from another college, catalog year of enrollment that guides general education course requirements, financial aid, and encumbrances or blocks. Your address and phone number are accessed for important communication; thus, it is important that you notify the records office immediately if your address changes.

In the student database each student is a *record*, and each category of information is a *field*. Student names would be divided into three fields—last name, first name, and middle initial. The records could be sorted in alphabetical order by last name as the primary sort, by first name as the secondary sort, and by middle initial as the third sort. A numeric sort by ZIP Code field would arrange addresses for processing a bulk mailing.

Databases commonly used by college students are online computerized card catalogs, special subject indexes (such as *Newspaper Abstracts*), and commercial databases (such as *CompuServe*). Computer databases are available on CD-ROM and by online connections through networks, the most popular being the Internet.

Exercise 4 Viewing College Databases

On your college website access the following databases. For each database, specify the database name, explain its order of data, describe one record, and identify three of its respective fields. An example is given. Be prepared to share your findings in class.

TYPE OF INFORMATION	DBASE NAME	ORDER OF DATA	A RECORD	EXAMPLES OF THREE FIELDS
Students	STDT	Alpha by last name	One student	Address, Phone, GPA
Schedule of Courses				
My Academic Summary				
Academic Calendar				

Presentations

Presentation software enables you to create attractive, easy-to-read slides and overhead transparencies for dynamic presentations. Pictures, charts, and graphs can be inserted to simplify information and to emphasize key points. Most software packages have templates within which text, data, and graphics can be placed to facilitate the production process.

Design consultants recommend that users apply simplicity and consistency in color, scheme, type style, headings, and artwork. Text lines should be short, and the font should be at least 24 points. For bulleted text, the proper technique is to use a minimum of two bullets and a maximum of five bullets per slide. A handout can be prepared that displays the slides in miniature size with nearby lines on which to write notes.

Presentation software enables you to enhance the professional quality of your speeches. Well-designed visuals can aid you in driving home the most important points or conclusion.

Explore Internet Capabilities

What is the difference between an internet and the Internet? An *internet* is a large network made up of two or more connected local area networks or wide area networks. The largest worldwide internet made up of connected networks is the *Internet*, a huge library of information or "information superhighway."

By accessing the Internet, you can send e-mail messages, research topics, download files, exchange information, view video clips, or listen to music. You can send e-mail to anyone who has a computer, a network connection, and a modem.

Domains

The addressing scheme of connected computers includes identification about where a computer resides—its *domain*. For example, the *edu* domain is the distinct category of colleges and universities in the United States that are connected by the Internet. Major domains include the following:

Domain	Type of Organization
com	Commercial/business entity
edu	Educational institution
gov	Government agency or department
mil	Military organization
net	Network administrative site (resources)
org	Other type of organization, usually a not-for-profit

One of the most popular and widely used Internet resources is the World Wide Web (WWW), often called the Web. In browsing (moving around through linked documents), you are working with hypertext and hypermedia.

Hypertext

If you were reading this page on your computer screen, each of the six domains listed above might be underlined or appear in a different color or font than adjacent text. If you clicked on *edu*, for example, a new document would appear on your screen that explains what *edu* domain means. Other words and phrases on which you could click would take you to other documents or to other places in the same document. *Hypertext* is the presentation of text that lets you move from idea to idea by following associated pathways. The clickable words and phrases are *links*, and the moving around through linked documents is called *browsing* (or surfing) the Net.

Hypermedia

Hypermedia is the presentation of a variety of media—including graphics, sound, and full-motion video as well as text. When you click on a link, the document you get does not have to be on the same computer as the original document. The primary *protocol* (rules that networks use to understand each other) for the World Wide Web is HTTP (HyperText Transfer Protocol), which enables you to access documents on any public Web server on the Internet.

Servers and Browsers

Special computers and software known as World Wide Web servers and *web browsers* make the linked hypermedia documents accessible to the public. Examples of Web browsers include Netscape Navigator and Microsoft Internet Explorer.

Search Engines

A *search engine*, like an online catalog, enables you to locate sites indexed by category or keyword. Popular search engines include AltaVista, Google, HotBot, Lycos, and Yahoo.

Internet Service Providers

To connect to the Internet, a person must have dial-up connection to a server. As a college student, your Internet service is available through your educational institution. Most individuals and businesses access the Internet through a commercial Internet service, for which a monthly service fee is charged. Two categories of commercial Internet services are Internet service providers and online services. *Internet service providers* offer direct access to the Internet, including e-mail service, but do not provide special subscriber content. Examples include AT&T Worldnet, MCI, and Netcom. *Online services* are large, private networks that provide to subscribers special content and other services in addition to access to the Internet. Examples include America Online, CompuServe, Microsoft Network, and Prodigy.

■ Conduct Research on the Web

You can access nearly unlimited information from the World Wide Web. The task of conducting research on the Web is quick but not always easy, because you have to sort through volumes of information. The information is neither categorized like a library database nor controlled for quality (accuracy and objectivity) as are peer reviewed articles identified in a library database. The following steps should help you as you conduct research on the Web.

Step 1: Preparation

If you know the Web address, called a *URL (Uniform Resource Locator)*, you merely key it at the browser's address box. The text must be keyed accurately, including capitalization. Here are the parts of the following typical URL: **http://www.usatoday.com/life/front**

http://	Protocol
www.usatoday.com	Domain name (home page of the website)
life/front	Directory path
	life–Collection of pages (the Life section of *USA Today*)
	front–A page on the site (front page of the Life section)

When you do not have a Web address, the first step is to define the type of information you want and to circle or list the keywords of the search. For an example, we want to get biographical information about Henry Louis Gates, Jr, who has promoted Afro-American studies at Harvard University. The keywords would be *Henry Louis Gates, Afro-American studies,* and *biography.*

Step 2: Selection of Search Engine

Among the easy-to-use, popular search engines are Google (**http://www.google.com**) and Yahoo (**http://www.yahoo.com**). Once you have mastered these computerized indexes to information on the Web, you can explore these search sites: AltaVista, Ask Jeeves (**www.ask.com**), Dogpile, Exite, HotBot, LookSmart, Lycos, and MetaCrawler.

Step 3: Keying of Search String

The manner by which you key your search string will determine the number of entries resulting from the search. As you review the following techniques, note which ones expand the results and which ones limit the results.

- *Boolean operators* are the words AND, OR, NOT (or AND NOT), and NEAR:

environment AND energy	Limits number of resulting entries by requiring that both search terms appear
environment OR energy	Expands number of resulting entries by requiring only that either search term appear
environment NOT energy	Limits number of resulting entries by forbidding the search term following NOT from appearing
environment NEAR energy	Limits number of entries by requiring that search terms appear within a certain number of words of each other (usually between 1 and 20)

- *Quotation marks* denote words that should appear together as a phrase:

  "Henry Louis Gates"
  "Afro-American studies"

- *Plus signs* are used before words that must appear in all resulting entries:

  "Henry Louis Gates" AND "Afro-American studies" +biography

- *Minus signs* are used before words you do not want to appear in resulting entries:

  "Lawrence Roberts" AND "data systems" –basketball –politician

(Of three people named Lawrence Roberts, you want information on the one who has developed efficient data systems and switching systems to make possible video and voice transmission over the Web.)

Step 4: Selection of Quality Entries

Realizing there is no editor, reviewer, or referee of information that is available on the Web, you have to decide which entries appear to be the highest quality.

- Consider the credibility of the author and/or publisher. An author writing for a well-known organization or publisher is more likely to be respected than an unknown author. Observe the site's host; addresses that end with .com are less likely to be objective than those that end with .edu, .gov, or .org.

- Look for reliability of information. If your search results in eight entries with six entries reporting the same information and the other two giving conflicting facts, you probably should eliminate the two from consideration.

- Observe the date of the information presented. For topics such as medical advances and computer technology, the most current dates are important.

- Check for other citations or references. A helpful entry is one that offers additional citations and references for a researcher to review.

Conducting research on the Web can be enjoyable and productive. The more you practice different types of searches, the more proficient you will become.

Exercise 5 Doing Research on the Web

For each of these topics write your search string, choose your favorite search engine, and conduct Web searches. Print the best and final search results page.

Lawrence Roberts, a leader in the design and use of the Internet, has developed a switching system that makes possible video and voice transmission over the Web.

Search string: _____

Mary Oliver, an American poet who celebrates the spirit of nature, has earned a Pulitzer Prize and National Book Award for expressing the beauty of the growing world.

Search string: _____

Robert Redford, actor, film maker, and environmentalist who has been a proponent of the Clean Air Act, Energy Conservation and Protection Act, and regulation of strip mining.

Search string: _____

Finally, for the topic of your choice: Select two of the best-quality entries to access, review, and print. Bring them to class so you can share the results with classmates.

◾ Be Aware of Ethical and Legal Issues

Where are judicial programs housed?

Any action that is unethical or illegal remains unethical or illegal in the Internet world. Being on a network does not change the legality of an action. Special laws concerning computer crime and networking are being developed as cases evolve. Among the issues of recent concern are research plagiarism, software piracy, unauthorized computer access, and unsuitable websites.

Whether information in your reports was derived from a published document or from the Internet, you are responsible for its accuracy and for giving proper credit to the source. To give proper credit for information researched by the Internet, you would give the search address. For example: **http://abcnews.com**.

Your college has discipline procedures in the event a student is involved in academic dishonesty. Actions that fall under the category of academic dishonesty include cheating, fabricating, plagiarism, and facilitating academic dishonesty for another person. *Cheating* is defined as using or attempting to use unauthorized materials, information, or study aids in an academic exercise. *Fabricating* is the unauthorized falsification or invention of information or citation. *Plagiarism* involves using the published or unpublished work of another person (by paraphrasing or direct quote) without full and clear acknowledgment. Plagiarism includes the unacknowledged use of materials prepared by another person or agency engaged in the selling of term papers or other academic materials, including material taken from or ordered through the Internet. All forms of academic dishonesty have been discovered among computer users.

Another issue of concern for student researchers is the lack of controls and standards on the Internet. Though some articles, books, and newspapers publish biased and inaccurate information, generally some editing and review have taken place to meet professional standards. On the Internet, however, each network has its own user policies and procedures. With no editorial or review body, the information may not have met any standards. In fact, some websites are deemed unsuitable—those that illustrate pornography, for example.

Exercise 6 Studying Legal and Ethical Issues of Net Use

Research one of the following issues and present your position in a two-page, double-spaced paper; include your references; use word processing software.

- Downloading a research paper from the Internet
- Reading another person's e-mail messages
- Infringing on copyrights (intellectual property, such as music and film) by software piracy
- Using the computer on company time for personal needs
- Identifying unsuitable websites

Computers are powerful tools that can assist us in doing many academic activities, in communicating with others, and in acquiring information for personal interests. As users, we are challenged to keep up to date with technology but excited about the vast capabilities and volumes of information available. At the same time, we must exercise ethical and legal behavior to be responsible citizens of our academic community.

Solve This Case—Wendy's Use of the Computer

Students in Dr Smith's advanced computer applications course were required for all assignments and exams to submit both the paper document and the media file. The paper document would show whether the final document was formatted properly for ease of reading. The media file would reveal whether the students performed the functions according to instructions (in the most efficient manner and conducive to revision later).

At the end of the term after all assignments and exams had been graded, the students were to close out their account—delete all files. Professor Smith was responsible to computer services for seeing that all student accounts were in fact closed and deleted from the computer system. To avoid deleting an important document, Professor Smith checked the contents of each file to see if the document was an assignment that should have been deleted or a document (such as a résumé) that the student would not want deleted (for which the student would be notified).

In checking each of the students' accounts, Dr Smith found only Wendy's account to have files not deleted—a research paper for another course, two computer assignments that should have been deleted, and this message to a friend: "I am applying for the computer lab assistant position but will have to work with Dr Smith. Do you know what she gave me on my final project? a D!!!"

1 How would you describe Wendy as a computer user?

2 Do you think she will get the computer lab assistant position? Why or why not?

My Reflections Journal

For this journal writing you are invited to describe your computer background and access to computer equipment. Provide two- or three-sentence answers for the following questions. Using your computer, you may either print the pages and turn them in on paper or e-mail the pages to your instructor. Ask your instructor which method he or she prefers.

1 What computer courses have you had before this term? Are you enrolled in a computer course this term? If so, what is it?

2 With which computer application software are you the most proficient? Describe the types of documents you have prepared, including the most advanced level of tasks.

3 Which aspects of computer usage would you like to develop further?

4 Describe your access to computer equipment. Do you have a computer at home?

5 What is your biggest frustration in using computers?

Website Practice Test

On the website at http://www.casadyenterprises.com/collegeedgebook/practicetests.htm you can access a practice test to check on your understanding of the chapter concepts. You may print the results of this self-test to review before taking the respective in-class exam.

11 DOING RESEARCH AT THE LIBRARY

Objectives

Upon completing this chapter, you should be able to:

- Locate the major areas of the library

- Identify the basic steps and protocol of library research

- Conduct electronic searches

- Develop a system of taking and organizing notes

- Document sources of reference

LIKE MINING FOR GOLD, using the library can make you rich if you know where to dig. You can become rich with knowledge, and wealth will be reflected in the grades you earn on assignments. The mission of the college or university library is to provide information services in support of the teaching, research, and public service missions of the school. Materials within the collection include books, periodicals, government documents, maps, videotapes, and indexes to support research efforts.

Where is your campus library?

What are its hours?

In studying this chapter and doing the exercises, you will benefit the most by going to your campus library or visiting its website. Obtain a map of the library, the library hours, the phone numbers of main departments, and handouts for convenient references (available at the reference desk or online). You might make a copy of the library hours and phone numbers for your desk and for each course notebook.

In preparation for your library visit, you can check to see that you have these items:

- Your student ID card—to verify student status and to check out materials
- Coins, $1 bills, or an account card (student ID card in many colleges)—to make photocopies or microform copies
- Your assignment—to support doing the most specific searches
- Supplies (including pens and paper)—to be prepared to work

■ Locate the Major Areas of the Library

Being familiar with high school and city libraries has prepared you to use your college library. Like visiting another's home, you find the same types of rooms as in your own house; but each room has a unique arrangement and accessories. Libraries house a circulation desk, a reference desk, indexes, books, periodicals (including newspapers), government documents, maps, microforms, and audiovisual materials. Open stacks can be accessed by users, whereas closed stacks can be accessed only by library personnel or by special permission.

Circulation Desk

The circulation desk, located close to the entrance and exit doors, is the area where you check out books and materials from the library. Your ID card is required for checking out books and for requesting various other services; be sure to have it with you. Teachers may have books, magazines, or photocopied articles placed on reserve at the circulation desk for students to use. Reserve materials are available for a limited time.

Reference Desk and Reference Area

Which items at the reference desk are most helpful to you?

If you need help in your searches, go to the reference desk. Printed handouts with instructions and illustrations can help you locate information, and librarians or library assistants are there to guide you and answer questions. If you need an item that is not in your library, it can be borrowed from another library (through *interlibrary loan*) for a small fee or at no cost. You would request the item at your reference desk or from an online form. It then will be delivered by the outside library. You will be notified by the library when the item is ready for pick-up.

Among the books located in the reference area are specialized dictionaries, almanacs, directories, encyclopedias, yearbooks, and consumer guides. Reference books that are most frequently requested are located at the reference desk. An example is the *Occupational Outlook Handbook*, which you would want to use for researching career options.

Located near the reference desk are computer terminals where you can access the online catalog—the primary access point to the library's holdings. Each terminal gives you access to a number of databases. Terminals are located in various areas of the library for your convenience. Look for instructional cards or sheets for step-by-step directions. If you need assistance, ask the librarian or library assistant at the reference desk for help.

In addition to on-site access to the online catalog and the library's various databases, you can log in from any computer by accessing the library's website address. Many campus computer labs, residence hall rooms, and homes are equipped to save you from going to the library for initial searches. These computers, however, might not have the capacity to download advanced searches and results. Performing research at the library enables you to perform advanced searches and to readily access the respective materials.

Indexes (in Reference Area)

The library subscribes to various indexes (in paper or by electronic access) that are either general or subject specific. An example of a general index is *The Readers' Guide to Periodical Literature*, which indexes magazine articles on many subjects. Subject indexes give rapid access to special subject reference sources—including business, education, literature, and psychology. Indexes that specialize by subjects include *ERIC, MLA Bibliography, Sociological Abstracts*, and *MasterFile Elite* on EBSCOhost. Major newspaper indexes include *The New York Times, USA Today,* and *The Wall Street Journal*.

Periodicals (Newspapers, Magazines, and Journals)

A periodical is published at regular intervals—weekly, monthly, or quarterly. The library keeps magazines and journals until a volume has accumulated a certain number of issues (typically six months or a year) and then has them bound for permanent keeping. Periodicals on reserve are located at the circulation desk.

Current issues within this year are located in the current periodicals area. Older issues that have been bound are in the periodical stacks (back issues) area. Those that have been microfilmed or microfiched can be viewed in the microforms area.

The library subscribes to many local, regional, national, and international newspapers. The most current newspapers are on display in the current periodicals area. Previous weeks' issues are boxed and labeled by the week at some libraries. After several months certain newspapers, such as *The New York Times* and *The Wall Street Journal*, can be located on microfilm or microfiche in the microforms area.

Books

Shelves of general collection books occupy much of a library's space. Libraries arrange general collection books by subject—using either the Dewey Decimal Classification System shown in Table 1 (Arabic numerals with decimals) or the Library of Congress Classification System shown in Table 2 (combination of alphabetic letters and Arabic numerals).

Books can be located quickly by using the online catalog. Terminals are located throughout the library for your convenience. The online catalog tells you how to find a book and whether it is available or has been checked out. If the computer system is down or a terminal is not available, you may have to search for your books by using a card-based catalog or asking a librarian for assistance.

Table 1 Dewey Decimal Classification System

THE DEWEY DECIMAL CLASSIFICATION SYSTEM

000	General (bibliographies, encyclopedias, newspapers, and magazines)
100	Philosophy and Psychology
200	Religion
300	Social Studies
400	Languages
500	Natural Science
600	Technology
700	The Arts
800	Literature
900	Geography and History

Table 2 The Library of Congress Classification Systerm

What is the classification of books you use most often for your discipline?

THE LIBRARY OF CONGRESS CLASSIFICATION SYSTEM

A	General Works	N	Fine Arts
B	Philosophy, Psychology, Religion	P	Language and Literature
C	History: Auxiliary Sciences	Q	Science
D	History: World	R	Medicine
E-F	History: America	S	Agriculture
G	Geography and Anthropology	T	Technology
H	Social Sciences	U	Military Science
J	Political Science	V	Naval Science
K	Law	Z	Bibliography and Library Science
L	Education		
M	Music		

Letters I, O, W, X, and Y are reserved for further expansion.

Table 3 shows the Science subheadings of each classification system.

Table 3 Science Subheadings of Each Classification System

EXCERPTS FROM DEWEY DECIMAL SYSTEM		EXCERPTS FROM LIBRARY OF CONGRESS SYSTEM	
500	Sciences	Q	Science
510	Math	QA	Mathematics
530	Physics	QB	Astronomy
534	Sound	QC	Physics
535	Light	QD	Chemistry
536	Heat	QE	Geology
540	Chemistry	QH	Natural History
580	Botany	QK	Botany
590	Zoology	QL	Zoology

Microforms

The microforms area contains microfilm, microfiche, and microcards of both old and new materials. Many libraries have old issues of *The New York Times* and *The Wall Street Journal* back to the late 1800s. A copy of any page can be made at a reader-printer for a nominal charge.

Audiovisuals

At the audiovisual area you can check out audiotapes, videotapes, CDs, and DVDs. Many items are reserved for use in the library only. Professors might put certain materials on reserve for students to access so that they can complete a course assignment. For example, if you missed class when a videotape was shown, you could go to the audiovisual area to view it (provided a copy was placed on reserve).

Curriculum Resource Center

The curriculum resource center, in colleges that have education majors, has textbooks and curriculum guides used by grades K-12 in nearby schools. Students also may find juvenile and young adult books, posters, and other supportive materials to use for methods course assignments, student tutoring, and student teaching.

Government Documents

Government publications inform citizens about government activities, operations, and services. Recognized as primary sources, these publications include annual reports, bibliographies, census data, directories, statistical analyses, and transcripts of congressional hearings. The *Statistical Abstract of the United States* is one of the more popular U.S. government documents.

The U.S. government makes this information available to nearly 1,400 "depository" libraries, which are required to select publications that best meet the needs of their constituents. These documents are available in several formats—paper, microfiche, and electronic. Many of these same libraries also receive their own state documents by virtue of being state depository libraries.

Even some local governments send their official publications to libraries. In addition, there are forty-six United Nations depository libraries in the U.S., which provide valuable information to those studying international relations.

Some colleges and universities keep their official school publications, including catalogs and yearbooks, in the government documents area or in a special collections area in the library. A number of college libraries even offer voter registration and tax forms as a service to their patrons.

Special Collections

Many libraries have received gifts of unique collections, which are housed in one or more areas named Special Collections. Examples would be an author's works (publications by Will Rogers) and books and materials on a specific topic (publications about the Civil War).

Some libraries house their rare book collections in the same area. Rare books often cover a wide variety of topics such as literature, histories of Europe and America, religion, and the printing industry. Rare books are located in special collections departments because of their age, format, subject matter, scarcity, or fragile condition. The special collections area is also where some libraries maintain the college archives such as catalogs, yearbooks, presidential papers, faculty papers, student theses, and campus photographs. A college archives area serves as the institutional memory by identifying, acquiring, preserving, and providing access to records of enduring value that chronicle the history and development of the institution.

Exercise 1 Locating the Major Areas

Go to each of these areas of the library and obtain the information requested. Use a computer to prepare your answers, and staple the attachments together.

Reference Area	a Names of three encyclopedia sets b Names of three special subject indexes in paper format c Names of three electronic indexes that can be used for your particular discipline
Periodicals Area	Select a popular magazine published this month. Read one article and write a one-paragraph reaction; give the source.
Books and Circulation Desk	Find a book on the subject of your favorite hobby or interest. Check it out to read. Type the complete source.
Newspapers	Read one of today's local or regional newspapers. Write a one-paragraph reaction to an article on the front page.
Microforms	Search a newspaper on the date of your birth. Find a noteworthy article on the front page. Make a copy of it.
Government Documents	Pick a topic with which the government would be involved, and search for a document located in the government documents area or published by a government agency. Write down the call number, the title, and the search strategy used to find this item.

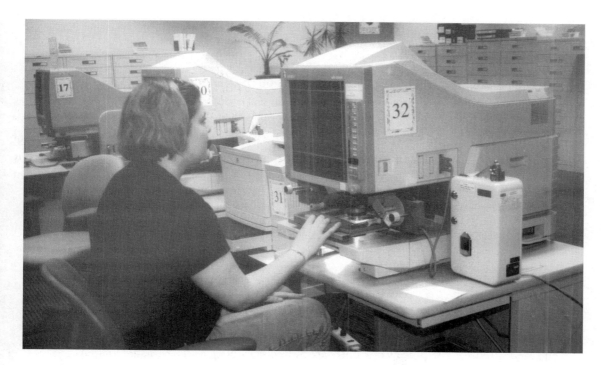

◼ Identify the Basic Steps and Protocol of Library Research

Library research involves finding out what has been studied and written by others. With the ability to access the vast information available in libraries and their electronic resources, we can grow in knowledge and wisdom throughout our lives. Each research topic is somewhat unique and requires the use of different resources. However, most library research projects have at least some elements in common. To do library research efficiently, consider following these basic steps:

1 Know the purpose of the research, and state the problem in your own words.

2 Narrow your topic, and define key terms.

3 Prepare an outline to organize major points.

4 Search for information in the library by locating reference material, books, and articles.

5 Develop a system of taking notes and putting them in order.

6 Document the reference sources while taking notes.

The amount of time required for a research project depends on the professor's assignment (which may or may not designate number of pages), the amount of information available on the topic, the ease of locating viable library sources, and your expertise. An interlibrary loan likely would extend the time. Another factor is whether you are working on an individual assignment or a group project.

Reference Collection

The reference collection is a good starting point in conducting research because of the easy access to materials. The materials are arranged alphabetically and indexed. Reference articles are relatively short, and they contain definitions of some of the vocabulary you will encounter during the research process. They also give you an overview of the topic. Each reference article usually gives a list of sources cited for the topic.

Books

Books relevant to your topic can be located by using different methods. One method is to use the bibliographies or list of cited sources found at the end of reference articles. These bibliographies or list of cited sources will direct you to material on your topic. Another method is to search the library's online catalog, which allows you to search the library's holdings. If you are trying to find material on a certain subject, type a couple of the keywords that describe the subject. After obtaining some material from the catalog, pay attention to the subject headings listed on the records you search. These subjects will help you to narrow your search topic and find relevant information about your topic.

If you need a book that the library does not have, complete an interlibrary loan request form or contact the reference desk for assistance.

Articles

Articles are found in periodicals (commonly called magazines, journals, or newspapers). Articles are good to use for research because they contain the following common features: frequency of publication; specific subject matter; relatively current information; and usually short, brief documents. Hundreds of periodicals currently are available in print and electronic formats.

Articles can be difficult to find. The best way to locate periodical articles is to use indexes and abstracts in electronic or paper format. (Browsing through stacks can be tedious and unproductive.) Indexes and abstracts, found in print and electronic formats, contain citations that provide the information to locate the particular articles. Some periodical databases contain full-text articles, which you can print or e-mail to yourself. If an article you want is not available in full text, check the library's holdings.

If the issue you need is not in the library's collection, complete an interlibrary loan request form or contact the reference department for assistance.

In your search for information and supporting facts, look for sources that are the most current (or at the time of the historical occurrence) and are written by the most reputable authors. For information on technological advancement, you would look for articles written within the last six months. For the acceptance of personal computers in office systems, you would look for articles written in the early 1980s—when corporations first were orienting and training employees on using computers.

In searching for the most reliable and valid data, you would choose an article from a refereed journal rather than a trade magazine. Articles that appear in a refereed journal have undergone blind reviews (the name of the author is not revealed) by at least three experts in the field. In contrast, articles that appear in trade magazines typically undergo acceptance by an editor only. If the article was written by a vendor, you can expect a biased view; probably the magazine includes an advertisement of the vendor's product.

In conducting research or using the library for any other purpose, feel free to ask the library personnel for assistance. Your campus library personnel look forward to helping you with your research. The reference desk and other library staff are there to serve your information needs. Your question is not an interruption; it is the main focus of their work.

Library users are expected to be quiet, courteous, and considerate of the library staff as well as fellow researchers. Return materials promptly so they will be available to other users. Follow instructions on whether to return items to the respective shelves or to a depository table. Do not tear out pages.

If you are assessed a library fine (for late returns or lost items), pay promptly. In many colleges, library fines are encumbrances or blocks; students cannot register or have their transcript mailed until the fines are paid. Also check the rules on copying materials and obtaining copy permissions to protect yourself in the event of ethical and legal scrutiny.

Conduct Electronic Searches

Electronic searches can be conducted using the online catalog as well as any electronic database to which the library subscribes or has a site license, including magazine and journal indexes. The online catalog has the records of materials the library owns and is not used to find periodical articles. Use the online catalog to find only the local library's holdings. To conduct electronic searches, go to a computer terminal.

The introductory screen enables you to select the online catalog, categories of indexes, and various other types of information. Select your library's catalog, where you can search by author, title, subject, keyword, or call number. Each screen has instructions to guide you onward. Though your library's system probably is unique from the examples given, the search process is similar and the monitor will display similar information only in a unique screen format.

Search for a Book by Author

Our example will be to search the online catalog for writings by Mark Twain. To search by author:

1 Key Twain Mark or Twain, Mark (depending on your system's software).

2 Displayed will be a list of books he has written (see Figure 1). In this example, the search found 334 records and displayed the first 12 records.

3 To see detailed information about *The Adventures of Huckleberry Finn,* click on the box to the left of the desired entry or on the title link.

4 Displayed will be the record, which can be printed (see Figure 2). The screen will show the location, the call number, and the status of the copies the library has on record.

Exercise 2 Searching by Author

To learn about the writings of a favorite author, conduct a search by author.

1 Print the screen that lists all the documents on record at the library.

2 Select one of the entries to display detailed information on the screen.

3 Print the screen that gives detailed information about the document.

4 Write your name on the printout sheet(s) as evidence of your search.

5 Find the document in the library, and scan the pages to get an idea of the writing.

Figure 1—Search by Author (Mark Twain)

AUTHOR ▾	Twain, Mark	SMSU	▾	Search

Result page:**1** 2 3 4 5 6 7 8 9 10 11 ... 28 Next

Save Marked Records	Save All On Page

Num	Mark	AUTHORS (1-12 of 334)	Medium	Year
		Twain Mark 1835 1910		
1	☐	**1601.**	BOOK/JOURNAL	1938
2	☐	**'1601' : A Tudor Fireside Conversation** / as Written By The Ingenuous, Virtuous, And Learned Mark Twain, Wit ; Embellished By The Worthy Alan	BOOK/JOURNAL	c1969
3	☐	**1601 ; And, Is Shakespeare Dead?** / Mark Twain ; Foreword, Shelley Fisher Fishkin ; Introduction, Erica Jong ; Afterword, Leslie A. Fied	BOOK/JOURNAL	1996
4		**"1601", or, Conversation as it was at the fireside in the time of the Tudors -- See 1601**		
5		**1601, or, Sociall fireside conversation in ye time of ye Tudors -- See 1601**		
6	☐	**The £1,000,000 Bank-Note And Other New Stories** / Mark Twain ; Foreword, Shelley Fisher Fishkin ; Introduction, Malcolm Bradbury ; Afterword, James D.	BOOK/JOURNAL	1996
7	☐	**The $30,000 Bequest, And Other Stories,** / by Mark Twain [Pseud.]**	BOOK/JOURNAL	1917
8	☐	**The $30,000 Bequest And Other Stories** / Mark Twain ; Foreword, Shelley Fisher Fishkin ; Introduction, Frederick Busch ; Afterword, Judith Ya	BOOK/JOURNAL	1996
9	☐	**The Adventures Of Colonel Sellers : Being Mark Twain's Share Of The Gilded Age, A Novel Which He Wro** / now Published Separately For The First Time And Comprising, In Effect, A New Work ; Edited And With	BOOK/JOURNAL	1965
10	☐	**Adventures Of Huckelberry Finn.**	BOOK/JOURNAL	1986
11	☐	**Adventures Of Huckleberry Finn** / Mark Twain [I.E. S. L. Clemens] ; Edited, With An Introd. And Notes, By Henry Nash Smith.	BOOK/JOURNAL	1958
12	☐	**Adventures Of Huckleberry Finn** / Mark Twain ; Introduction By Justin Kaplan ; Foreword And Addendum By Victor Doyno.	BOOK/JOURNAL	c1996

Save Marked Records	Locate In Results
Save All On Page	334

Figure 2—One Record (The Adventures of Huckleberry Finn)

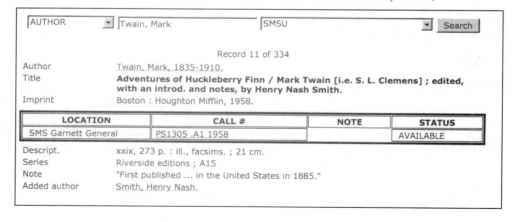

AUTHOR ▾	Twain, Mark	SMSU	▾	Search

Record 11 of 334

Author	Twain, Mark, 1835-1910.
Title	**Adventures of Huckleberry Finn / Mark Twain [i.e. S. L. Clemens] ; edited, with an introd. and notes, by Henry Nash Smith.**
Imprint	Boston : Houghton Mifflin, 1958.

LOCATION	CALL #	NOTE	STATUS
SMS Garnett General	PS1305 .A1 1958		AVAILABLE

Descript.	xxix, 273 p. : ill., facsims. ; 21 cm.
Series	Riverside editions ; A15
Note	"First published ... in the United States in 1885."
Added author	Smith, Henry Nash.

Search for a Book by Subject

To search by subject, it helps to be familiar with the topic so you can be specific. The terms of the *Library of Congress Subject Headings* must be used. Assume you want information about freshman students at colleges and universities in the United States. For this example, first we will be general; then we will be specific:

1 Check the *Library of Congress Subject Headings*.

2 Key *college freshmen* and click on Submit Search.

   Notice that 24 subject titles were found (the first 12 displayed); the 24 titles generated 47 entries (see Figure 3).

Figure 3—Subject Search (college freshmen)

Num	Mark	SUBJECTS (1-12 of 24)	Year	Entries 47 Found
1	☐	College Freshmen		9
2	☐	College Freshmen Attitudes		2
3	☐	College Freshmen Counseling Of United States	1989	1
4	☐	College Freshmen Education United States Statistics	1996	1
5	☐	College Freshmen Health And Hygiene		3
6	☐	College Freshmen Health And Hygiene Middle West	2000	1
7	☐	College Freshmen Mental Health	c1997	1
8	☐	College Freshmen Missouri Springfield	1988	1
9	☐	College Freshmen Montana Mathematics	1989	1
10	☐	College Freshmen Nutrition	1967	1
11	☐	College Freshmen Oregon Eugene Health And Hygiene	1959	1
12	☐	College Freshmen Oregon Health And Hygiene	1966	1

Starting over, this time we will be more specific:

1 Key *college freshmen united states*.

2 Notice that 6 subject titles with a total of 16 entries were found (see Figure 4).

Figure 4—Subject Search (college freshmen united states)

Num	Mark	SUBJECTS (1-6 of 6)	Year	Entries 16 Found
1	☐	College Freshmen United States		6
2	☐	College Freshmen United States Conduct Of Life		6
3	☐	College Freshmen United States Information Services Congresses	2002	1
4	☐	College Freshmen United States Periodicals	1998-	1
5	☐	College Freshmen United States Testing	1987	1
6	☐	College Freshmen United States Transportation	c1991	1

In using two-part words as descriptors, such as *United States* or *New Mexico*, you need to know how your library's system works. Does it search for every instance of *United States* as a phrase, or does it search for every instance of *United* and every instance of *States*? The reference desk can help you.

Exercise 3 Searching by Subject

Conduct a search by subject of *college freshmen*.

1 View the screen(s) listing the documents in your library.
2 Choose one of the entries to examine individually.
3 Print the screen of the individual entry, and label it with your name.
4 Find the document on the shelf and glance through it.
5 On the printout (step 3), write reaction comments.

Search for a Book by Keyword

Keyword searching looks for the word or phrase you enter in titles, in topics, and in the text of documents. If you do not know how to spell a name or word, key only the first part about which you are confident.

Assume you want to acquire information about water pollution in California. Upon selecting Keyword, you would type the words to identify your search. If you were to key *environment*, in the library for this example you would find 12,252 titles. Keying *water* would result in 23,481 titles; *pollution*, 8,739; and *California*, 16,567 titles.

The "Boolean operators" *and, or,* and *not* are helpful in defining keyword searches. To widen a search (generating more titles or entries), you would use *or;* to narrow a search (generating fewer titles) you would use *and* or *not* as part of the search string. In the accompanying example, keying *environment and pollution* resulted in 1,200 titles; adding *California* reduced the number of titles to 26; and adding *water* to the keyword search reduced the number to only 11 entries.

Figure 5—Keyword Search (environment and water and pollution and California)

| WORD | environment and water and poll | SMSU | Search |

Sorted by Date

| Save Marked Records | Save All On Page |

Num	Mark	WORDS (1-11 of 11)	Medium	Year
1	☐	Water pollution risks of methyl tertiary butyl ether (MTBE) : field hearing before the Committee on	BOOK/JOURNAL	1998
2	☐	Karst waters & environmental impacts : proceedings 5th International Symposium and Field Seminar on	BOOK/JOURNAL	1997
3	☐	Mercury pollution : integration and synthesis / edited by Carl J. Watras and John W. Huckabee.	BOOK/JOURNAL	c1994
4	☐	Energy & pollution control opportunities to the year 2000 / [compiled and edited by Marilyn Jackson]	BOOK/JOURNAL	c1994
5	☐	Race to save the planet [videorecording] : level I videodisc.	VIDEO/FILM	c1993
6	☐	Review of ground water contamination : hearing before the Subcommittee on Environment and Labor of t	BOOK/JOURNAL	1991
7	☐	Delineation of a hydrocabron (weathered gasoline) plume in shallow deposits at the U.S. Naval Weapon	BOOK/JOURNAL	1991
8	☐	Toxics A to Z : a guide to everyday pollution hazards / John Harte ... [et al.].	BOOK/JOURNAL	c1991
9	☐	Health implications of toxic chemical contamination of the Santa Monica Bay : hearing before the Sub	BOOK/JOURNAL	1986
10	☐	Water rights : scarce resource allocation, bureaucracy, and the environment / editor, Terry L. Ander	BOOK/JOURNAL	c1983
11	☐	Feasibility of recovering useful salts from irrigation wastewater concentrates produced by power pla	BOOK/JOURNAL	1980

| Save Marked Records | Save All On Page |

Using specific terms and Boolean operators enables you to narrow your search. For efficiency you want only the documents most relevant to your research topic. Selecting the eleventh entry of the keyword search example (Figure 5) would produce the information presented in Figure 6. The search string window on the screen might limit the display to only the first words of the search string; the rest of the words are in the background.

In addition to Boolean searching, truncation provides you with another search feature. Truncation especially is good if you are unsure of the spelling. Truncation allows you to retrieve documents containing variations of the spelling of a search term. To conduct a truncation search, type the first letters of the word followed by an asterisk (*) or a question mark (?). For example, *improvi** would retrieve *improvidence, improvident, improvisation,* and *improvise.*

Electronic indexes, databases, and library catalogs contain a vast amount of information. These resources cannot understand your search idea when you type your search words. However, these resources will produce exactly what you type in your search. Many searches fail because of typos or spelling errors; always go back and check for any of these problems.

Figure 6—One Record (Feasibility of recovering useful salts . . .)

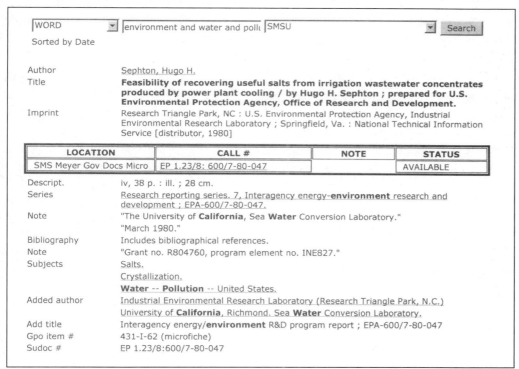

Exercise 4 Searching by Keyword

Conduct a search by keyword to learn more about water pollution.

1 Print the search results.
2 Select one entry to view for detailed information.
3 Print the screen that gives detailed information about that entry.
4 Print the full text as shown on the screen, or find the document on the shelf.
5 Scan the document to find three interesting facts. On a sheet of paper list the three facts and the respective page numbers. Attach the screen printouts (steps 3 and 4) to your sheet.

Search for Magazine and Journal Documents

Your library subscribes to or pays a site license fee for a number of commercial databases. Among the popular magazine and journal indexes are EBSCOhost, FirstSearch, Gale Research, and Lexis/Nexis Universe.

▶ *EBSCOhost* gives access to over 3,100 periodicals and documents, of which 1,500 periodicals have full text. This general interest database is updated daily.

▶ *FirstSearch* is linked to bibliographic records that represent the holdings of 20,000 libraries worldwide. It includes indexes to books and periodicals on many topics. Materials can be ordered by using the interlibrary loan system.

▶ *Gale Research* provides databases about authors, science, and history—helpful in researching biographies or literary critiques.

Which magazine or journal index do you use most often?

▶ *Lexis/Nexis Universe* indexes legal and business resources plus late-breaking news. You can access federal and state case law, United States Code and law review articles, company profiles, and business forecasts. Full text of newspapers can be viewed.

Electronic database searches can be conducted at home by accessing the library's web page, which can be accessed either on campus or off campus by the college's proxy server. The reference desk will provide information and instructions on how to connect to the college's proxy server.

■ Develop a System of Taking and Organizing Notes

When using the library computer databases, have your search results printed. Keep the printouts as records of your search pattern and the sources to reference in your paper.

Once you have narrowed your topic, you will draft an outline of your research paper. An outline is like a road map, enabling you to reach your destination by the shortest route. In the process of doing searches at the library, you might revise your outline. Your system of taking notes, whether on cards or paper, hinges on your outline. You might write notes on cards, half-sheets of paper, or full sheets of paper (see Figure 7).

Figure 7—Research Note Card

> II   Causes of Pollution
>   A   Agricultural Runoff
>   Herbicides
>   Pesticides   } Spills into groundwater
>   Fertilizer
>   Nitrates — from pesticides, corn, soybeans
>   Deprive fish of oxygen
>   Corrupt drinking wells
> (Jeff Glasser and Kenneth Walsh, US News
> and World Report, 7-17-2000, Vol 129 Issue 3 p 27)

Figure 8—Outline Overlaid on Marked Text of Source Document

Environmental Pollution

I   Major Environmental Factors
   A Air
   B Water

II   Causes of Pollution
   A Agricultural Runoff
   B Urban Development
   C Industrial Waste
   D Exhaust Fumes and Smoke

III   Government's Influence
   A Environmental Protection Agency
   B Legislative Acts

veto the measure. He has indicated he'll sign it, but also has signaled environ- ...alize the rules before he does. That maneuver would give Clinton and Vice Pres ... whose No. 1 environmental concerns, polls say, are cleaner water and air. But ... a political fast one could backfire. It would be mostly for show, which means ... enforce the new rules. The strategy also could so inflame congressional ...s, that they might retaliate by abolishing water cleanup slots at the EPA and ...rcement efforts. Either way, "It's not going to change," admits Clean Water ...ws how long [Congress] will delay it?"

II Causes of Pollution
A Agricultural Runoff

In the ...ing passage of the Clean Water Act, the EPA largely succeeded in stemming the "point source" discharges of big industrial and municipal offenders, whose pipes spewed chemicals directly into oceans, rivers, lakes, and streams. It has become clear, however, that "point source" pollution is only part of the problem. As farmers sprayed more herbicides and pesticides and spread more fertilizer on their crops in the late 1970s and early 1980s, increasing levels of "nonpoint source" contaminants spilled into the ground-water. The pesticides—and corn and soybean crops naturally—spawn nutrients such as nitrates, which move easily in water and deprive fish of much needed oxygen. The nitrates also corrupt rural drinking wells and can lead to blue baby syndrome, in which infants essentially suffocate.

The Midwest Corn Belt provides a perfect example of the perils of agricultural runoff. The nitrates from the farms leak into the Illinois, Ohio, and Missouri rivers, which empty into the Mississippi River and eventually into the Gulf of Mexico. When the weather gets hot, the accumulation of nitrates triggers a "dead zone" the size of New Jersey in the gulf.

The agriculture lobby says that unlike industrial polluters, who control the amount of chemicals they produce, farmers cannot easily contain the problem. They can't do anything, for instance, about rain, which they view as the top reason nitrates dribble into the water supply. John Hall, who runs a Wisconsin agricultural institute that promotes ecofriendly farming, says the answer is for farmers to branch out. If the Corn Belt grew other crops such as winter grain and alfalfa, which suck up water during the rainy spring season, less water would run off and fewer nutrients would creep into it.

Farmers say they're being unfairly blamed for the nation's water woes. Says Orford, N.H., tree farmer Tom Thomson: "They should focus on soil runoff from the development shopping malls and housing, the gasoline dripping out of cars, and the other ills of urban sprawl instead of beating up on the best land stewards in the country."

PHOTO: Fertilizer such as this being sprayed on a Mississippi farm is a major cause of river pollution.

~~~~~~~~

By Jeff Glasser with Kenneth T. Walsh

Source: U.S. News & World Report, 07/17/2000, Vol. 129 Issue 3, p27, 1p

Original Source

To facilitate organizing your note cards and inserting them at strategic places within the text draft, limit each card or sheet of paper to one main idea, point, or subtopic. Then label the card or paper to include the corresponding outline entry number and/or letter and a phrase that describes its main idea, point, or subtopic. Identify the source, including the page number (see Figure 8).

You might choose to photocopy the article or excerpt from a book and highlight the important points. For each photocopied page:

1 Label the top of the sheet to include the corresponding outline entry number or letter and a phrase that describes its main idea, point, or subtopic.
2 Attach it to the respective note card or sheet (if applicable).
3 Identify the source, including the page number.

By keeping your notes and photocopies labeled to coincide with your outline, you will be able to compose your draft efficiently.

Exercise 5 Preparing Note Cards of Paraphrased Text

From the sheet of paper on which you wrote three interesting facts about water pollution (Exercise 4), prepare three note cards—one for each fact.

1 At the top of the card write a descriptive phrase to label the fact.
2 Paraphrase the text as you transfer the fact from your sheet of paper to the card.
3 At the bottom of the card in parentheses write the source, including the page number.

In small groups share the three most interesting facts your learned.

■ Document Sources of Reference

A reference might be a *direct quote* (word-for-word text) or *paraphrased text* (information rewritten in your own words). A direct quote is put within quotation marks; if it is four or more lines, indent the text block, and omit the quotation marks. Paraphrased text, though it has been reworded, needs to be referenced. Conscientious writers who are aware of ethical and legal issues about copyrights give credit where it is due and are careful not to lose the author's intended meaning.

For the reader of your report or research paper to know the sources referenced, you will list the sources at the end of the document. The format will depend on the manuscript style your professor assigns. Among commonly used manuscript styles are those outlined in the *Publication Manual of the American Psychological Association* (APA style) and the *MLA Handbook for Writers of Research Papers* (MLA style—published by the Modern Language Association). A major difference between the two styles is whether the date appears as part of the reference in the body of the paper: For APA, the date of the source document appears as part of a reference note in the body; for MLA, the reference note does not have the date.

APA style is preferred by the business, education, psychology, and science disciplines. MLA style is the choice of writers in the humanities—art, history, literature, music, and theater. For source documentation the two styles differ in many ways, as the examples show.

Which manuscript style are you to use for this course?

Documenting Periodicals
APA

Benson, H. & Proctor, W. (2003). Triggers for a happier life. *The Saturday Evening Post*, 275 (4), 38-39.

MLA

Benson, Herbert, and William Proctor. "Triggers for a Happier Life." *The Saturday Evening Post* 275.4 (2003): 38-39.

Documenting Books
APA

Agatston, A. (2003). *The south beach diet.* Emmaus, PA: Rodale Press.

MLA

Agatston, Arthur. *The South Beach Diet.* Emmaus: Rodale Press, 2003.

Documenting Internet Sources
APA

Jacobson, J. (1995). A history of facilitated communication: Science, pseudoscience, and anti-science. *American Psychologist, 50,* 750-765. Retrieved May 2, 2001 from http://www.apa.org/journals/jacobson.html

MLA

Barry, Dave. "How to Handle the IRS." *HeraldLink.* 2 May 2001 <http://www.herald.com/archive/barry/archive/98mar19.htm>.

Regardless of style, each reference must be documented accurately and completely. Then you can format it according to the instructions of the style manual.

For Book Documentation

1 Each author's last name, first name, and middle initial
2 Name of book
3 Name of publishing company and its city and state
4 Copyright year
5 Page numbers of specific references

For Government Publications

1 Name of department or division
2 Name of bureau or agency
3 Name of publication
4 Copyright year
5 Page numbers of specific references

For Periodicals

1 Each author's last name, first name, and middle initial
2 Title of the article
3 Name of magazine, journal, or newspaper
4 Volume number and issue number
5 Date of issue's publication—month and year; month, day, and year; season and year
6 Page numbers of special references

For Electronic Sources

1 Name of the author of the article
2 Title of the document
3 Title of print version of work
4 Date (copyright date) of print version
5 Title of electronic work
6 Medium
7 Information supplier
8 Electronic address, or URL, of the source
9 Access date

Exercise 6 Doing Library Research

Choose a public affairs issue from this week's news.

1 State the public affairs issue in your own words.
2 Narrow your topic, and define key terms.
3 Prepare an outline to organize major points.
4 Search for information in the library. Conduct a subject search or keyword search at an online terminal; print the search results.
5 Choose three records to access from the shelves or from full-text online display.
6 Either photocopy or prepare note cards on the reference information; label the references to parallel your outline.
7 Write the complete source of the reference on each photocopy or note card.

Self-Assessment: Assessing Ability to Do Library Research ✓

On a scale of 1 (low) to 5 (high), assess your knowledge of the campus library and the ability to perform each of the tasks described.

	KNOWLEDGE OF THE LIBRARY AND ABILITY TO DO RESEARCH	LOW 1	2	3	4	HIGH 5
1	Getting help at the reference desk and reference area					
2	Using the newspaper indexes					
3	Locating this week's issues of newspapers and magazines					
4	Finding your discipline's general collection books					
5	Getting a copy of an article in the microforms area					
6	Viewing a videotape, CD, or DVD in the audiovisual area					
7	Obtaining census data in the government documents area					
8	Searching for a book by author					
9	Searching for a book by subject					
10	Searching for a magazine or journal article by keyword					
11	Taking and organizing research notes					
12	Documenting sources of reference					

If any of the items were assessed as 1 or 2, review those sections of this chapter and seek additional help from a librarian or library assistant.

Solve This Case—Hank's Research at the Library

In researching the topic of unhealthy dieting, Hank wanted to discover the differences between the symptoms of anorexia and bulimia. He tried searching by subject, keying *dieting*, but did not get any listing. Then he searched by the keyword *anorexia or bulimia or dieting*, which generated 162 entries—most of which were not related to his topic.

1 Why do you think Hank could not complete a successful search by subject?

2 How could Hank get better results in searching by keyword?

My Reflections Journal

In this journaling opportunity, respond to three of the following five questions, writing a short paragraph for each answer. Using your computer, you may either print the page and turn it in on paper or e-mail the page to your instructor. Ask your instructor which method he or she prefers.

1 How comfortable do you feel about performing research in your college library?

2 How adept are you in performing electronic searches either at home or in the library?

3 Describe your background and experiences in using a public or a school library.

4 What are the most challenging aspects of doing research for college assignments?

5 What is most enjoyable about using your college library?

Website Practice Test

On the website at http://www.casadyenterprises.com/collegeedgebook/practicetests.htm you can access a practice test to check on your understanding of the chapter concepts. You may print the results of this self-test to review before taking the respective in-class exam.

12 WRITING AND SPEAKING

Objectives

Upon completing this chapter, you should be able to:

- Work in small groups for collaborative projects

- Organize your thoughts and compose a draft

- Use word processing software aids

- Complete a research paper and learn from the results

- Speak to a large group

AMONG THE TOP SKILLS employers value most highly are teamwork, writing, and communication. The importance of these three skills is documented by a joint survey conducted recently by the U.S. Department of Labor and the American Association of Training and Development. Successful college graduates who have advanced to administrative and managerial positions in their careers can attest to the value of these skills.

Because employers value communication skills, higher education emphasizes small-group work, writing, and speaking. Many of your professors, including those outside the departments of English and communication departments, will incorporate these three types of assignments. English composition, interpersonal communication, and public speaking courses cover these topics in depth. The tips in this chapter should help you in the meantime.

■ Work in Small Groups for Collaborative Projects

Working in small groups helps build teamwork skills, which can be further refined throughout life. There are both benefits and challenges to such work, as various backgrounds, goals, and abilities are used for one project. You will learn from each experience.

Benefiting from Team Projects

Working with other classmates on a project offers a number of benefits. Each person has expertise the others might not have. Pooling together the creativeness and talents of several classmates can result in a better "product," provided each person puts forth maximum effort. A project can be done in less time when each team member carries part of the load than when one person has to do everything. For example, a research project could be divided into these five parts: conducting library research, developing and administering a questionnaire, tabulating the results and preparing summary charts, composing and keying the report, and preparing visual aids.

Undergoing Challenges

Teamwork might not always go smoothly. In addition to differences in abilities and backgrounds, personal characteristics and problems can be obstacles to the group process.

Finding a time outside the class period when all members of the group can meet is one of the biggest challenges. Students with a tight schedule of attending classes and working or commuting to campus or caring for children are juggling a number of responsibilities. If a member misses a group meeting, extra time is required to bring that person up to date on the project. An added risk can be miscommunication between members absent and those present.

If one member does not do his or her part of the project or does the part inadequately, everyone's grade can be affected, depending on how the professor grades the project. Some professors evaluate only the project; if the grade is a B, everyone on the team gets a B. Some professors have the team members evaluate each other's contributions to the project as well as working relationships as part of the project grade. Other professors grade each student on the specific part he or she prepared.

The final risk of a group written project is malfunction of the computer used by the student doing the word processing. Of course, keying the final paper the night before it is due indicates procrastination and poor time management. One reason for group assignments is to help students become better team players—to overcome challenges by solving problems and to apply critical thinking skills. "How can we get Ted to do his part and to get it done on time?" "The final paper that Kelly keyed and printed is not formatted correctly and has errors. What shall we do?"

You might want to use the Group Project Agreement form shown in Figure 1 when you work in small groups for collaborative projects.

Figure 1—Group Project Agreement

GROUP PROJECT AGREEMENT

MEMBERS	#1	#2	#3	#4	#5
Name					
Address					
Phone					
E-Mail					
Area(s) of Expertise					

Division of Responsibilities and Tasks

Responsibility or Task	Team Member	Completion Deadline
_____	_____	_____
_____	_____	_____
_____	_____	_____
_____	_____	_____
_____	_____	_____

Group Meetings

Date	Time	Place
_____	_____	_____
_____	_____	_____
_____	_____	_____

Agreement on what to do if any team member does not carry his or her load:

Plans to celebrate the completion of the project:

Participating Effectively in Small Groups

Group work might be oral discussion or collaborative efforts for a written report. Each type of process requires special considerations. Typically, small groups work more effectively if there is an odd number of participants (to avoid a tie vote on a decision)—preferably three or five. Oral discussions could involve seven members, but for a written report seven would be too many to assemble for meetings and to coordinate.

Oral Discussions If you are part of a small group (assume five members) in an oral discussion, you would find these approaches of participation to be helpful:

- Members should take turns speaking. The group leader is expected to monitor the time and turns so that everyone participates. In groups without a leader, everyone is responsible to see that each member has a chance to speak.

- Determine the maximum number of minutes anyone should speak. To do so you would divide the minutes allowed for discussion by the number of members in the group; for example, 15 minutes) 5 members = 3 minutes for each member to speak.

- No one should monopolize conversation, speaking longer than the maximum allowed. At the other extreme is the person who barely speaks; each member should participate and contribute to the discussion.

- Use tact in voicing an opinion or soliciting an opinion of others. Do not take offense when someone's opinion differs from yours.

- Commend team members with sincere compliments about their contributions to the discussion. Use eye contact, and address each group member by name.

Collaborative Writing Because of the difficulty of getting people together, the ideal group size is three. More commonly, professors tend to assign four or five students to a group. You might apply the following tips to succeed in a group writing project. Consider filling out the Group Project Agreement form to facilitate these steps, and make copies for all team members.

- As the project tasks are divided, offer to do the task that calls on your strengths. You tend to do best on the tasks you enjoy doing and feel confident about handling.

- Prepare a list or a table of members' names, addresses, and phone numbers (including best times to call).

- Organize the project, making an outline or preparing lists. For each part write the name of the person(s) responsible and set a deadline.
  a   Establish a reward for timely completion of the project—perhaps a pizza party.
  b   Discuss the dilemmas of anyone not doing the work or meeting the deadline, and determine the consequences to a group member who does not do his or her share.

- Once the best meeting time and place are determined, write the information on your weekly calendar. Going to a group meeting should be your priority. If a problem prevents your attending, contact all the other members and get yourself caught up.

- Do your part and meet your deadline. In a group project everyone depends on another person's task completion. If one person gets behind or does not do the work, the others are delayed and burdened by having to do more than their share.

- Appreciate the contributions and participation by your team members. Commend them and acknowledge their contributions, both in private and in public.

Exercise 1 Working in Small Groups

1   Describe a small-group discussion or project in which you enjoyed participating and experienced satisfaction. Include the benefits of working in a small group.

_____

_____

2   Describe the challenges and problems you have experienced in small-group work including oral discussions or written projects.

_____

_____

3   How could the challenges and problems have been avoided? What are your suggestions for improving the coordination of teamwork in small-group discussions or written projects?

_____

_____

Many companies in the workplace are moving toward utilizing digital and electronic media for collaboration, problem solving, and creative team work. Working with a team in the online environment can be both a challenging and rewarding experience. Because the bandwidth on many personal computers does not support reliable audio-visual exchange, the most accessible tool for working in a virtual team is e-mail file sharing.

■ Organize Your Thoughts and Compose a Draft

Writing is easier for some people than for others, depending on personal interests and experiences. If you are among those who do not like writing or who feel they are not good writers, you have resources to help you conquer the challenge. Writing can become enjoyable and rewarding if you are willing to try and to get help.

Even for experienced and successful authors, writing is a challenge and a process. Writers have to be in the mood for writing and in an atmosphere conducive to writing. Except for short (half-page) documents, no successful report, article, essay, letter, or book has been completed in one draft—called a *first-time final copy*. Articles and reports generally undergo several revisions. Collaboration by others who are qualified helps to improve the writing.

Setting the Environment

Establish a comfortable writing environment by asking yourself "Where and under what conditions can I do my best writing?"

- At the dinette table, at your desk, or on your lap?
- With warm or cool temperature?
- Using a pen and tablet or a computer with word processing software?
- In the morning, afternoon, or evening?
- By yourself or with a partner (collaborative effort)?
- With quietness or soft music?

- Dressed in formal attire or casual clothes?
- Eating snacks or drinking a favorite beverage?
- Working ahead of the deadline or under last-minute pressure?

Consider what enhances your best and most enjoyable writing experiences. By arranging for a comfortable and pleasing environment, you can maximize your writing potential.

Realizing That Writing Is a Process

Writing is not like doing a math problem, whereby you plug numbers into a formula to get a right answer. Responding to an essay question is not quick or something at which you can guess, as in choosing between *true* or *false* on a test. Writing is a process that involves many steps: interpreting the professor's assignment, brainstorming (discovering ideas), organizing and developing a draft, revising, editing, and documenting sources. The percent of project time for each step varies among writers and depends on the difficulty of the topic.

Interpreting the Assignment
Be sure you understand what you are expected to do before you begin. If any part of the assignment is unclear, ask the professor.

Brainstorming and Discovering Ideas
Brainstorming involves spontaneous thoughts without limit or qualifications. Think freely and write your ideas promptly. Discovering ideas requires being in a creative mood. Choose the best time of day and a pleasurable location. Use your imagination rather than relying on other writings. Then you can take ownership and pride in your paper.

Organizing and Developing a Draft
Nearly every writer is challenged by this step. If you do not know much about the subject, you might be tempted to start reading resources and writing the paper before making an outline. Organizing thoughts before writing the paper is the better approach. By drafting an outline or making a list of major points and subpoints, you will have a plan on which to focus. The outline or list can be modified as you develop the paper; it will aid you in reorganizing the content and in keeping a focus on the main goals and points. Figure 2 illustrates outline format and explains the procedures.

Figure 2—Illustration of Outline Format and Procedures

OUTLINE FORMAT AND PROCEDURES

I IDENTIFYING DIVISIONS (OUTLINE LEVELS)
   A Roman Numerals for First-Order Division (Level 1)
   B Capital Letters for Second-Order Division (Level 2)
   C Arabic Numerals for Third-Order Division (Level 3)
   D Lowercase Letters for Fourth-Order Division (Level 4)

II CAPITALIZING HEADINGS
   A First-Order Headings: ALL CAPS or Larger Font in Bold
   B Second-Order Headings: First Letter of Principal Words Capped
   C Third- and Fourth-Order Headings: First word capped

III SPACING
   A Horizontal Spacing: Leave two spaces after identifying numeral or letter.
   B Vertical Spacing: Follow the example of this outline or use additional spacing between divisions, following a consistent pattern.

IV PUNCTUATION
   A After Identifying Letter or Numeral: Omit periods.
   B At End of Entry
      1 If a word or phrase, use no ending punctuation mark.
      2 If a complete sentence, use the appropriate ending punctuation mark.

In doing research for a paper, you will have accessed a number of sources. Some of the facts and information are more pertinent and valuable in supporting your topic than others. Any library or Internet source could be biased or contain inaccuracies. Evaluate the sources by asking these questions:

1 When was the information published? For time-sensitive topics, such as political races of the current election year, you would want a publication date within the last few weeks. For historical events the date might be irrelevant, unless you want an editorial that was written at the time of the event.

2 Who is the author? What are the qualifications of the author(s)? On the topic *"Is Milk Good for Adults?"* an article written by a research chemist probably would have more credibility than one written by the head of a dairy farmers association, who likely would have a biased view and less experience in conducting research.

3 Who is the publisher or Internet source provider? A *refereed journal article* (peer-reviewed article) will have been reviewed by experts in the field (peers), whereas a trade magazine might have had only one editor involved.

Select only the best sources to incorporate into your paper. No doubt you will eliminate the less relevant note cards and printouts when you compose your first draft.

In writing the first draft, express your thoughts without worrying about perfect formatting or mechanics. Take a break between major sections of the paper; do not try to draft the entire document in one sitting. After the first draft is completed, set aside the paper for a day or two.

Revising Good writing undergoes *"re-vision"* (another vision of the paper by you or a reviewer). Plan on several revisions to polish the composition, check the format, and get feedback from qualified reviewers. Choose people who are knowledgeable about the topic and who will be honest in giving feedback and their reactions—a professor, classmates or partners on the project, or the campus writing center. You will gain audience awareness: Is the paper clearly understandable? Does it offend anyone? Consider the reader(s) of the final document.

Revision is critical to moving a paper from the C or D category to a B. Welcome suggestions from reviewers. Do not interpret constructive criticism as a personal offense. Remember, the document is in the revision stage. You still can make changes or leave the text as originally written. You do not have to accept the suggestions, for you are the author—the authority on the paper.

Editing After a paper has been revised and printed, it needs to be edited—the fine-tuning stage. Proofread the document at least two times, once for content, asking: Does it make sense? Does it parallel the outline? Mark Twain said, "The difference between the right word and the almost right word is the difference between lightning and the lightning bug." Second, proofread for mechanics— grammar, spelling, punctuation, word usage, and capitalization.

Editing is critical to improving a paper from a B to an A. Even if you used spell check, some errors may not have been caught by the word processor's dictionary. Moreover, the numbers in figures and tables need to be proofread for accuracy.

Where is the writing center?

What are its days and hours of service?

As you assess your writing process, note the most difficult steps and seek assistance for them from the campus writing center. Once you improve a deficiency, you will derive more satisfaction from writing and will get better grades on assignments.

The amount of time to schedule for a writing assignment will depend on the professor's requirements (including minimum length), your ease of access to library resources, your previous experiences in writing similar types of assignments, and the environment in which you are working. The identical assignment might take three weeks for one student but five weeks for another. In writing two papers of the same length, you might devote twice as much time on one as on the other. In estimating the time, you are wise to plan for a longer period than anticipated.

Self–Assessment: Assessing Your Writing Needs ✔

Assess your writing needs in terms of the ideal conditions or environment and the percentage of time required to do each step of the process.

Part A Describe the ideal environment within which you can do your best writing:

Place (desk, dinette table, lap, or ____) _____

Tool (pen and tablet, computer, or ____) _____

Time of day (morning, afternoon, or evening) _____

Background noise (quietness, soft music, or ____) _____

Type of clothes being worn _____

Beverage and/or snacks desired _____

Meeting deadline (ahead or last-minute pressure) _____

Part B   For these major steps in the writing process, designate the percentage of time you typically devote to each:

Interpreting the assignment	___%
Brainstorming/discovering ideas	___
Organizing and developing a draft	___
Revising	___
Editing	___
Total	100%

The purposes of this assessment are to help you recognize the features that maximize your potential and to allot appropriate time for the entire writing process. You might adjust the time percentages depending on the project.

■ Use Word Processing Software Aids

In preparing a printed report, use the helpful features of your word processing software. For reports and research papers, first refer to the manuscript style the professor requires. Though software packages differ by vendor, the following tips apply to most word processing software.

Specifying the Format

Word processing software has standard settings, called *default settings*, that format all documents unless you instruct the computer differently. To change standard settings within a document, first position the cursor at the screen or page, line, and character position where the change is to begin. Then proceed with the commands.

Font and Size The type is a choice of fonts, depending on the printer's capability. The size of print on a typewriter is designated by pitch; on a computer the size is designated by points. Point sizes vary somewhat according to the specific font.

Figure 3—Samples of Print Styles and Sizes

	Small Print	*Large Print*	*Effects for Headings*
Typewriter	12 Pitch Elite	10 Pitch Pica	ALL CAPS <u>Cap & Underline</u>
Computer Word Processing	9 Point	11 Point	**14 Point and Bold** ***12 Point, Bold, & Italic*** <u>*10 Point, Italic, Underline*</u>

In Figure 3, the typewriter print is Courier, a common type style of typewriters. The computer print is Times Roman, which is an appropriate family of fonts for letters, memos, reports, newsletters, and brochures. A Times Roman font is easy to read in the smaller print sizes. In preparing visual aids (such as slide presentations and transparency masters) with large print to be viewed from a distance, choose a Letter Gothic or Helvetica font. Notice the difference between Times Roman and Helvetica in Figure 4.

Figure 4—Samples of Times Roman and Helvetica Fonts

Times New Roman	**11 pt**	**Letters/memos, reports, newsletters, brochures**
Helvetica	15 pt	Overhead transparencies

Margins The default settings typically are 1 inch for the top, bottom, left, and right margins. In a multipage document you will need to make these adjustments:

- *First Page* Most manuscript styles require a 1.5-inch or 2-inch top margin for the first page. For a half-inch more than the standard inch, press the Enter key three times; for a 2-inch top margin (another inch), press Enter six times—assuming the line spacing is single spaced.

- *Left Margin* If the document is to be bound on the left, another half-inch is needed for the left margin. Change the left margin from the standard 1.0-inch to a 1.5-inch setting.

Page Numbering Of the various options for positioning page numbers, the simplest and easiest to set is center bottom. Unless the style manual suggests otherwise, choose center bottom page numbering to appear on all pages. You do not need to suppress printing the page number on the first page. The page number will fit within the bottom margin; change the bottom margin setting from the standard 1.0 inch to .5 inch.

Line Spacing Letters and memos are single-spaced. Reports can be single-spaced or double-spaced. If the report is to be double-spaced, leave the standard 1.0 setting for line spacing until the first line of the first paragraph after the title. At that position change the line spacing to 2.0 for double-spacing.

Justification In letters and memos the preferred justification setting is *Left*; the left margin is even, but the right margin is ragged (depending on the length of a line). If a letter or memo also were justified at the right margin, the recipient would assume the message is a form document for a mass mailing rather than a personalized message. In books, reports, and newsletters (documents written for many readers) the typical justification is *Full*; both the left and the right margins are even.

Hyphenation (Word Division) If the manuscript guide specifies no word division, leave the default setting at *Hyphenation Off*. If the document is to have a relatively even right margin, long words need to be divided so the right margin will not be extremely ragged. Turn on *Auto Hyphenation*. If the document is to have right-margin as well as left-margin justification (Full justification setting), long words need to be divided to avoid big gaps between words.

Widow and Orphan Line Protection Only one line of a paragraph at the bottom of a page is called a widow line; a single paragraph line at the top of a page is called an orphan line. At least two lines of a paragraph need to appear at the bottom and at the top of a page. For automatic page breaks to prevent widow or orphan lines, change the format setting to *Widow/Orphan Protect On*.

Indent Feature In outlines and numbered items that extend beyond one line, use the *Indent* feature (rather than at the end of each line depressing Enter and Tab). Should you insert or delete text thereafter, the computer will automatically realign the text. The Indent feature depends on a Left Tab set at the first position of the indentation.

Tab Sets The default setting has a tab set every five positions (see the tab scale or ruler bar). Learn to change tab settings. In Figure 5 the tab settings were changed to every three positions and the Indent feature is used for numbered paragraphs within an outline format.

Figure 5—Headings

HEADINGS

Reports have main or primary headings and subheadings. Emphasis is shown by the position, size, and treatment of headings. Follow these guidelines:

1 Text (at least two sentences) needs to appear between headings.

2 Be consistent in vertical spacing before and after side headings. Some style manuals require a triple space (TS) before a side heading; others require a double space (DS). Spacing after a side heading is a DS by all style manuals.

3 A main/primary heading is centered horizontally and emphasized over secondary headings. Never use all caps and underline (<u>HEADING</u>) for any heading.

  a In short reports the main heading is the title; use a larger font or all caps plus either bold or italic: **Title of Report**

  b In reports with primary headings in the body, the title should be emphasized over the primary headings. Use a larger font or all caps, bold, and italic: ***Body Heading***

4 Secondary or subheadings in order of emphasis are the following:

  a Side Headings—Use initial cap and lowercase; add underline, bold, and/or italic for more emphasis: **<u>Initial Caps, Bold, and Underline</u>**; ***Initial Caps, Bold, and Italic***

  b Paragraph Headings—Use one of these treatments consistently: <u>Initial Caps and Underline</u>, **Initial Caps and Bold**, or *Initial Caps and Italic*.

Headings If you are not required to follow a manuscript style manual, you may format the headings of a document according to your choice. Levels of emphasis are designated by the font size, type style choices such as bold and italic, as well as underscoring. Review the guidelines for the treatment of headings given in Figure 5 to have professional-looking documents.

Numbered Items Numbers (whether Arabic or Roman numerals) need to align at the right (the unit's position). You must set a *Right Tab* for numbered lists that advance from single digits to double digits. Notice the differences between correct and incorrect formatting as illustrated in Figure 6.

Figure 6—Numbered Items

Correct Format of Numbered Items

Right   Left

Tab   Tab

| |

  8 Some word processing software packages have default settings positioned incorrectly for numbered lists that advance from single to double digits.

  9 You must turn off the default settings and customize the tab settings.

10 In this example, standard tab settings were changed from appearing every five spaces to appearing every three spaces. A *Right Tab* was set for the unit's position of the numbers, and a *Left Tab* was set for the first word of the text.

11 Notice that the numbers align at the right (the unit's position).

Incorrect Format of Numbered Items

  8 Item eight

  9 Item nine

10 Item ten

11 Item eleven

Checking the Spelling

The *Spell Check* feature is helpful in catching most keying errors and misspellings. Use it as the first step in proofreading and editing a document. To use Spell Check, position the cursor at the beginning of the document. Though some software will check the entire document regardless of the cursor's position, be safe and begin at the top of the first page.

Spell Check flags words not in its dictionary as errors. Some words flagged are not misspelled; they merely are not in the dictionary. Numbers are not flagged, so you must check them against the source document. Many proper nouns are not in the dictionary. Moreover, errors in grammar and word usage are not detected; examples include *there* versus *their*, *are* versus *is*, *you* versus *your*, *to* versus *too*, and *its* versus *it's*. Nor does Spell Check catch keying errors that result in a dictionary word: *form* for *from*, *the* for *they*, and *on* for *no*. In the poem "Ode to Spelling," notice the errors that were not caught by Spell Check. After using Spell Check, you should proofread your documents carefully.

ODE TO SPELLING

I have a spelling checker,
It came with my PC;
It plainly marks four my revue,
Mistakes I might not sea.

I've run this poem threw it,
I'm sure your pleased too no;
Its letter perfect, in its weigh,
My checker tolled me sew.   —*Roger E Herman* (Reprinted by permission of the author.)

Using Proofreaders' Marks

In revising and editing papers, reviewers and writers use proofreaders' marks. Your professors will use many of the marks shown in Figure 7. As you revise papers, use bright colored ink so the editorial marks stand out from the print.

Figure 7—Proofreaders' Marks

Mark	Meaning	Rough Draft	Final Copy
∧ or ∨	Insert text	to college	to the college
	Insert comma	Read the book too.	Read the book, too.
	Insert apostrophe	a students paper	a student's paper
⊙	Insert period	to the game They will	to the game. They will
	Insert hyphen	the three year old child	the three-year-old child
	Insert dash	See Ty my oldest son	See Ty—my oldest son
	Delete	are very considerate	are considerate
STET or	Restore it	toy is dirty and worn	toy is dirty and worn
∩	Transpose	She was then called	She was called then.
≡	Capitalize	to rsvp by may 27	to RSVP by May 27
lc or /	Use lowercase	the Winter term	the winter term
C + lc	Cap & lowercase	SANDRA DARST	Sandra Darst
bf ∼∼∼	Boldface	Remember, take Exit 82	Remember, take **Exit 82**
ital ___	Italic	Read USA Today.	Read *USA Today*.
#	Add/insert space	see alot at St.Louis	see a lot at St. Louis
C	Close up space	over see the study	oversee the study
¶	New paragraph	he did. The next step	he did. The next step
No ¶ or ⌐	No new paragraph	it ended. Then they	It ended. Then they
sp	Spell out	860 4th Street	860 Fourth Street
+++++	Delete underline	read the story	read the story
ALL CAPS	All caps	see the Stop sign	see the STOP sign
SS	Single space; press Enter once; change line spacing to 1.0		
DS	Double space; press Enter twice; change line spacing to 2.0		
TS	Triple space; press Enter three times; change line spacing to 3.0		

Exercise 2 Using Word Processing Software

Key the following report—double-spaced and pages numbered at bottom center. Select a Times Roman font and 12-point size. Correct any errors not marked.

Significant Factors in GPA Achievement

The survey of freshmen, which has been administered to over 17,000 first semester students at the authors university, reveals significant factors leading to college success. First-year students who achieved the highest GPAs at the very end of their first term:

1 Carried at least 15 credit hrs a semester
2 Studied more then two hours outside class for every hr in class
3 Limited employment to fewer than twenty hours a week
4 Attended classes regularly (no more than one absence in a 3 credit hour course)
5 Got seven to eight hours of sleep a night
6 Ate three nutritious meals each day
7 Had a positive experience with academic advisement
8 Used a campus computer lab
9 Used the college library
10 Attended and participated in a Religious Center
11 Used the writing center
12 Attended outside class activities and events
13 Knew at least one faculty or staff member for advise and help
14 Had a positive relationship with their family

Known as the *Key Points to Achieving Academic Success*, this list of significant factors is shared with all new students. Other factors of interest, though not directly related to GPA, are the following:

Employment In the fall term 60 percent of the freshmen were not employed; in the spring term 60 percent of the freshmen were employed.

Socializing Part time students and those employed spent less time socializing than their counter parts.

Sleep Nearly half the freshmen reported getting at least seven hours of sleep a night. Of those who got five or fewer hours of sleep most were part time students and those who were employed.

Attendance Full time students had better attendance than part time students.

Campus Activites Freshman who participated in outside-class activities and events on campus were more committed to returning to college the next year The findings of this research probably are similar to that of many institutions and regions of the country.

Colleges are interested in helping their freshmen succeed.

Being Responsible

In preparing written documents, you are expected to know how to use word processing software. Most professors are not sympathetic to excuses that begin like "My computer wouldn't . . ." or "My printer is not working" or "My disk is ruined." *You are responsible for knowing how to prepare a document, for accessing a computer and printer that function properly, and for getting any required supplies not available in the computer lab.* For example, you might have to supply good-quality bond paper; formal reports generally have to be printed on higher-quality paper than computer lab paper.

Where can you get help with using your word processing software?

Where can you buy good-quality bond paper?

■ Complete a Research Paper and Learn from the Results

Upon completing a paper, you will experience a real sense of satisfaction. Yet two more tasks need to be done:

• Save the document or file onto a second disk.

• Make a photocopy of the paper for your course file folder or notebook.

You no doubt will be anxious to see how the professor evaluates your writing. When you receive the paper, you might see many comments from the professor or only a few marks. Professors and reviewers who write comments and editorial marks on your paper are taking an interest in helping you. Moreover, reading and editing take substantial time. When teachers have several classes of papers to review or grade, they sometimes neglect to give enough positive comments to balance constructive criticism. If you have such an experience, focus on appreciating the input, however it sounds. To receive a grade without any comments is worse, because you might not know how the grade was determined.

Appreciate every opportunity to develop your writing skills, for you likely will have to write many important papers in your future. Just as one cannot learn to swim without swimming, a person cannot learn to write without writing. The only way to improve writing skill is to write.

Exercise 3 Writing a Research Paper

For the topic you researched in Chapter 11, Exercise 6, write the paper. Include these steps:

1 Brainstorm and discover ideas to incorporate into your paper.
2 Organize and develop a draft—include library research and use all the word processing features that are applicable.
3 Request others in your class and/or the writing center to read your paper.
4 Revise your paper.
5 Edit your paper by using proofreaders' marks, and prepare the final draft.
6 Print the paper, copy the document onto a disk, and make a photocopy.

■ Speak to a Large Group

Most people shy away from speaking to a large group. Even expert speakers become nervous as the event nears. So being apprehensive or fearful about speaking to a large group is not uncommon, and you need not feel badly about it.

A public speaking course will help you develop various types of talks and deliver them effectively, but you might not be enrolled in that course until later. Meanwhile, you might be assigned to give a presentation in some of your classes or in a campus organization. By following these basic principles of public speaking, you can do a good job. With each experience you will gain confidence and improve your speaking skills.

Getting Prepared

Where can you go to get help in preparing a visual aid?

If you are well prepared to speak, you probably will be less nervous and will have more poise in your delivery. Research and study the topic. Anticipate questions from the audience. Overlearn the material. Like a written report, an oral presentation has an introduction, body, and conclusions or recommendations. Organize your thoughts with an outline format or list of key points.

Consider preparing at least one visual aid—a transparency, presentation slides, the chalkboard or whiteboard, a flip chart, a brochure, a handout, or a physical object. Visual aids can help you get the attention of the audience and clarify or emphasize main points. Using a visual aid also reduces nervousness because it gives your hands something to do. If the transparency or slide includes the main points of your talk, you have a tool to help you stay focused on the message.

Prepare note cards or half-sheets of paper (in a vertical position) with an outline of your talk or a list of the key points. Write only short phrases. During the talk you can glance at the cards quickly and be reminded of the next point. Do not write complete sentences, or you will be tempted to read word-for-word from the card. You cannot get a quick reminder from having to read a complete sentence.

Speakers who read their talk often fall into a monotone voice, which is boring to hear and difficult to remember. Neither should you try to memorize your speech and recite it; when you are nervous, you easily can forget a portion and experience the disaster of embarrassing silence.

Being well dressed and groomed will give you confidence. Wear a favorite outfit that is accented by your best color.

Practice giving your speech. Perhaps a fellow classmate or your roommate would be a practice partner. You could listen to each other's presentation and give helpful comments. Another option would be to videotape or at least tape your speech. You might be amazed how your voice sounds.

Giving Your Talk

Speaking to a large group becomes easier with practice. You can improve your public speaking skills by practicing the following:

✓ Stand with good posture and both feet on the floor. Do not lean on the podium. Do not shuffle your feet or be a "dancing bear."

✓ Speak distinctly; do not mumble.

✓ Glance occasionally at your notes (an outline or lists of short phrases).

✓ Use voice inflection and breathe regularly. Pause at times. Like a symphony, an oral presentation has major impact when the voice becomes louder, softens, and pauses.

✓ Give verbal examples (cases and short scenarios) to enhance important points. Unless you are a talented humorist, be careful about using humor or telling jokes. You do not want to offend anyone.

✓ Use visual aids to emphasize main points or to illustrate parts. Help your audience follow the visual aid or to observe the part about which you are speaking.

✓ If you are citing important dollar amounts, numbers, or percentages, write them on the board or transparency. Numbers presented only orally are not easy to remember. As you point sideways to the numbers, keep your eyes on the audience. Do not face and talk to the board.

✓ Use good eye contact, looking from one section of the audience to another casually. Include the people at your far left and far right from time to time. Poor eye contact includes looking only at the ceiling or at the floor, staring at one or two people, and rotating your eyes in a continual and even pattern (which causes dizziness).

✓ Avoid distracting mannerisms—such as chewing gum, jiggling coins in your pocket, clicking on and off the top of a ballpoint pen, and adjusting your eyeglasses.

✓ Use appropriate and helpful hand gestures to emphasize points or to help the audience follow your message.

✓ Do not talk down to the audience. Using "we" helps to position yourself on the same level as your audience: "As students, we . . ." "We can profit from her research."

✓ Stay within your time limit. Practice giving the talk at home, and time yourself so you can make appropriate adjustments to its length.

✓ If you have a handout, distribute it after the presentation unless the audience needs to use it while you are speaking. If the audience has a handout during your talk, some people will read ahead, write unrelated text, or draw on it instead of giving you undivided attention.

✓ Plan when and how to involve your audience.

✓ Remember that people can listen (from 400 to 700 WAM) much faster than you can speak (from 150 to 180 WAM). You may speak at a comfortable speed as long as your words are articulate and understandable.

✓ Be gracious in answering questions. You can be pleased that the audience was listening and was interested in your presentation enough to ask questions.

Following Up After the Presentation

Oral presentations in class might be evaluated by only the professor, or comments from classmates might be part of the evaluation. In a public speaking course the professor will have a formal evaluation process, but in other courses evaluation typically is more informal. In fact, many professors just want you to get experience speaking and are lenient in grading oral presentations.

Getting honest feedback after a talk is helpful. If a formal evaluation is not in place, ask the professor to give you suggestions for improvement. Ask several classmates whose opinions you respect to comment on your talk. You might ask these questions:

1 What were the three most effective techniques of my talk?
2 To improve my speaking skills, on which two or three techniques should I focus?

3 On a scale of 1-10 (with 10 being high), how would you rate these techniques:

   a Eye contact
   b Rate of speech (listening speed)
   c Voice inflection
   d Use of notes
   e Visual aids

Each speaking experience helps you to develop self-confidence and leadership skill. Welcome each opportunity so you can polish your skills.

Exercise 4 Speaking to a Large Group

Give a two-minute oral presentation on one of these topics:

My Best Vacation
My Favorite Novel or Movie
A Significant Life Experience
A Famous Person Whom I Admire
My Hobby

As you listen to your classmates' talks, make notes of their strengths in speaking and commend them personally. Begin your constructive feedback with positive comments, embed a suggestion for improvement, and close with another positive point. Seek feedback on your speaking skill so you can continue improving.

Solve This Case—Maria's Dilemma in Preparing a Speech

Maria knew several weeks ago that her turn in class to give an oral presentation would be the day after tomorrow. Having followed her term-at-a-glance sheet and planner, she was on schedule. But this afternoon Maria's daughter had an appendicitis attack and had to be taken to the hospital. While surgery to remove the appendix is occurring, Maria sits in the waiting room and tries to study for the exam to be taken tomorrow.

She keeps worrying about the oral presentation. Which topic from Exercise 4 should she choose? How can she get ready most efficiently under these circumstances? She starts writing her speech word for word.

1 If you were Maria, on which topic would you choose to speak? Why?

2 In what way is she approaching the oral presentation incorrectly?

3 What suggestions do you have for Maria?

My Reflections Journal

Choose any three of the following questions to answer for this journal entry that describes your writing and speaking experiences. Using your computer, you may either print the pages and turn them in on paper or e-mail the pages to your instructor. Ask your instructor which method he or she prefers.

1 On a scale of 1 (low) to 10 (high), how well do you like to write? Why?

2 Recall comments teachers have written on your papers. What type of suggestions have been given? What compliments have you received?

3 What are some of the challenges you have with word processing software?

4 How do you feel about speaking in front of a group? Are you gaining confidence?

5 How important do you think writing and speaking skills will be in your future?

Website Practice Test

On the website at http://www.casadyenterprises.com/collegeedgebook/practicetests.htm you can access a practice test to check on your understanding of the chapter concepts. You may print the results of this self-test to review before taking the respective in-class exam.

Objectives

Upon completing this chapter, you should be able to:

- Anticipate various backgrounds and experiences among people
- Practice good human relations skills
- Handle difficult circumstances
- Resolve conflict with others
- Show leadership qualities

"About 15 percent of one's financial success is due to one's technical knowledge and about 85 percent is due to personality and the ability to lead people."—Dale Carnegie

BIOGRAPHIES OF SUCCESSFUL people reveal a common characteristic—positive relationships with others. In *See You at the Top*, Zig Ziglar illustrates a stairway that leads to success. The steps are in this order: a good self-image, a positive relationship with others, goals, a positive attitude, willingness to work, and the desire to succeed. In college our positive relationships with classmates, living mate(s), professors, staff personnel, administrators, friends, and family members are important.

If you anticipate that others will have a variety of backgrounds and experiences, you can enhance your human relations skills and leadership qualities. Getting along with people is relatively easy when conditions are pleasant, but complications may occur. How we overcome or respond to difficult circumstances is a major factor in lifetime achievements and maturity development.

Higher education gives you the tools to become a lifelong learner of human behavior and relationships. Self-development is like achieving a "personal best" in an athletic event. Successful people never cease striving for a personal best. You will compete within your environment and according to your personal qualities and ideals.

■ Anticipate Various Backgrounds and Experiences Among People

If everyone were alike, the world would be dull and mediocre. In your classes you probably have observed a variety of backgrounds and experiences among classmates. Each person's actions are affected by many factors—including health, personality, financial security, education, talents, interests, skills, appearance, heritage, values, genes, and environment.

How do you get along with those who have unusual ways and backgrounds that are quite different from yours? Prejudiced by the persuasion of others or because of a negative experience, many people form quick opinions. An educated person, on the other hand, studies and researches issues before drawing a conclusion. Before speaking or writing, he or she asks, "How does my comment or thought reflect my own experiences?" In this way the person contributes honestly and positively to everyone's knowledge.

In college you become acquainted with classmates, roommates, and professors whose characteristics vary within such extremes as the following:

Sensitive; feelings easily hurt	Inconsiderate of others' feelings; tactless
Extended periods of moodiness	Happy-go-lucky; takes nothing seriously
Conservative and stingy with money	Generous and extravagant with money
Chooses a few close friends	Chooses many casual acquaintances
Bonded to closely knit family	Separated from family; loose family ties
Stronger academic than social goals	Stronger social than academic goals
Messy	Neat
Sedentary	Physically active
Conceited and egotistical	Modest and humble
Strong religious conviction	No religious conviction
Supported by wealthy parents	Self-supported
An only child	One of many siblings
Gets angry easily	Easygoing

Building healthy relationships requires awareness without judgment as well as tolerance without endorsement. Though unlike you in many ways, most people need affection and appreciation for achievement.

Exercise 1 Observing Differences Among Associates

Identify by a letter or pen name (to protect confidentiality) three people with whom you associate regularly. You might include professors, classmates, your employment supervisor, and living mates (family members, roommates, or suite mates). In the second column, briefly describe one or two ways by which that person is quite different from you.

Associate   *Major Ways by Which Person Differs from You*

_____   _____

_____   _____

_____   _____

Which of the differences among associates challenge your relationship the most?

_____

_____

Which of the differences do you admire and wish to emulate?

_____

_____

■ Practice Good Human Relations Skills

Everyone has many positive characteristics that deserve attention. The pluses generally far override any differences or negative factors. Successful people look for the good in others and practice good human relations skills.

Smile

As though you were looking in a mirror, what you send out comes back. What you see in others exists in you. Usually a big smile will generate a smile in return. Frowning is said to take 72 muscles; smiling takes only 14 muscles. A smile reveals happiness in the home and fosters goodwill in business; it cheers those who are discouraged, and it is the countersign of friendship.

Be Pleasant and Positive

You are about as happy as you want to be. Cheerfulness can be reflected in your speech and in your actions. Discussing your disappointments and problems will depress others. You should also avoid complaining and criticizing, which are negative behaviors that pull others and yourself down. Instead, if you think positively, positive things will happen to you. The language of speaking varies by countries, but the language of attitude is universal. Helen Keller once said, "If you are looking at the sun, you seldom will see any shadows."

Nurture Friendships

Actions often speak louder than words. A friend is a person who will go out of the way to help someone who cannot do the favor in return. Being a genuine, loyal friend is a virtue beyond measure.

Address People by Name

The best sound is someone calling you by name (and pronouncing it correctly); the best print is your name that has been written accurately. Learn the names of people you meet. Cordially address them by name in correspondence, on the telephone, and in personal conversation. Make an effort to pronounce and spell names correctly, for most people notice. Likewise, most people are offended by errors of pronunciation and spelling.

A Most Important Question

During my second month of nursing school our professor gave us a pop quiz. I was a conscientious student and had breezed through the questions, until I read the last one: "What is the first name of the woman who cleans the school?"

Surely this was some kind of joke. I had seen the cleaning woman several times. She was tall, dark-haired, and in her 50s; but how would I know her name? I handed in my paper, leaving the last question blank.

Before class ended, one student asked if the last question would count toward our quiz grade. "Absolutely," said the professor. "In your careers you will meet many people. All are significant. They deserve your attention and care, even if all you can do is smile and say hello."

I've never forgotten that lesson. I also learned her name was Dorothy.

—JoAnn C Jones, Brockville, Ontario
GUIDEPOSTS. January 1996, page 8

Be Genuinely Interested in Others

What are the special interests of your professors?

Where are your closest classmates from, and who is in their family?

Charles Schwab was paid $1 million a year by Andrew Carnegie, not because he was a genius about manufacturing steel, but because of his ability to communicate and work with people. Let your associates know they are important. Ralph Waldo Emerson said, "Every man I meet is in some way my superior in that I can learn of him."

When you converse with another person, talk about his or her interests. Be interested in your classmates' progress in course work, in their hobbies, and in their families. Also be interested in your professors' campus activities, and in your family's work and accomplishments. A salesperson's success is not in selling a product but in helping customers solve their problems. Dale Carnegie said, "You can make more friends in two months by becoming interested in other people than you can in two years by trying to get other people interested in you."

Use Eye Contact

Direct eye contact reveals a healthy self-image and sincere interest in others. We should look people in the eye as we communicate with them, for eyes are expressive. Glancing down, up, or away from the other party indicates deceitfulness or shyness. (In some countries outside Canada and the United States, however, indirect eye contact is a sign of respect.)

Listen Attentively

Good listeners usually are good conversationalists. By encouraging others to talk about themselves and not interrupting anyone who is speaking, you demonstrate attentive listening skill.
Barbara Bush said, "I listen and then give input only if somebody asks."

Empathize with Others

Show empathy and understanding toward others' experiences and feelings. When you see someone acting in an unusual manner, you might be confused or critical. Upon learning about the
problem or its cause, however, you likely will revise your interpretation of the person's actions.

   Unless you are a pro, be cautious in sharing humor and wit to avoid hurting anyone's feelings.
Refuse to gossip and talk about people's vices; to do so is destructive and hurtful. When you
want to be persuasive, cultivate a low and quiet voice. How you speak is more impressive than
what you say.

Commend People

Recognize the positive behaviors and characteristics of others. Giving a sincere compliment is
powerful motivational fuel for generating positive actions. Compliment people on their abilities
and appearance, commend their achievements, and praise their good work. Believe in the potential of your associates, and help them live up to the image that is expected of them.

Exercise 2 Commending a Classmate

Compose and send an e-mail message of commendation to a classmate; designate a copy to go to your teacher. Perhaps the following starters will trigger some ideas for you in developing your paragraph.

I liked what you said in class today. You presented a new viewpoint to consider.
You gave a great presentation today, and you got all of us involved.
I enjoyed the concert last night. Your clarinet solo was a highlight.

Have an Open Mind

Educated people are open to the ideas and opinions of others. Realizing a controversy has at least two sides, they avoid arguments. They are able to disagree without being disagreeable. They try to see an issue from the other person's point of view. If you question the professor's evaluation of your paper, for example, you should first put yourself in his or her position. Given your professor's level of knowledge and his or her status as an objective outside reader, what is valid about his or her evaluation?

Ignore Bad Remarks

Whenever you hear an ill-natured criticism or remark about you, ignore it. If you simply live in a way that proves the comment was inaccurate, nobody will believe it. Many criticisms and uncomplimentary remarks are made because the person has an unhealthy self-concept. Being condescending gives the person a feeling of importance. Consider the remark as impetus to doing something better—not as a reason to be hurt.

Show Humility

People admire those who are humble and modest about their achievements. They do not need publicity to be remembered. A certain dignity is attached to modesty, and no one likes a braggart. John Wooden, NCAA coach once said, "There is no limit to what can be accomplished when no one cares who gets the credit."

Practice Courtesy and Good Manners

Evidences of courtesy include refusing a request gracefully, showing respect for what others revere, treating even unpleasant people with consideration, being calm under provocation, and being at ease under pressure. You can be considerate of others and apply good manners.

You learned long ago to say *please* when asking for something and *thank you* when given a compliment or a gift. Proper manners include acknowledging RSVPs. Upon receiving an invitation with an RSVP notation, say "Yes, I can come and look forward to the event" or "No, I am sorry I'm not able to attend." If a reply date is not given, see that your RSVP is received at least three days before the event. Expenses of food, flowers, and table settings depend on the number of reservations—commonly required at least forty-eight hours in advance of the event.

Keep Promises

Do not make a promise unless you are sure you can keep it. If you make an appointment to see a professor, be there on the agreed upon date and time. If you offer to bring refreshments, remember to bring them. If you replied *Yes* to an RSVP notation, attend the function. People are counting on you, and they easily become annoyed by irresponsible and thoughtless behavior.

Keep Confidences

People who can be depended upon to keep a confidence are admired, trusted, and appreciated. To be entrusted with important information is a compliment to your integrity and relationship.

Admit Mistakes

Everyone makes unintentional mistakes occasionally. Feelings of guilt and frustration usually follow. Typically, we wish we could correct the act so that no one would know. Or, we would like to think it really was not our error but the fault of someone else. The best way to handle a mistake is to apologize and admit it with sincerity. Neither ignore an error nor pass on the blame to someone else.

IMPORTANT WORDS OF GOOD HUMAN RELATIONS
Six important words: *I apologize for making a mistake.*
Five important words: *You did an outstanding job.*
Four important words: *What is your opinion?*
Three important words: *I am sorry.*
Two important words: *Thank you*
One important word: *Please*

Exercise 3 Getting to Know a Professor

Choose one of your professors to interview. In making an appointment, request 15 minutes of his or her time. To prepare for the interview, check your college catalog to learn where the professor earned degrees and when he or she was hired by the college, so you can apply good human relations skills. Make a list of questions to ask, including the following:

1 What type of students are most enjoyable to teach?

2 What characteristics of students in general are most challenging for professors?

3 If you have been a student organization sponsor, what were the characteristics of the best leaders? of the weakest leaders?

4 When you were a college student, what were your major difficulties or obstacles to overcome? How did you overcome them?

5 Why did you decide to become a teacher? What were your major influences?

6 To what do you attribute your success?

7 What advice do you have for students to succeed in your classes?

Share your reactions and summary. What one thing most surprised you during the interview? What advice did you receive?

_____

_____

_____

_____

_____

_____

■ Handle Difficult Circumstances

As long as everything is going well, relationships are relatively easy to maintain on a positive level. When we are challenged by hardships, however, relationships are more difficult to keep on an even keel.

College students encounter many types of challenges in their personal lives as they are trying to excel in their academic lives. Freshmen undergo enough challenges in adjusting to college life that they should not have to cope with additional obstacles in the path. Yet many students do experience difficult circumstances: adjusting to being away from home, maintaining long-distance relationships, learning that a parent has a major illness, being informed that their parents are divorcing, handling grief upon the death of a loved one, receiving low grades, running out of money, being pressured by an employer to work more hours, becoming ill or coping with a disease, or discovering an unwanted pregnancy. Upon returning home at the end of the term, many students realize they have changed (grown up); but their parents still treat them as high school students.

Overcoming obstacles gives us an opportunity to develop our character, to learn, to cultivate empathy, and to mature. Knute Rockne said, "The way a man wins shows much of his character; the way he loses shows all of it."

Letting Obstacles Overcome You

All students face obstacles in the path to reaching their goals. You do not want problems to overcome you and ruin important relationships. Inappropriate ways to handle academic dilemmas are revealed in these authentic cases, for which the names have been changed:

Bob and Jill were in the same history class, which required essays. Not liking to write, Bob had avoided professors who assigned much writing; but this term he had to take Dr Day's class. Jill did well in writing assignments and got a B on the first essay; Bob got a D. On the second essay Bob copied Jill's paper. With over seventy students in class, Bob thought Dr Day would not detect the same words. Before that paper was returned, a third essay was assigned. Again Bob and Jill turned in identical essays except for their individual handwriting. When the last two papers were returned, Bob's essays each had a question mark with a copy of Jill's paper attached. Jill's essays had a question mark with a copy of Bob's essays. Dr Day told them to come to his office.

Lana was enrolled in a computer applications class for which she was also scheduled to attend lab. Three weeks into the semester (after the add/drop period), she told Professor Frens she had gotten a job, which she needed in order to pay expenses and stay in college. Claiming her work hours conflicted with the designated lab time, she asked Professor Frens to help her individually at another time each week. Being sensitive to her needs, Professor Frens met with Lana on an individual basis two hours a week in her office. Six weeks later she learned that Lana really did not have a job. Lana had told a lie in order to get one-on-one help from the professor at Lana's choice of time. The next day Lana came to Professor Frens's office a conference was held.

Bob and Jill both were given an F in the course, which they appealed. The student judicial system determined both to be guilty. The actual writing was proven to be Jill's, for which she was put on disciplinary probation. Bob was suspended from the university for one term; upon returning he would be put on disciplinary probation. Bob's and Jill's academic records were encumbered (blocked).

Lana received no formal disciplinary action. The professor explained to Lana her disappointment and emphasized the seriousness of not telling the truth: *Once a person loses credibility for either words or deeds, trust is not regained easily.* Highly respected by employers, Professor Frans helped place many students in jobs. One consequence of losing credibility was the loss of a job reference from Professor Frans, who was known for her detailed and positive reference statements.

Positive relationships are built on honesty, sincerity, consistency, and trust. If you undergo difficult challenges, get help from campus resources and services. Bob could have overcome his fear of writing by getting assistance from the writing center and by seeing Professor Day for help at the start of the course. Lana could have utilized services of the counseling center, the financial aid office, and the student employment office.

Overcoming Obstacles and Winning

The ability to keep going in the face of obstacles and defeat leads to success. If you encounter a road block, do not change your goal; just change your direction to get there. After trying an experiment 10,000 times, Thomas Edison said, "I have not failed 10,000 times. I have successfully found 10,000 ways that will not work."

The following authentic cases describe first-semester freshmen who overcame obstacles and *won*—earning at least a B average and maintaining positive relationships with their associates. All three were nominated by their professors for the Outstanding Commitment Award—which recognizes freshmen who have overcome adversity or challenges in the first semester of the freshman year. (Names have been changed.)

Cindy had to take maternal leave for the birth of her second child during her first term in college. Upon being diagnosed with postpartum depression, she began to dislike everything she had loved—including her husband, children, and schooling. Medication did not relieve the depression, so she withdrew from college. She separated from her husband and began the struggle to raise two children on her own. Fortunately, after about six months her depression lifted. Cindy attempted two different jobs but missed the intellectual challenge of college, so she avidly read books every day. Then she returned to college for evening classes. Upon being offered a freshman academic scholarship, she became a full-time student. Cindy focused on another chance—to make good grades, to get a satisfying job, and to be proud of herself. At the end of her first term, she earned a 4.0/4.0 GPA.

Eric started college with personal problems. On the day he left home, his girlfriend informed him she was pregnant. Eric was the oldest of nine children. When his father died, he felt he needed to fill that role. Being over 200 miles from home, he was homesick and felt guilty about not being able to help his mother with his siblings. The first week on campus he could not eat in the cafeteria because he had not purchased a meal plan; he had only $5. Though he had been recruited to play football on scholarship, he declined in order to be able to work and provide for his family. Through campus employment services, he got a job working in a cafeteria. His mother, who had been struggling to make ends meet, was injured on the job and out of work. Several weekends Eric traveled home to work on repairing the family house so it would not be condemned. Eric got married two weeks before final exams and studied for finals on his honeymoon. Against all odds, he earned a 3.6/4.0 GPA.

Jean returned to college after many years and found herself with classmates the same age as her youngest child. She had a number of obstacles to overcome to gain the self-esteem needed to pursue college studies. By the age of 24 she had been married and divorced twice, had two small children, had lost both parents (killed in a car wreck), and had succumbed to alcohol and drugs. Then she moved to a new city, enrolled in night classes to earn a medical assistant's certificate, became employed at a hospital, and found Alcoholics Anonymous. An injury at work resulted in her inability to continue her job. With the decision to return to school and pursue a degree in social work, she applied for vocational rehabilitation and was able to enroll in college. During her first term, Jean was active in church, volunteer work, and Alcoholics Anonymous. She earned a 3.4/4.0 overall GPA.

The freshmen who overcame obstacles and became "winners" in their first term of college share these common characteristics:
- Goals on which to focus
- Determination to succeed
- Appreciation for college education
- Positive relationship with professors
- Use of campus resources and services
- Good human relations skills, including a positive attitude
- Support (friendship and encouragement) from the freshman success class

By comparing the two sets of case studies, you can tell a winner from a loser: A winner goes through a problem; a loser goes around it and never gets past it.

Exercise 4 Accepting Responsibility as a Winner

For each statement made by a student who does not accept responsibility (a "loser"), convert the statement to that of a student who accepts responsibility for actions (a "winner"). The first one is given as an example.

1 I couldn't come to class because I had to meet with my advisor. (Loser)
Winner: *I chose to meet with my advisor instead of going to class.*

2 I would have called you, but I had to go to work. (Loser)
Winner: _____

3 I tried calling my professor, but he is never in his office. (Loser)
Winner: _____

4 I did not have time to do the report. (Loser)
Winner: _____

5 I don't have class notes because I was absent. (Loser)
Winner: _____

6 I couldn't attend the conference because I didn't have the money to go. (Loser)
Winner: _____

■ Resolve Conflict with Others

According to recent and repeated research conducted by The Nierenberg Group, the most important skills needed for career success are fostering strong relationships, motivation, and ability to communicate. Interpersonal skills ranked three times higher than technical skills. The respondents named the most essential business skills to be communication, motivation, and conflict resolution.

Open and tactful communication is the key to success in most relationships. Theoretically, if you express your personal needs and expectations at the onset of an association or relationship you can avoid conflict. In actuality, however, the combination of undergoing stress in college and associating with people of varying backgrounds easily can result in conflict. The conflict might originate from a misunderstanding, an error, or ignorance of the circumstances surrounding a situation. In discussing a problem and resolving it, you might consider these suggestions from professional counselors:

Does any office or group offer a seminar or workshop on conflict resolution and/or relationships?

Begin with Praise Begin with the positive aspect of the person's actions or behavior. Express honest appreciation and sincere praise.

Use the Indirect Approach Call attention to people's mistakes indirectly; use passive voice. Instead of "You did not turn off the iron," say "The iron was not turned off."

Discuss Your Own Shortcomings Before the Other Person's Talk about your own inadequacies and mistakes before discussing the other person's mistake or problem. Then the other person will be more ready to accept a criticism or complaint.

Ask Questions to Get the Facts Find out from the other person his or her side of the story before passing judgment and expressing disenchantment. Instead of saying, "Why didn't you give me Jane's telephone message?" ask "Did Jane call and leave a message?"

Let the Other Person Save Face Even if you know the other person was wrong or made a mistake, give the person the benefit of any doubt. Never correct or criticize someone in front of others. Discuss problems one-on-one in a private office.

Help the Other Person Maintain Pride and a Good Reputation Inspire the other person to do what is right. Instead of "Don't be late to class," say "As you rush to be on time, . . ."

Offer Alternative Solutions If people have an opportunity to choose from alternative solutions, they are more likely to feel they participated in the decision and will accept responsibility to perform accordingly. Instead of "Because my weekly residence floor meeting and pizza gathering are on Wednesday nights, let's change our weekly phone call to Thursday night," it would be better to say, "Because my residence floor meeting and pizza gathering on Wednesday evenings often extend too late for us to phone each other, shall we change to Tuesday or Thursday nights? Which would be better for you?"

Many conflicts can be resolved by being honest, open, and specific. Clarifying guidelines and procedures beforehand can prevent many problems, but often the situations resulting in a conflict cannot be predicted. Keep options of compromise and negotiation open. Try to regain a good relationship with the other person. Respect people for their unique characteristics, and appreciate challenges as opportunities to improve human relation skills.

Exercise 5 Resolving Conflict

Describe a conflict you have experienced with another person and tried to resolve. Explain what you said or did that was effective in resolving the problem. Also, discuss any actions or words you would not repeat should a similar situation occur.

_____

_____

_____

How would you try to resolve a similar situation in the future? What would you say?

_____

_____

_____

■ Show Leadership Qualities

If you aspire to leadership positions, you will practice all the human relations skills just described and will advance further. You show leadership qualities when you lead a group discussion, chair a committee, serve as a peer leader, or train new employees. In all these situations, you are observed by professors and employers for your ability to direct or guide a group.

Leaders build teamwork by soliciting cooperation from members of the group and treating them as associates. The way you see others is the way you treat them; the way you treat them is the way they will become. A coach sees the total person in an athlete; he or she is concerned for the player's health and character as well as for his or her athletic ability.

Does any office or group offer a seminar or workshop on leadership development?

An effective leader:

- Is friendly to all members regardless of their differences
- Understands people's needs and what motivates them
- Has confidence in the group's abilities
- Shows competency in helping with a project
- Knows how to delegate
- Demonstrates fairness
- Represents the group well to superiors
- Overcomes defeat and resistance to change
- Seeks the opinions of group members
- Respects and values each person who contributes to a project
- Gives credit to those who accomplish the work
- Praises good work publicly and gives criticism privately

Leaders show initiative. They understand their responsibilities, and they learn what needs to be done and then begin. As an officer of an organization, you would perform your duties in an exemplary manner. You would not rely on the sponsor to get you started or to prod you along, reminding you of your responsibilities and deadlines. As a leader, you would come up with new ideas and would suggest ways to improve any inadequate procedures.

Good leaders also know how to delegate. From the responsibilities of your position, select the jobs that can and should be delegated. Organize projects that will be turned over to the group. Select the best people for the job, be fair in assigning tasks, and both prepare and motivate them for the assignment. They should fully understand what is to be done before they start. Encourage independence but maintain supervisory control by monitoring the project.

Leaders show their greatness by the way they treat lesser-known people and their team of subordinates. They are not antagonistic, condescending, domineering, or jealous. They are generous in extending goodwill, in showing appreciation, and in rewarding achievers.

Is there a peer leadership or peer mentorship opportunity on campus?

Self-Assessment: Assessing Leadership Qualities

For the following situations, circle the letter of each response that describes your actions. Each question may have one or more answers.

1 For a dinner social sponsored by my organization, I
   a replied *Yes* to RSVP but did not attend.
   b did not reply to RSVP but went to the event.
   c called on the day of the event to RSVP.
   d replied *Yes* to RSVP the next day and went to the event.

2 Following the dinner social for my organization, I
   a said *thank you* to the host and to the keynote speaker.
   b wrote *thank you and commendation* to the host and to the keynote speaker.
   c expressed criticism about the dinner and/or program to the host.
   d did not say or write any communication.

3 As president of an organization, I would
   a rely on the sponsor for reminders.
   b delegate tasks fairly.
   c commend members publicly for club accomplishments.
   d resist changes suggested by members.

4 As a committee chair, I would
   a do all committee tasks myself so they would be done right.
   b delegate all tasks and not participate in the group.
   c organize projects, delegate tasks, and work with the group.
   d ask the president to organize the project.

5 As a peer leader to host or to moderate large-group presentations, I would
   a appreciate experience speaking in front of a large group.
   b be excused from being late or absent because of other commitments.
   c learn some procedures of handling large-group meetings.
   d be concerned about having to serve more times than some of the others.

6 As president of an organization, I would
   a select committee members at random.
   b use the same procedures (good or bad) as those of the previous president.
   c have members start on projects and then check to see if they know what is to be done.
   d treat all members, committee chairs, and other officers as people of equal importance.

7 Should a class and an organization or work have a time conflict, I would
   a tell the professor I must participate in the organization or work.
   b tell the organization or employer I must attend class.
   c skip the committee meeting or work without contacting the chair or employer.
   d skip the class without contacting the teacher.

8 Without having been given instructions on what is expected of a peer leader, I would
   a wait for the teacher to tell me what I should do.
   b tell the teacher what I want to do.
   c offer to lead an activity or topic in an area that is not among the teacher's strengths.
   d look upon it as an opportunity to be creative and to show initiative.

You may check your answers with the key that is given at the end of this chapter. If you have 7 of the 8 correct responses, you are well on your way to leadership development.

You can be a *winner*—developing positive relationships and succeeding in college as well as in life. Following the examples of role models, you can anticipate varying backgrounds and experiences among people, practice good human relations skills, handle difficult circumstances, resolve conflict with others, and show leadership qualities.

Solve This Case—Challenges of a Long-Distance Relationship

In his second month of college, Juan is encountering the challenges of a long-distance relationship. His hometown girlfriend, Liliana, is a high school senior whom he has dated for two years. Being 240 miles from home, he has been going home every weekend. But this Saturday he would like to attend the football game with friends.

Liliana has asked Juan to attend a party with her on Saturday night. With midterm exams approaching and a research paper due the next week, Juan does not want to go home this weekend. He feels he needs the time to study and finish the research paper. With very little homework in high school, Liliana does not understand why Juan cannot come home this weekend.

In the freshman success course an announcement has been made that the Counseling and Testing Center is sponsoring a seminar on handling long-distance relationships. Later in class the professor has the class work in small groups to discuss challenges they were experiencing in the first term of their freshman year.

1 As a member of Juan's small group, what personal challenges would you identify for this week? for this term?

2 What would be your suggestions for Juan to consider? to say to Liliana?

My Reflections Journal

Choose two of the following questions to address in this journal entry, writing one to two paragraphs for each. Using your computer, you may either print the pages and turn them in on paper or e-mail the pages to your instructor. Ask your instructor which method he or she prefers.

1   Of the human relations skills discussed, which ones do you practice most successfully? Which skills do you plan to work on to improve?

2   Recall a problem or obstacle you experienced years ago. Did you learn from the experience? Did something positive occur thereafter that might support the saying "Out of every bad happening, something good evolves"?

3   What have been the most difficult challenges or obstacles you have faced this term? Have you sought help from any campus resources or services? If so, describe. Are you making progress in overcoming the challenges or obstacles? How do you know?

Website Practice Test

On the website at http://www.casadyenterprises.com/collegeedgebook/practicetests.htm you can access a practice test to check on your understanding of the chapter concepts. You may print the results of this self-test to review before taking the respective in-class exam.

Key to Self-Assessment—Assessing Leadership Qualities: 1—d; 2—a & b; 3—b & c; 4—c; 5—a & c; 6—d; 7—b; 8—c & d.

14 PLANNING FOR A SATISFYING CAREER

Objectives

Upon completing this chapter, you should be able to:

- Gain knowledge of yourself through assessments

- Learn about the career services office

- Obtain occupational information

- Get career-related experience

- Prepare application documents

LIKE MOST COLLEGE STUDENTS, you probably want to enter a career that interests you and that matches your needs and values. The more education and skills you gain, the better prepared you will be to compete for jobs in your field. As you focus on career goals, realize that career development is a process that should begin during your freshman year.

The career development process begins with assessing your personality, interests, and values. You can obtain occupational information by visiting your career services office. Another important step is to find out how regional and national employment trends will affect your career choice. You can gain the skills that your career requires by getting related work experience through the options of an internship, a cooperative education job, a practicum, or a volunteer position. You might enroll in courses that will improve your skills or offer you new skills. The skills used to apply for awards and scholarships also apply to an effective job search (researching employers and industries, writing résumés and cover letters, interviewing, and developing a portfolio).

The office of career services can assist you with each stage of your career development. Career counselors help students clarify their career goals as well as research related employment opportunities. Career services include hosting career fairs, sponsoring workshops, and helping students individually with the job search.

■ Gain Knowledge of Yourself Through Assessments

Understanding your own personality, interests, goals, aptitudes, skills, and work values is an important part of the career development process. The more you know about yourself, the better you can make decisions that affect your life. Two popular assessments are Career Dimensions' *FOCUS II* and Holland's *Self-Directed Search*.

Using a Computer-Assisted Career Guidance Program

Where is your career services office?

What are its hours?

Which career-guidance and self-assessment programs are offered by the career services office?

FOCUS II is a computer-assisted career guidance program (Minor, F J, [2003] Career Dimensions, Inc, NH. http://www.focuscareer.com). The program enables you to assess your interests, educational preferences, personality, life values, leisure time preferences, and skills. Then you can discover and explore occupations that are compatible with these factors and your needs. Finally, you can consider the experiences and training needed to achieve your career goals.

As you go through self-assessment software, typically you can print a screen of your work for future reference. By taking several types of self-assessments, you should be able to narrow your choices and begin concentrating on just one or two career areas.

Taking Holland's Self-Directed Search

Categories of People The *Self-Directed Search* created by John L Holland describes six general categories of people (their approaches to life). They are based on interests, skills, values, and personality characteristics and are illustrated in "Holland's Hexagon." See Figure 1.

Categories of Disciplines Holland groups disciplines, too, into six main categories. They are grouped according to the skills and personality characteristics associated with success in those fields as well as the interests and values associated with satisfaction. As you read the examples, mark the careers you have considered or still consider pursuing.

▶ *R ealistic* Agricultural business, cartography and map technology, community and regional planning, construction management, criminal justice studies, dietetics, drafting and design technology, horticulture, industrial safety, industrial technology, manufacturing technology, mechanical drafting and design, mechanical technology, medical technology, printing technology, radiography, wildlife conservation or management.

▶ *I nvestigative* Agronomy, animal science, audiology, biochemistry, biology, cell and molecular biology, chemical engineering, chemistry, computer science, earth sciences, economics, electrical-electronics technology, engineering physics, environmental and natural resources, general science, geography, geology, industrial chemistry, manufacturing technology, marketing research, materials science, mathematics, physics, psychology.

Figure 1—Categories of People

R   I

Realistic People who have athletic or mechanical ability and who prefer to work with objects, machines, tools, plants, or to be outdoors. Practical doers; assertive and competitive; prefer action—using motor coordination, physical strength and, skill.

Investigative People who like to observe, learn, investigate, analyze evaluate, or solve problems. Analytical, logical, and rational problem solvers; intellectuals who prefer to think and understand rather than to take action and persuade; interested in physical, biological, or social sciences.

Artistic People who have artistic, innovative, or intuitive abilities; they like to work in unstructured situations, using their imagination or creativity. Independent; use artistic means to express themselves and relate to others; emotionally expressive; interested in cultural and aesthetic activities.

C   A

Social People who like to work with people—to inform, enlighten, help, train, develop, or cure them—or are skilled with words. Helpful, kind, and understanding of others; contribute to society; enjoy one-to-one and small-group interaction; like to teach, counsel, and advise.

Enterprising People who like to work with people—influencing, persuading, performing, or leading/managing for organzational goals or economic gain. Assertive and persuasive; pursue power, prestige, and status; like to direct and supervise; willing to take risks.

Conventional People who like to work with data, have clerical or numerical ability, enjoy working with details, and follow through on instructions. Detail-minded, organized, and neat; persistent and self-disciplined; value order, structure, and status; can plan and schedule.

E   S

▶ *A rtistic* Advertising or commercial art; art; art history; clothing or apparel design, production and merchandising; crafts; dance; educational media; electronic media; English; film studies; graphic design; instrumental music; literature; media operations; painting; printmaking; public administration technology; sculpture; studio art; theater; vocal music; writing.

▶ *S ocial* Anthropology, antiquities, child and family development, classical studies, communications, consumer and family studies, corrections, elementary and secondary education, foods and nutrition, foreign languages, gerontology, history, nursing, organizational communication, philosophy, physical education, political science, prelaw, recreational and leisure studies, religious studies, respiratory therapy, social work, sociology, special education.

▶ *E nterprising* Administrative management (mgmt), advertising, agricultural business, business mgmt, computer information systems, electronic media production, entrepreneurship, fashion merchandising, finance, hospitality and restaurant administration (admin), human resource mgmt, industrial mgmt, insurance, international business admin, law enforcement, marketing mgmt, production and operations mgmt, real estate, retail marketing, sales mgmt.

▶ *C onventional* Accounting, administrative office systems, computer science, computer technology, legal office management, medical office management, power and transportation management, technology, word processing.

After studying this synopsis of the *Self-Directed Search*, you might want to take the entire self-assessment. Once you have assessed your people category and ranked yourself in the top three discipline categories, you can access Holland's *Occupations Finder* for a classification of 1,335 occupations. They are arranged by three-letter codes that use R (realistic), I (investigative), A (artistic), S (social), E (enterprising), and C (conventional). For example, occupations listed under ESC are for people who assessed themselves first as **E**nterprising, second as **S**ocial, and third as **C**onventional.

Self-Assessment: Assessing Yourself ✓

Review Holland's categories of people in Figure 1. Then return to the beginning and circle the individual descriptors within each category that describe you. The category with the most circled descriptors ranks in first place; second place has the next most circled descriptors, and so forth. Finally, for each of your top three people categories, list the disciplines given in Holland's categories of disciplines you consider pursuing. Include the respective letter codes.

Categories of People / Code   *Disciplines Being Considered and Code*

_____   1st Place   _____

_____   2nd Place   _____

_____   3rd Place   _____

Transfer this information to your Career Planning Worksheet in the Personal References section at the end of this textbook.

■ Learn About the Career Services Office

In preparing for your career, become acquainted with an important campus resource—the office of career services. Begin visiting and using the resources of this office as a freshman, and intensify your relationship with these professionals each year. As a graduating senior, you could have a job offer in one hand as you receive your degree certificate in the other hand.

What You Will Do as a Freshman

▶ Clarify your interests, values, aptitudes, skills, and personality through assessments.

▶ Research various majors or disciplines and occupations.

▶ Create a résumé and cover letter to apply for awards, employment, or scholarships.

▶ Seek ways to enhance career-related skills.

▶ Begin developing a portfolio.

Career counselors can assist with occupational information and career assessments. In addition, you can access publications and outlooks for nearly every career field. By taking these steps during your first year, you will enter the sophomore year with much clearer goals as you begin taking classes within your intended major.

Self-Assessment: Assessing Career Choice

You might have decided on a career, or perhaps you are considering two or three. Even if you have decided on a general category, you probably are not sure about the specific area you want to pursue.

Self-directed career guidance software can assist you in confirming your career choice or narrowing your choices—perhaps to two. Go to the career services office to find out which self-directed career guidance software is available. Allow approximately an hour to go through the program. Most of the programs allow you to exit at various points and to return to the program should you need more time to complete it or to spend more time in a certain section.

If a career counselor is available, make an appointment with him or her to discuss the results with you.

What resources at the career services office are available to help you?

Is a career counselor on staff to assist you?

If so, what functions could he or she perform for you?

What You Will Do as a Sophomore and as a Junior

▶ Narrow your career options, find out which jobs fit your major, and collect information about the careers of interest.

▶ Continue developing your portfolio.

▶ Revise your cover (application) letter and résumé; arrange for their critique by a career counselor and your academic advisor.

▶ Document your leadership activities in professional organizations.

▶ Gain practical experience in your field through cooperative education, internship, part-time or summer employment, and volunteer opportunities.

▶ Interview people in positions of your career choices to learn more about those occupations.

▶ Practice your interviewing skills.

The office of career services provides mock interviews so that students can practice their interviewing skills and learn about what results in employment offers. A mock interview, which can be videotaped and later reviewed, is a chance to see what areas need improvement before an actual employment interview takes place. *Do I express myself well? How do I respond to difficult questions? How is my appearance? How is my posture?*

What You Will Do as a Senior

▶ Register early with the career placement division of career services.

▶ Learn how to conduct a thorough job search.

▶ Revise and update your résumé.

▶ Revise and update your portfolio.

▶ Write an effective application (cover) letter for a full-time position.

▶ Read publications (job listings, newspapers, and journals) in your field.

▶ Further develop interview skills with prospective employers (including mock interviews).

▶ Compile information on potential employers and keep records of employers you contact—dates, method of contact, and results.

▶ Write follow-up letters.

When is the next career day or career fair scheduled that you could attend?

Career days and teacher placement days are scheduled for students to explore opportunities with many different companies. As a senior, you will bring copies of your résumé and have preliminary interviews. Many employers schedule a follow-up interview at a later date. Check with the career services office for the dates and location of these events.

Exercise 1 Becoming Acquainted with Career Services

Fill out the Career Planning Worksheet in the Personal References section in the back of this textbook. You will have a handy reference on the location of career services, name of the director and/or career counselor, findings from self-assessments, resources available to help you, and dates of upcoming career days or career fairs open to freshmen.

■ Obtain Occupational Information

Beginning now and continuing throughout college, keep abreast of job market trends. Check publications that are updated regularly, and interview people in occupations or companies you are considering. Fine-tune your decision about a major and respective course selections so you can meet employment competition with intelligence, rigor, and success.

Updates appear throughout the year in newspapers such as *USA Today, The New York Times,* and *The Wall Street Journal.* Recent reports by the U. S. Department of Labor, Bureau of Labor Statistics; America's Career Info Net; and the National Association of Colleges and Employers reveal the following facts:

▶ *What are the fastest growing occupations requiring a bachelor's degree or higher?* Computer software engineers, network and computer systems administrators, network systems and data communications analysts, database administrators, computer systems analysts, physician assistants, information systems managers, audiologists, computer/information scientists, and teachers

▶ *Which industries are expected to have the fastest wage and salary employment growth by 2010?* Computer and data processing services, residential care, health services, cable and pay television services, personnel supply services, miscellaneous business services, as well as management and public relations

▶ *What skills and abilities are employers seeking?* Communication skills, technical and computer-related skills, teamwork abilities, interpersonal skills, and work experience (cooperative education and internship experiences, part-time jobs, and summer jobs)–for definitions see the "Get Career-Related Experience" section that follows

▶ *How do employers obtain most of their entry-level new hires?* By recruiting on college campuses

▶ *Which skills give candidates the competitive edge?* Oral communication skills, interpersonal skills (ability to communicate and interact with others), technical skills (computers and software packages), and work experience in team environments

▶ *How can students prepare to find satisfying jobs upon graduation?* Maintain excellent grades, get a well-rounded education, get cooperative education or internship experience, and be involved in extracurricular activities (work with a team and accept a leadership role)

▶ *Where do employers often look for new hires?* Among their own cooperative education and internship programs (first) and from another organization's program (second)

Accessing Up-to-Date Publications

What sources on the Internet could help you?

The library and the career services office have timely publications. An excellent reference is the *Occupational Outlook Handbook*—in the government documents section of the library, in the career services' library, and on the Internet: http://www.bls.gov/oco. The *Occupational Outlook Handbook* describes for each career: the nature of the work; working conditions; employment; training, other qualifications, and advancement; job outlook; earnings; and related occupations.

Other good references include the *Dictionary of Occupational Titles*, the *Encyclopedia of Careers*, and *Peterson's Job Opportunities*. Reference books and a list of websites can be found in the career services office.

Interviewing People in Your Chosen Occupations

You can learn more about career options by talking with people experienced in the field. You might ask to be a guest at a professional organization meeting, where you could talk with a number of people. You could make an appointment to visit an experienced person who is in the type of job you are considering. *Job shadowing*, another approach, involves going to a place of employment and observing both the employee(s) and the work environment.

Interviewing several people and visiting more than one company would give you a broader view of the career choice. A person with all the qualifications for a specific position can be satisfied working in one company but dissatisfied with the identical position in another company. Your interests, aptitudes, skills, personality characteristics, and values might be different from that of the person you interview. Overall, you will gain new perspectives from talking with people in the field.

Exercise 2 Interviewing a Person in a Career You Are Considering

Contact a person in a career you are considering to request an information interview. The alumni office or career services office might have a list of alumni who offer to serve as mentors. In making the appointment, explain the purpose of the interview and indicate you will be prepared to take no more than 15 minutes of the person's time. List the questions you plan to ask. You might include any of the following:

1 What are your major tasks and responsibilities?
2 What is most satisfying and rewarding about your position or career?
3 What is most dissatisfying, frustrating, or challenging about your position or career?
4 Which college courses do you suggest to best prepare a person for your career?
5 What was the most difficult part of college for you as a student?

Summarize your findings. What one thing most surprised you during the interview? What advice did you receive?

_____
_____
_____
_____
_____
_____

■ Get Career-Related Experience

Many college students are employed part time during the school year. In getting a part-time job, students typically are concerned that the hours are convenient with their class schedule and that the job pays well. As you approach your junior and senior years, the type of job should become more important than the wages.

Career-related work experience is important. Cooperative education and internships provide both academic education in the classroom (with academic credit for most majors) and practical education (with pay) in the workplace. In addition, you learn about a company's work relationships, ethics, and politics. Here are three options:

1 Working part time in the local area (up to twenty hours a week) while taking classes.

2 Working full time for a semester. Though graduation will be delayed, excellent experience can lead to an offer for a permanent job after graduation.

3 Working full time or part time during the summer.

Both cooperative education arrangements and internships offer supervised work experience in conjunction with course credit. In cooperative education you typically attend a class that parallels the term of employment, whereas internships may require no more than a seminar meeting at the beginning and at the end of the term. In cooperative education the college supervisor usually assists students in finding a job site and sees that the employer assigns job tasks that progress in

Where would you go to get information about cooperative education and/or internship opportunities?

responsibility. For internships students generally have to find their own job site, and the college supervisor serves as a monitor of the employer-employee relationship. Many cooperative education experiences and internships lead to full-time employment upon graduation from college.

Citizenship and service learning (CASL) courses (combining academic study and community service) prepare students to participate in society as effective citizens and to develop a lifelong service ethic. Students get real-world work experience and earn course credit. Your academic advisor can help you pursue this option.

Some students work on a volunteer basis to develop job related skills. Community service opportunities are available through many campus organizations. Your college might have a campus volunteer center to coordinate these efforts.

Peer leadership (peer mentorship) is another option. Working with the teacher and students of a freshman class would help you refine your career goals and learn about the teaching profession. The director of the freshman seminar or student success course (and program) would welcome your inquiry about becoming a peer leader or mentor.

Exercise 3 Relating Work Experience to Career Choice

Identify two types of jobs that would give you relevant work experience, and explain how each would help prepare you for your career choice.

Type of Job

Relationship to Career Choice

_____   _____

_____   _____

If you are currently employed, describe why you chose or accepted the job opportunity:

_____

For your current and previous work experiences, list the job position, company, and tasks that demonstrated your dependability, responsibility, trustworthiness, and leadership:

Job Position	*Company*	*Tasks of Responsibility and Trustworthiness*
Salesperson	XYZ Dept Store	Closed store, deposited money, trained new employees
_____	_____	_____
_____	_____	_____

■ Prepare Application Documents

During college you will be applying for awards, scholarships, and jobs (including cooperative education and internship positions). The basic documents prepared for applications are a résumé, application (cover) letter, and application form. After the interview you should send a follow-up letter. To maximize your chances for selection, you might also prepare a portfolio.

Creating a Résumé

Your résumé and application (cover) letter might be your first contact with a potential employer and the only contact with award or scholarship reviewers. To make the best impression possible, use high-quality bond paper (25 percent cotton)—white or ivory color and perhaps a linen finish—and laser print. Use the same paper for both the résumé and the letter. Though the letter is placed on top, the résumé is prepared first.

A *résumé* (data sheet or vita) is a record of one's personal history that lists qualifications and positive characteristics. A typical résumé consists of six sections. For freshmen and sophomores the information usually will fit on one page; a senior's résumé probably would be two pages. Notice the following features in Figure 2.

Does career services offer help in preparing a résumé?

Name and Address The name, address, phone number, and e-mail address are arranged in an attractive heading. A larger font is used for the name than for the address, phone number, and e-mail address.

Education Beginning with the most recent, list the schools you have attended: name of college or school, city and state, and years of attendance or the diploma (or certificate) year. As a freshman or sophomore, include the degree and major you are pursuing, the number of credit hours completed, and your GPA (if a B average or better). For high school give the month and year of graduation (the diploma) and special achievements. If you state your class rank, include the class size. When you become a college senior, your high school information will be less important and should be minimized.

Work Experience Beginning with the most recent job, list for each: name of employer, city and state, inclusive dates, designation of whether the job was part time or full time, your position title or a generic job title, and a specific description of your tasks and responsibilities. Specify how employers depended upon and trusted you (closing office or store); show leadership (training new employees); and explain team effort.

Skills Describe your employment skills. Examples include equipment you can operate, your keyboarding rate, computer software you can use, as well as language(s) in addition to English you can speak and write.

Activities and Honors Show leadership ability by listing the organizations you have joined. Include information about committees you have chaired and officer positions you have held. If you have done volunteer work, explain how you have served your campus and community. For the high school years, give only the most significant facts.

References Choose teachers or coaches and employers or supervisors as your references; do not list friends or relatives. For each reference give the complete business address: name of person; company or school name; street address or box number; and city, state, and ZIP code. Include the person's business telephone number so he or she can be contacted easily. Home addresses are appropriate if you performed work at the home, such as babysitting and mowing lawns. If a reference has retired, list the home address but include a qualifying phrase: *Former supervisor at XYZ.* In the résumé example you will notice these features:

- Only one typeface (Times Roman) is used.
- The format is easy to read.
- Style is consistent—in spacing between parts, in names of schools and employers, and by application of boldface and italic for emphasis.
- Accuracy is perfect; no keyboarding or spelling errors appear.

Figure 2—Résumé

Lynn A Rutledge

4611 East Valley Lane
Boston MA 02116

Telephone 617-888-777
E-Mail lar444s@university.edu

Education

State University, Boston, Massachusetts
Pursuing a Bachelor of Science Degree with a major in Marketing
Have completed 16 semester credit hours with a 3.6 GPA (on a 4.0 scale)

Glendale High School, Albany, New York
Earned diploma in June 2003; ranked among the top 10 percent in a class of 323
National Honor Society, AFSI (Foreign Language Club)—Secretary

Work Experience

The Style Shop, Boston, Massachusetts—*Sales Associate*   September 2003 to present
Assist customers, handle exchanges & returns, and train temporaries.   Part time

Green Hills Swim Club, Albany, New York—*Lifeguard*   Summer 2003
Monitored swimmers, helped instructor, and judged competitive events.   Part time

Dawn Schultz, Albany, New York—*Nanny*   Summers 2001 and 2002
Played with, prepared meals for, and supervised children aged 10 and 7.   Part time

Skills

Keyboarding (65 NWAM)
Word processing (WordPerfect and Word)
Desktop publishing (Microsoft Publisher)
Spanish (speaking and writing)

Activities and Honors

Phi Eta Sigma—Honor Society
Dean's List and Honor Roll
Marketing Club—Publicity Committee
Superintendent's Leadership Award

References

Dr Edith S Dell, Professor
State University
901 South National Avenue
Boston MA 02116
Phone 617-888-6666

Mr Gene Hatton, Manager
Green Hills Swim Club
3100 West Lake Road
Albany NY 12207
Phone 518-777-1111

Ms Elaine Tindell-Wright
The Style Shop
2729 East Oakridge
Boston MA 02104
Phone 617-444-3333

You should update your résumé each year. Give a copy to your references when you ask them to write on your behalf. With information about you, they can write a better letter.

Exercise 4 Preparing a Résumé

Using the suggestions on the design and content of a résumé, prepare one you could use in applying for an award, scholarship, internship, peer leader position, or employment.

Composing an Application (Cover) Letter

An *application letter* is a persuasive request to be invited for a job interview, approved for credit or financial aid, or selected to receive an award or scholarship. Because this letter is positioned on top of the résumé, often it is called a *cover letter*. Figure 3, an application for a summer job, illustrates these techniques:

Format The simplified letter style is attractive, contemporary, and easy to read.

Letter Address and Personalization The letter is addressed to a person—not to a department or position. This person is addressed in the first and last paragraphs as in a conversation. (Other letter styles have a salutation and a complimentary close instead.)

Subject Line The subject line specifies the position for which the application is being made, making it easy for the employer to process the application.

Body of Message The body is organized into four paragraphs:

¶1 Introduces applicant to the employer, explains how applicant learned about the job opportunity, and states the job position of the opening.

¶2 Describes education that has prepared the applicant to do the job—is specific in stating qualifications and tells what the applicant can do for the employer. The employer should be able to visualize the person's working and doing a commendable job.

¶3 Describes how work experience has prepared the applicant to serve the employer. "You approach" (how the applicant can help the employer) is emphasized. The writer refers indirectly to the résumé. Included are the characteristics of dependability and honesty.

¶4 Requests action—an interview. Even for part-time jobs, employers want to meet and talk with you before making a decision. The applicant states possible times (probably when she is neither in class nor at work)—indicating she is a responsible person.

Closing Lines Gives complete mailing address, telephone number (plus the best times to call), and e-mail address—making it easy for the employer to respond.

Mechanics Uses correct grammar, spelling, punctuation, capitalization, and word usage.

Figure 3—Application/Cover Letter

7 May 2004

MS ELLEN HERRILL
FASHIONS UNLIMITED
468 CONCORD STREET
BOSTON MA 02114

APPLICATION FOR SALES ASSOCIATE POSITION

The Career Services Office at State University informs me you will be hiring a full-time sales associate this summer, Ms Herrill. I am enthusiastic in applying for that position.

As a sophomore, I am seeking a Bachelor of Science degree with a major in marketing. Business Communication class has taught me to use courtesy, psychology, and tact in talking with your customers. In the fall I will take Marketing Principles, which should prepare me to help you forecast sales, price goods, and promote product lines.

My two most recent jobs, as described in my résumé, have prepared me to provide excellent service for your customers. At The Style Shop efficient ways to handle exchanges and refunds were learned. Being dependable and honest, I was entrusted to close the store. You would find me to be pleasant and tactful in helping customers select appropriate colors for their hair shade and skin tone. At the Green Hills Swim Club the latest fashions in swim wear were observed, and my ability to learn names was sharpened. Making your customers feel important would help to increase your sales volume.

Having shopped often at Fashions Unlimited, I would like to meet with you to learn more about your expectations in hiring a cooperative education student for the summer. Would a Tuesday or Thursday after 3 PM be convenient to have an interview, Ms Herrill?

Lynn Rutledge

Miss Lynn A Rutledge
4611 East Valley Lane
Boston MA 02116

Phone 617-888-7777 (Best times: 3-5 PM on TR and 8-10 AM on MW)
E-Mail lar444s@university.edu

Studies show that at least 90 percent of job applications go in the wastebasket. Initial screening typically is for appearance and accuracy. A keyboarding error or misspelled word can cause an application to be rejected. The theory is: *If this is how the person performs when trying to make a good impression, how would he or she perform on the job when no longer trying to impress us?*

Exercise 5 Writing an Application (Cover) Letter

Write an application (cover) letter for one of these situations:

- A professor tells you about a part-time job opportunity on campus.
- You have been nominated for a scholarship in your major department.
- A letter invites you to apply to be a peer leader or mentor for the freshman success course or program.
- A cooperative education or internship opportunity is announced in class.

Filling Out an Application Form

In filling out an application form, use a typewriter if you cannot access the form on the website so your form will look professional and will be easy to read. Handwritten applications, the last choice, need to be legible. The employer or scholarship reviewer is looking for standard information from all applicants. In addition, the evaluator is scrutinizing your work to determine the following characteristics:

- *Are you detail minded?* Did you answer all the questions? Do not leave any blank; if a question does not apply to you, write *Not applicable* or *None*.

- *Can you follow instructions?* Did you place your answer on the correct line? Is your full name in the requested order? Did you sign your name?

- *Are you neat or messy?* Handwriting should be so legible there is no question of any word or its spelling. No erasures, marks, or smudges should appear.

To do the best job on an application form, you first might make a photocopy and fill it out as a draft copy. Then fill out the original form. Be sure to sign the form—writing legibly.

Being Interviewed

In arranging for an interview, be sure of the date, time, and place. As you are getting ready, allow plenty of time. Have a good physical appearance—paying attention to your hair, grooming, clothes, style, and cleanliness. Take a pen, paper for notes, and your résumé with you. Review the interviewer's title and name so you can pronounce it correctly. Practice entering and leaving a room—sitting down and getting up—gracefully.

Keeping your appointment and being on time are very important. In fact, you would be wise to arrive about ten minutes early. Introduce yourself to the receptionist. While waiting, sit with good posture and read professional publications. Selling yourself during the interview includes these tips:

◗ Let the interviewer initiate the conversation and hand shaking.

◗ Make the interviewer feel important by using his or her name in the conversation, looking directly at him or her, and giving sincere compliments about the position or job atmosphere.

◗ Have your education and work experience on the tip of your tongue.

◗ In answering questions be honest and tell the truth; do not lie or bluff.

◗ Be a good listener.

◗ Do not criticize others or run down a previous employer or teacher.

◗ Do not air your prejudices.

◗ Watch for indications from the interviewer of the meeting's end—shuffling papers or getting up from the chair. Thank the interviewer. Leave with courtesy and poise.

Typical questions asked during job interviews include: Tell me about yourself. How would your previous employers and teachers describe your strengths? How would your teammates describe you? If you have any weaknesses related to this position, what might they be? Why should we hire you? Describe an obstacle you have had to overcome and how you accomplished the challenge. What abilities and skills make you qualified for this position?

You should have some questions ready to ask during the interview. They might include: *Is this a new position, or are you filling a vacancy? What qualities are most important to you in filling this position? Could you describe the orientation and training for this position? When do you plan to make a hiring decision?*

Writing a Follow-Up Letter

The day after an interview, write a letter to express appreciation for the meeting and to let the interviewer know your desire for the position or award. Your paragraphs would be:

¶1 Express thanks for the interview and any courtesies extended (introductions to employees, a tour of the facility, office, or business, and refreshments).

¶2 Refer to specifics that were said, done, or shown during the interview. Give sincere compliments about positive aspects of the company or position.

¶3 Indicate your desire for the position.

  As a simple but important courtesy, a follow-up letter should be written within two days of an interview. Even if you do not want the position, inform the employer so your name can be eliminated from consideration. Likewise, the employer promptly should notify all applicants who were interviewed but not chosen when a job has been filled.

Figure 4—Follow-Up Letter After Interview

27 May 20004

MS ELLEN HERRILL
FASHIONS UNLIMITED
468 CONCORD STREET
BOSTON MA 02114

APPRECIATION FOR INTERVIEW

Thank you, Ms Herrill, for the interview on Tuesday for the Sales Associate position to begin in June. I enjoyed meeting Mr Charles and others at your store.

Your full line of clothes/accessories and limited inventory are impressive. Efficient and friendly customer service was evident as I observed shoppers come and go.

I would be delighted to serve as one of your full-time sales associates this summer, Ms Herrill. Your decision by June 10 is anxiously awaited by Clyde Aker (from our Career Services Office) and me.

Lynn Rutledge

Miss Lynn A Rutledge
4611 East Valley Lane
Boston MA 02116

Phone 617-888-7777
E-Mail lar444s@university.edu

  Upon getting a job or receiving an award, a _winner_ expresses appreciation to all the people who made the _win_ possible. One day you will need reference letters again. Continue to practice your excellent human relations skills.

Develop a Portfolio

A *portfolio* is a professional exhibit of your achievements—outstanding papers, major projects, awards, grade sheets, publicity items, application (cover) letter, résumé, and letters of praise. Portfolios are popular among decision makers and screening committees of awards, scholarships, jobs, and leadership positions. Create your portfolio now by setting up a file for collecting items and a notebook for displaying your materials attractively. You should revise and update it throughout college and during your employment years.

Exercise 6 Developing a Portfolio

Prepare a portfolio that both describes and illustrates your freshman year. Include your best papers and projects, résumé, application (cover) letter, publicity items, awards, grade sheets, letters of praise, and other noteworthy items. You might include programs of special activities and major events you attended or chaired. The design should be flexible so you can expand and revise its contents throughout college.

Your early planning for a satisfying career will give you a competitive edge in college and in the job market. Should you change your career plans during college, you have the tools to adjust your plans.

Solve This Case—Career Planning

Elana is a computer science major who is having difficulty with college algebra. Her father, a systems analyst, wants her to become a partner in his firm. He often reminds her about the high salaries in the computer industry. Elana enjoys art and music, but her father warns her against careers in the fine arts because of their low pay and highly competitive nature.

Doug thinks he might want to become an elementary teacher, but he is holding off the step of declaring a major until his junior year. Meanwhile, he is working thirty hours a week at a fast-food restaurant.

1 In what ways are Elana and Doug off track in planning for satisfying careers?

2 What suggestions do you have for each?

My Reflections Journal

For this journal writing opportunity choose three of the following questions to answer, writing a paragraph or two on each. You may either print the pages and turn them in on paper or e-mail the pages to your instructor. Ask your instructor what he or she prefers.

1 How do you feel about your educational preparation for your career plan?

2 What kind of work experience would enhance your career opportunities?

3 How has this chapter and your class activities affected your career preparation?

4 Describe your experiences in interviewing for jobs. How might you improve this step in the job application or scholarship application process?

5 What would you like to share about your career planning decisions?

BECOMING INVOLVED ON CAMPUS

Objectives

Upon completing this chapter, you should be able to:

- Participate in a variety of campus events
- Find collegiate organizations to join
- Serve as an active organization member
- Organize and conduct meetings
- Apply basic parliamentary procedures

TO COMPLEMENT YOUR STUDIES, campus events and organizations offer various means to develop friendships, interests, and leadership skills. Becoming involved on campus gives you short breaks from the stress of studying and enables you to further develop social skills. You can have fun while helping to make your campus community a better place.

Participating in team efforts builds interpersonal skills that are important in leadership positions. By chairing a committee or serving as an officer in an organization, you develop the kind of leadership experiences sought by employers. As a leader, you need the ability to plan and organize programs as well as to conduct meetings in a professional manner.

Being active on campus opens doors to new friendships and the satisfaction of helping others. You form networks with professors, administrators, and staff personnel as well as classmates. You also enhance your leadership skills as you become well-rounded in academic and social skills. Memories of special events and associations will be treasures in your life's scrapbook.

Self-Assessment: Assessing Campus Involvement ✔

Place a check mark to the right of each entry that describes your campus involvement.

Part A   Categories of Campus Activities and Student Organizational Opportunities

I have attended or participated in at least one on-campus activity or event as follows:

1   Athletic event (baseball, basketball, football, hockey, tennis, swimming, etc)   ____

2   Cultural event (art exhibit, music/theater/dance production, literary reading)   ____

3   Convocation sponsored by the college or university   ____

4   Student organization meeting or sponsored event   ____

5   Intramural sport   ____

6   Lecture sponsored by an academic department   ____

7   Program or workshop presented by the counseling or health center   ____

Total your number of check marks. If you have at least three check marks, you are on the road to adequate and healthy campus involvement. By the end of this chapter you should have at least four check marks to identify categories of participation.

Part B Reasons to Become Involved on Campus

My reasons for being involved on campus or to become more involved are to:

1	Make new friends	____	8	Improve time management	____
2	Share similar interests	____	9	Build interpersonal skills	____
3	Have fun	____	10	Get to know faculty and staff	____
4	Relieve stress of studies	____	11	Network with community leaders	____
5	Enhance social skills	____	12	Provide service to campus	____
6	Develop leadership skills	____	13	Develop teamwork abilities	____
7	Become well-rounded	____	14	Create college memories	____

Total your number of check marks. The closer your total is to 14, the more aware you are of the intrinsic value of campus involvement.

■ Participate in a Variety of Campus Events

The academic, athletic, and student activities departments on campus offer many types of events to broaden your college experience. A variety of events are offered to bolster your school spirit, to expose you to the liberal arts, and to provide recreational opportunities. Your campus no doubt offers some of the following entertainment and informative events from which to choose:

Where is your athletics department?

★ *Athletic Competition* Competitive events of the athletic department—football, basketball, swimming, tennis, soccer, baseball, softball, track, hockey, golf, and volleyball

★ *Forums and Lectures* Issues or topics of business, economics, history, science, education, health, philosophy, and international concerns

★ *Cultural Performances* Programs presented by faculty and students of band, orchestra, choir, art, theater, and dance; literary presentations

★ *Convocations* Guest speakers and performers who entertain, inform, and motivate

★ *Recreation* Intramural sports, fitness and wellness programs, and outdoor adventure—bike riding, canoeing, hiking, rafting, rappelling, and rock climbing

Where is your campus recreation office?

Most college events are either free or offered at a reduced cost to students. Complimentary events usually are covered by departmental funds or student fees. Students indirectly pay for "free" events, so you are wise to reap some benefits.

Exercise 1 Attending Campus Events

Attend an outside-of-class event and write your reaction or a review that describes the program, performers, sponsor(s), and audience response.

_____

_____

_____

_____

■ Find Collegiate Organizations to Join

Studies show that students who are actively involved in campus organizations achieve higher GPAs and do better at impressing potential employers than their counterparts who do not get involved. When you participate in organizations, you interact with faculty, staff, administrators, and fellow students. Most important, you make new friendships. Sharing committee responsibilities and serving as an officer help you to develop leadership skills.

Campus organizations contribute to the social, intellectual, cultural, recreational, and spiritual aspects of college life. The following categories of student organizations (though they might be grouped differently) typically are found on college campuses:

College or University Help to represent a positive image of the college or university. Examples—Ambassadors, Cheerleaders, Residence Hall Association, Student Activities Council, Student Government Association.

Departmental or Professional Organizations for a specific degree or major to enhance professional development. Examples—English Society, Geological Society, Kappa Mu Epsilon (Mathematics), Nurses Association, Pre-Medical Society, Psychology Club, Spanish Club.

Greek Social Fraternities and sororities promoting Greek-related life that includes achievement, friendship, and service. Examples—Alpha Chi Omega, Delta Sigma Theta, Panhellenic Council, Phi Beta Sigma, Sigma Phi Epsilon.

Honorary Scholarly organizations focusing on academics and leadership. Examples—Chemistry Honors Society, Delta Tau Alpha (Agriculture), Kappa Delta Pi (Education), Phi Kappa Phi (Higher Education), Pi Omega Pi (Business), Sigma Pi Sigma (Physics).

Religious Organizations that enhance spiritual life. Examples—Baptist Student Union, Catholic Ministries, Gospel Choir, Muslim Students Association, United Ministries in Higher Education, Wesley Foundation.

Service Helping the local community. Examples—Gamma Sigma Sigma, Habitat for Humanity, Peer Educators, Sierra Club.

Social Sharing a common interest or culture. Examples—Association of International Students, Hispanic American Leadership Organization, Horseman's Association, Natural High Club, Veterans Club.

Sports Playing on a sports team. Examples—Bowling Club, Chess Club, Handball Team, Mountaineering Society, Rodeo Club, Tae Kwon Do Club.

Where is your student activities office?

Who is the coordinator of student organizations?

Student organizations are coordinated through the office of student activities, which has information about each organization's goals, the officers, meeting times, and membership costs. In choosing an organization to join, you will be most satisfied if you find out some basic facts about each group you are considering. When students discover unpleasant surprises, such as extra costs or time requirements, they become disenchanted and often quit attending or discontinue their membership. Answers to these questions will help you make wise choices:

1 What is the purpose of the organization? What are its specific goals?

2 When does the group meet? What are their standard meeting times and frequency of meetings?

3 What are the minimum expectations or responsibilities of a member? What is the potential for advancing to an officer position?

4 What are the major activities of the organization? When are they held? Are costs involved that are not covered by membership dues?

5 What is the annual regular membership cost?

6 When are new members accepted?

To learn more about an organization, you might talk to a member or officer and ask to visit a meeting. Consider joining only one organization and become active in it before joining another group. The time required to become a contributing member varies among groups, as you might expect.

Joining numerous clubs only to have the memberships listed on your résumé is not wise. Prospective employers are not impressed by a long membership list; instead, they want to know how you participated in organizations. What did you contribute? Did you chair a committee? Did you organize a worthwhile cause? Did you serve as an officer? Were you dependable in accepting your responsibilities? How did you make a difference? Put mementos and other exhibits in your portfolio to show prospective employers.

Because academic achievement is a priority, students usually limit the number of organizations in which they are active members. At first they join only one or two groups, so they can devote the time necessary to serve on committees and to develop leadership skills. Then if they are studying at least two hours outside class for every hour in class and are earning excellent grades, they consider joining a third organization the next year.

Exercise 2 Learning About Campus Organizations

Obtain a list of campus organizations from the student activities office. Select two organizations to review and evaluate.

Talk with an officer or member of each group to fill out the Campus Organizations form in the Personal References section at the end of this book. For each organization you will have:

Person contacted and respective phone number

Purpose and goals

Standard meeting times

Frequency of regular meetings

Minimum expectations or responsibilities of a member

Major activities

Cost of annual dues and other costs

When new members are accepted

Ask if you can visit the next regular meeting of the organization.

■ Serve as an Active Organization Member

Being an active member of an organization requires a commitment. You will be rewarded according to how much time, energy, and ability you invest to help the organization achieve its goals. As you review these cases, think about the kind of member you want to be in a campus organization.

Case 1—John As a high school student, John was modest and somewhat shy. Belonging neither to the popular cliques nor the academic achievers, he was just an average student. He was neither an athletic jock nor a lead performer in a drama or music production. Years later when times came for class reunions, none of the class officers (who were among the popular achievers) took initiative to organize a reunion; but John did. He organized and assembled alumni to celebrate class reunions for the 20th, 25th, and 30th milestones. He became an executive of a utility company.

Case 2—Deanna As a sophomore in college, Deanna was discouraged because she did not have a career focus. The next term she began to develop a career plan. She enrolled in courses and got part-time work experience as a customer support representative for a computer vendor. She joined the Information Processing Association (IPA) as a student member and served on committees. Deanna co-chaired the annual seminar and trade show two consecutive years. Upon graduating from college, she was promoted to a full-time position with the computer vendor and became the president of IPA. Within five years Deanna was promoted to manager of customer support for a seventeen-state region.

Case 3—Binh As a junior, Binh was a member in four organizations. Attendance at meetings was sporadic. After volunteering or agreeing to serve on a committee, she seldom attended its meetings. Classmates who worked with her on group projects for courses reported the same pattern. Binh was critical of the officers and of members with whom she shared committee responsibilities. In one organization she volunteered to co-chair an important social event. After the event it was discovered that the other co-chair had done most of the work with little help from Binh. In her résumé Binh listed the four organization memberships and embellished the descriptions of committee service.

Though the names are fictitious, the cases are authentic. Case 1 describes John's years after high school. Was his leadership ability developed after high school? Why was it not inspired during high school? Case 1 also reveals the character of the class officers; they never accepted the responsibilities of their office beyond high school. Case 2 explains how being an active member enhances a person's career opportunities. Case 3 tells about an irresponsible person who joined organizations only to list them in her résumé. Perhaps you know similar types of cases. How do you want to be known and remembered as a student and as an organization member?

Being an Active Member

Active and responsible members are noticed by others. Among the characteristics that are deemed positive and suggestive of leadership potential are the following. As an exemplary member, you would:

▶ Attend meetings regularly.

▶ Be on time for regular meetings and committee meetings.

▶ If late, open the door quietly and go to a side or back seat without drawing attention to yourself.

▶ Notify the chair or president if you cannot meet.

▶ Reply "Yes" or "No" to invitations that request RSVP; an accurate count is needed to plan for food and handouts; if you reply "Yes," be sure to attend.

▶ Renew membership dues on time.

▶ Use basic parliamentary procedures in meetings.

▶ Offer creative ideas and contribute to meeting discussions.

▶ Volunteer to serve on committees and to help with programs.

▶ Follow through; do what you say you will do and complete what you start.

▶ Take initiative rather than wait for the sponsor to remind you of your responsibilities.

Chairing a Committee

In chairing a committee, you demonstrate ability to lead a small group and the potential to become an officer. *Standing (permanent) committees* consider matters that need constant attention. *Special* or *temporary (ad hoc) committees* are created by the chair to handle short-term projects. Competent committee chairs do the following:

▶ Understand the specific charges and purpose of the committee.

▶ Establish meeting times and notify all members (at least two weeks in advance).

▶ Prepare an agenda and distribute it (with the meeting notice if possible).

▶ Involve all people of the group—offering participation to each member.

▶ Keep a record of dates and major actions of each meeting—reporting to the president.

▶ Meet the deadlines of committee responsibilities.

▶ Stay within the budget allocation.

▶ Acknowledge and thank the committee members for their services.

▶ Maintain a list of procedures used, steps taken, and costs expended; pass along this information to the next chair of the committee.

You might review these tasks and responsibilities upon accepting a committee chair position. Your conscientious efforts will be noticed by the officers and the sponsor.

Planning a Program

Being in charge of a program and/or speaker is another leadership experience. In many organizations the chair of the program committee is a vice president.

Inviting a guest speaker can promote good public relations for your organization. A 30-minute talk likely will require several hours of preparation in addition to time used for travel and the presentation itself. Local speakers typically do not expect reimbursement for travel, but out-of-town speakers might expect travel expenses (mileage or public transportation fare, food, and lodging) to be covered. Some speakers charge an *honorarium*—a presentation fee.

If your organization has limited funds for guest speaker expenses, you might check with another group on campus to see if you could share the speaker. You could schedule separate but closely positioned meeting times and divide the expenses.

Early planning is critical to ensuring a successful program. The following guidelines will help you in planning programs and scheduling speakers:

Six Weeks Before the Program

1 Extend the speaking invitation by telephone or in person. Discuss and explain:
   a The purpose of the talk and its topic—requesting the speaker to designate the title
   b The number of members expected to be in the audience
   c The goals of the members or students
   d The date of the program (Example: *Tuesday, November 9*)
   e The time of the meeting and the position of the talk (Example: *Meeting from 7:00 to 9:00 PM; 45-minute talk beginning at 7:05; questions and discussion from 7:50 to 8:00*)
   f The place (building and room)
   g Compensation (travel expenses and/or honorarium) if any

2 Send a confirmation letter, a printed reference for the speaker and you.

3 Upon learning of the speaker's acceptance, ask for biographical information or a résumé as well as a photograph (for publicity and introduction).

Two Weeks Before the Presentation

Where can you get a guest parking permit and a campus map?

Where can you arrange for audio-visual equipment?

1 Send a follow-up letter (see Figure 1):
   a Repeat the date, time, and place.
   b Enclose a copy of the meeting announcement or program (if applicable).
   c Send a guest parking permit and campus map (mark the location of the parking lot).
   d If the talk is scheduled near meal time, invite the speaker to be your guest.
   e If the speaker is unfamiliar with the campus, suggest a place to meet him or her.
   f Ask if any audiovisual equipment will be needed.

2 Invite the department chair and dean of a related area to attend (if applicable).

3 Publicize the meeting in the college newspaper and on the appropriate website.

4 If a question-and-answer period is to follow the talk, encourage the members to have questions prepared to ask (revealing interest in the talk).

Figure 1—Follow-Up Letter to Guest Speaker Two Weeks Before Program

25 October 2004

SGT LOREN RUSK
POLICE SUBSTATION

CONFIRMATION OF YOUR SPEAKING

Thank you, Sgt Rusk, for your willingness to speak on "Self-Defense" at the Student-Athlete Advisory Board on Tuesday, November 9. We shall meet in the Alumni Lounge of the Hammons Student Center beginning at 7:00 PM. You can plan 45 minutes to speak and 10 minutes for questions. Our business meeting will follow the program.

Our 22 members on the Student-Athlete Advisory Board represent all the men's and women's sports. One of our goals is to support student-athletes' welfare. After your talk we will apply the self-defense techniques you demonstrate and open the floor to questions.

The Alumni Lounge has an overhead projector and screen as well as a videotape monitor and player. Will you need any other equipment? Thanks for the biographical information, which has been included in the program announcement. We look forward to your visit, Sgt Rusk.

Marc Destor

Marc Destor, Ext 8696
Vice President of Programs
Wells Hall 308
E-Mail: MarcDestor@university.edu

The Day of the Presentation

1 Have audiovisual equipment ready and checked to be sure it is working.
2 Meet the guest speaker at the designated place and help carry materials.
3 Introduce the speaker to the group.
4 Invite questions and comments from the audience.
5 Present a token of appreciation to the speaker after the talk.
6 Invite the speaker for refreshments.
7 Assist the speaker in carrying materials to the parking lot.

Within Two Days After the Presentation

1 Write a thank-you letter to the speaker (see Figure 2) and to others who assisted with the program.
2 Send a copy of the letter to the speaker's boss and add a note of commendation about the speaker. The supervisor (and company) will be pleased to know:
   • Their employee did an excellent job.
   • The speaker's and company's time and energy were well spent and appreciated.
   • The organization and college promote good public relations.

Figure 2— Thank-You Letter to Guest Speaker

10 November 2004

SGT LOREN RUSK
POLICE SUBSTATION

APPRECIATION FOR YOUR TALK ON SELF-DEFENSE

Thank you, Sgt Rusk, for speaking at our Student-Athlete Advisory Board meeting on Tuesday. Your information should prevent our being at risk, especially at night.

Several members have commented positively about your demonstration of self-defense moves. A student-athlete who lives near campus on Delmar Street said he is impressed by the Police Substation personnel for being good neighbors.

Your desire to serve the campus community is appreciated, Sgt Rusk. The Police Substation is improving the safety of our students; you all are commended.

Marc Destor

Marc Destor, Ext 8698
Vice President of Programs
Wells Hall 308

c Lt C P Hill

3 Encourage members to write letters of appreciation.
4 Submit a news article to the college newspaper.

In planning programs and communicating with guest speakers, you can practice important courtesies expected in the professional world. Your abilities will be noticed by associates, the organization sponsor(s), and administrators who attend the meeting.

Exercise 3 Being Active in an Organization

1 List and describe your membership(s) in campus organizations.

_____

_____

_____

2 Evaluate your participation in organizations—as a member, in chairing a committee, and in hosting a guest speaker. In what ways have you demonstrated leadership? In what ways would you like to further develop leadership skills through membership in campus organizations?

_____

_____

_____

Organize and Conduct Meetings

As the chair of a committee or president of an organization, you will organize and conduct meetings. Basic preparation procedures can facilitate an efficient meeting. Follow-up is necessary to document the meeting's discussion and to record actions and decisions.

Preparing for a Meeting

Early planning is reflected in successful meetings. Members need to be informed in advance so they can come prepared to discuss issues and to present appropriate information. *For committee meetings*: Inform members of the purpose of the meeting, the date, the starting and ending times, the place, the agenda, and the role each member is to play. *For regular organization meetings*: At the beginning of the year, provide the members with the year's schedule—meeting dates, starting time, place, and programs.

Before a meeting, prepare a checklist of things to do. Send meeting notices or reminders so the members receive them at least a week before the meeting. You might consider telephone or e-mail reminders.

Prepare the *agenda*—a list or outline of topics to consider at the meeting. An agenda usually is sent to participants before the meeting so they can be prepared to discuss it and to offer ideas. An agenda helps the chair to conduct the meeting in an orderly way and to focus on the pertinent issues without veering off the important topics. The agenda could be an attachment to an e-mail message that notifies or reminds members of the meeting.

Figure 3—Functional Agenda

Student-Athlete Advisory Board
Agenda
9 November 2004

1 Call to Order
2 Program: "Self-Defense"—Sgt Loren Rusk, Police Substation
3 Approval of October 12 Minutes
4 Treasurer's Report—Roberto Salez
5 Report from Intercollegiate Athletic Committee—Kim Anderson
6 Diversity Training Workshop—Michelle Bryce, Equity Committee Chair
   Date   Tuesday, December 7
   Time   4:00 PM
   Place   Plaster Student Union, Room 309
7 Community Service Project
   What? _____
   Chair? _____
   When? _____
8 Adjournment

The functional agenda illustrated in Figure 3 includes announcements and key points of information, saving the time and effort to take notes during the meeting and ensuring accurate communication to members. Underscored blanks are places where group decisions can be written as they are made during the meeting.

For informal meetings, a functional agenda serves as both the agenda and the minutes. Thus formal minutes do not have to be prepared or mailed to the members who were present; the chair can make photocopies of the marked agenda after the meeting and mail it to the members who were absent. Both paper and time can be saved. Minutes of formal meetings can be composed easily from a functional agenda.

Handouts to be distributed must be prepared. If audiovisual equipment is needed, arrangements for delivery and setup need to be made.

Conducting a Meeting

As chair of a meeting, you are responsible for following the proper order of business. If a guest speaker is scheduled, a courtesy to the speaker would be to have the program precede the business meeting, especially if business will take longer than 15 minutes. The secretary is responsible for taking attendance and taking minutes. The proper order of business is as follows.

Calling of meeting to order
Approval of previous meeting's minutes
Treasurer's report
Standing committee reports
Special or ad hoc committee reports
Old business
New business
Adjournment

Following Up After the Meeting

Follow-up after a meeting includes writing acknowledgments and preparing minutes. Acknowledgments should be sent to members who have completed projects and chaired committees. Thank-you letters should be sent to guest speakers and special supporters.

Minutes document the organization's business proceedings (see Figure 4). They become a historical reference for consistency of action and for future decisions. The secretary will draft the minutes for your review. As chair or president, you will help edit and revise them for accuracy. The minutes then would be copied and distributed to the members by e-mail, by mail, or at the next meeting. Both the chair and the secretary should maintain a file of each meeting's agenda and the respective minutes.

Figure 4—Minutes of a Meeting

Student-Athlete Advisory Board
Minutes of November 9 Meeting
Alumni Center, Hammons Student Center

Call to Order The November 9, 2004, meeting of the Student-Athlete Advisory Board was called to order at 7 PM by President Jeff Shin. Of the 22 members, 19 were present.

Program Sgt Loren Rusk of the Police Substation spoke on "Self-Defense"; he showed moves to protect one from an attacker and to avoid being at risk when traveling alone.

Treasurer's Report Roberto Salez, Treasurer, reported a balance of $572.50.

Report from Intercollegiate Athletic Committee Kim Anderson reported the Athletic Dept passed certification by the NCAA. She thanked those who reviewed the Student-Athlete Handbook and helped distribute copies.

Diversity Training Workshop Michelle Bryce encouraged members to attend the Diversity Training Workshop to be held Tuesday, December 7, at 4 PM, in PLSU 309.

Community Service Project Jeff Shin asked for community service ideas. Moved by Ted Davis and seconded by Marty Jones, the vote was unanimous that our community service project be to participate in Adopt-a-Quad (campus clean-up). Harvey Kubie agreed to chair the project; members will begin participating on December 1.

Adjournment The meeting was adjourned at 8:45 PM.

Gertrude Carlberg
Gertrude Carlberg
Secretary

10 November 2004

Exercise 4 Attending a Meeting and Taking Minutes

Attend a committee or regular meeting of an organization. Take notes of the meeting and prepare typed minutes as though you were the official recorder or secretary. Attach a copy of the agenda to your minutes. You may use the format shown in Figure 4.

■ Apply Basic Parliamentary Procedures

An organization's business meeting provides a forum for discussing matters of concern to the members and for taking action on them. Business is conducted through motions, debate and discussion, and voting. An educated person uses parliamentary procedures during meetings, for which *Robert's Rules of Order* is the noted reference. You can enhance your contribution to a meeting, whether you are chair or president or a voting member, by reviewing these basic parliamentary procedures.

Motions

Motions are formal proposals for action. Once a motion has been made ("I move that . . .") and seconded, it is the only subject that can be discussed.

Debate

Debate follows the chair's statement of the pending motion. The first person to speak usually is the author of the motion. Then other members may seek recognition by the chair, typically by raising their hands. Members should extend respect to other members by not speaking until recognized by the chair. When discussion is encouraged, the facts and merits of the motion are brought out. Then members can vote more intelligently and are less likely to be dissatisfied afterwards.

Voting

After discussion, the chair repeats the motion and puts it to a vote by one of these four methods:

- *By Acclamation ("Aye" or "Nay")* Quickest method; appropriate for motions that likely will pass by a majority.

- *By Standing or Raising the Hand* Recommended for important matters where the result of voting by acclamation could be uncertain.

- *By Roll Call* Gives every voter a chance to register his or her choice as a record.

- *By Ballot* Takes more time but is secret and accurate; advisable for controversial issues.

Amendments

An amendment to a motion is made to change or modify the previous motion under consideration ("I move to amend the motion to read . . ."). Like the principal motion, an amendment (a subsidiary motion) must be seconded. The amendment must be voted upon before the original motion. If the amendment passes, the original motion must be voted upon as amended. If the amendment is lost, the motion is voted upon as originally stated.

Types of Motions

Among commonly used motions in business meetings are postpone indefinitely, limit debate, move the previous question, lay on the table, and rescind or repeal a previous motion.

- *Postpone Indefinitely* Make this motion if you believe or feel that the main motion is so awful the group could not adopt or reject it without bad consequences. This motion must be seconded; it is debatable but not amendable. A majority vote is required to approve indefinite postponement.

- *Limit Debate* The motion to limit debate takes two forms—to shorten the limit on individual speeches or to end debate at a specific time. "I move that debate be limited to . . . (or end at . . .)." The motion must be seconded and is debatable. It is amendable as to time only; a two-thirds vote is required.

- *Move the Previous Question* The purpose of this motion is to stop debate and vote immediately. "I move the previous question" or "I move to close debate" requires a second, is neither debatable nor amendable, and requires a two-thirds vote.

- *Lay on the Table* To postpone consideration to a more convenient time, this motion often is considered a polite way of defeating a motion with the assumption that it is to lie on the table permanently. If not taken from the table by the end of the next regular meeting, it dies. The motion requires a second and a majority vote; it is not debatable and cannot be amended.

- *Rescind or Repeal a Previous Motion* A motion to rescind annuls something previously adopted. "I move we rescind the motion that . . . which was adopted at our . . . meeting." The motion requires a second, is debatable, can be amended, and requires a two-thirds vote unless previous notice is given. The motion can apply only to the unexecuted part of something previously adopted.

Being able to organize and conduct meetings using parliamentary procedures is expected of all chairpersons. As an education person, you will use these skills throughout life as you participate in organizations.

Solve This Case—Becoming Involved on Campus

As a first-term freshman, Rachel was enjoying her college experience until she received her midterm grades. Instead of the A's and B's that she expected, her grades were mostly C's and D's. Following the advice of her college success course instructor, she had become involved on campus in various ways. She had thought that campus involvement would enhance her college experience. Instead, college life has become stressful and is disappointing.

Having been invited to join three organizations during her first term, Rachel became an active member of all three. Wanting to develop leadership skills, she volunteered to chair a committee for each organization. Involvement in student organizations totaled approximately twelve hours a week.

As a member of the marching band, Rachel is required to participate in band practice and to perform at the football games—for a total of approximately fifteen hours a week. In addition, she attends one cultural event (dance, music, or theater performance) a week. She carries a 15-credit-hour load, and she spends approximately eighteen hours a week doing homework assignments and studying for exams. Many nights she does not get to bed until 2 AM, which causes her to miss her 8 AM class.

At her wit's end, Rachel questions whether she wants to continue college.

1 Which part of the discussion about campus involvement did Rachel not follow?

2 What suggestions do you have for Rachel to help her get on a successful track in college?

My Reflections Journal

From the following questions, choose three to answer in this journal entry, writing one to two paragraphs for each. Using your computer, you may either print the pages and turn them in on paper or e-mail the pages to your instructor. Ask your instructor which method he or she prefers.

1 Describe your involvement in activities and organizations prior to coming to college.

2 Tell about your current involvement in campus activities and organizations.

3 After studying this chapter, how can you show better leadership skill as a committee chair or organization officer?

4 How confident are you in parliamentary procedures—applying *Robert's Rules of Order*?

5 What challenges in your personal life are obstacles to your campus involvement?

Website Practice Test

On the website at http://www.casadyenterprises.com/collegeedgebook/practicetests.htm you can access a practice test to check on your understanding of the chapter concepts. You may print the results of this self-test to review before taking the respective in-class exam.

16 MANAGING MONEY

Objectives

Upon completing this chapter, you should be able to:

- Compare resources with expenses
- Develop a budget plan
- Understand credit principles and terms
- Apply for financial assistance
- Express appreciation for financial assistance

MANAGING MONEY INVOLVES prioritizing goals, comparing resources to expenses, planning a budget, and adjusting your lifestyle accordingly. Once you set your goals, you compare financial resources with expenses. If your expenses exceed resources, you will have to adjust your priorities. Then you can develop a budget plan and make it work to live within your means.

If you are single without dependents, you have only yourself to manage. Living with and sharing expenses with a partner, roommate, or spouse adds a second dimension. Money management takes on a third dimension when you have dependents to support or have suffered a catastrophe (such as an accident, a fire, or hospitalization).

Most expenses will be paid by personal check on your bank account or by a credit card. As an enrolled student, you have an account at the college. Purchases billed to your student account number (student ID card) or to a credit card require an understanding of basic credit principles. Many colleges, however, do not accept payment by commercial credit cards.

By going to the financial aid office, you can investigate the possibility of grants, loans, and scholarships. You might check the department of your major and student organizations to learn about scholarship opportunities. Administrators, faculty, and staff can answer your questions and offer encouragement. Applying for financial assistance is worthwhile.

Self-Assessment: Assessing Money Management Awareness

For each of the following questions, circle the letter that best describes your money management awareness and practices.

1 My college expenses are discussed with
   a no one.
   b the person(s) who help(s) pay for my education.

2 At the bank that has my money I have
   a a checking account only.
   b both a checking account and a savings (or money market) account.

3 In paying bills I typically pay
   a a week in advance of the due date.
   b within three days of receiving the bill.

4 In purchasing textbooks my first choice is to shop
   a at the bookstore for new books.
   b for used books (at a bookstore or from former students of the course).

5 When I will be getting a refund on income taxes, I file my tax forms
   a by February 15.
   b on April 12.

6 If I plan to drop a course, I initiate the drop process
   a immediately.
   b the last day of the course-drop period.

7 In paying credit card bills, I typically pay
   a the minimum monthly payment required.
   b the entire balance in full each month.

8 When I need to make a purchase, I typically
   a take out a cash advance.
   b charge the purchase to my credit card.

9 If I need to borrow money, my first choice is
   a a student loan from the financial aid office.
   b a savings and loan institution.

10 For the financial assistance (grant, work-study, loan, and/or scholarship) received to support my college education, I have
   a written a special thank-you letter to the contributor.
   b orally thanked the contributor.

The key to sound money management is at the end of this chapter. If you have eight out of the ten best responses, your money management awareness is above average. Upon completing this chapter, you should score all ten correctly.

■ Compare Resources with Expenses

Managing your money as a college student establishes a pattern for the years ahead. Before developing a budget, take inventory of the available resources and anticipated expenses. Upon comparing the totals, you can make decisions about a budget plan.

Available Resources

Resources include money from a savings account, scholarship, employment income and educational benefits, financial aid (grants, work-study, or loans), and family or living mate financial support. If you need additional money, you probably would borrow from a bank, credit union, or savings and loan institution.

Anticipated Expenses

Education and living expenses include registration and tuition fees, the student services fee, books, computer equipment, supplies, housing, food, parking permit, utilities, clothing, laundry, automobile expenses, insurance, telephone, child care, medical costs, membership dues, magazines, newspapers, entertainment, contributions and gifts, taxes, and financial costs (checking account, interest payments, and administrative fees). You need to keep records of all your expenses with accompanying receipts to reconcile monthly statements, develop and maintain a budget, file income tax forms, apply for aid, and submit claims.

Comparison of Totals

Upon comparing the totals of resources and expenses, you can see whether you have surplus money or a shortage. Then you can make decisions about adjusting your standard of living, investing, or borrowing. Exercise 1 will help you identify your resources and expenses.

Shared Decision Making and Responsibilities

If you depend on parents or other family members for financial resources, you should share your personal business plan with them. Anyone who provides major financial support probably considers it an investment in your future and feels he or she has the right to participate in your budget plan.

If you share income and expenses with a partner, you want to discuss and perform the functions of personal business management together. Decisions about contributing to income and spending money need to be made jointly. Each party might be responsible for certain tasks, such as keeping receipts in order versus reconciling monthly statements. Both parties, however, need to cooperate and to compromise in making adjustments.

Exercise 1 Comparing Resources With Expenses

List your resources and expenses for six months (see Figure 1), including this school term (estimating the last weeks). Subtract the smaller total from the larger total.

Figure 1—Comparing Resources with Expenses

Designated Period: _____ **to** _____

Available Financial Resources		*Anticipated & Actual Expenses*	
Savings account	$____	Registration & tuition fees	$____
Family support	____	Student services fee	____
Employment	____	Books	____
Scholarship money	____	Computer equipment	____
Grant money	____	School supplies	____
Student loan money	____	Clothes	____
ROTC	____	Food & personal supplies	____
Veteran benefits	____	Haircuts	____
_____	____	Laundry	____
_____	____	Utilities and cable	____
_____	____	Telephone and/or cell phone	____
_____	____	Auto payments	____
		Auto gas, service, license	____
Total Resources	$ ____	Auto insurance	____
		Parking permit	____
		Housing	____
		Travel/transportation	____
		Health and life insurance	____
		Homeowner insurance	____
		Membership dues	____
		Newspaper, magazines	____
		Contributions and gifts	____
		Medical plus prescriptions	____
		Entertainment	____
		Taxes	____
		Financial costs	____
		Child care	____
		Savings	____
		Total Expenses	$ ____

Difference: $_____ (Shortage or Surplus)

■ Develop a Budget Plan

A budget plan sets the limits of your spending while you focus on short-term goals. It also guides you in saving and investing money for long-term goals. In developing a budget plan, consider ways to maximize resources, to reduce expenses, and to adjust living standards.

Maximizing Resources

In addition to having the maximum amount of cash available, you can have your money work for you. Some ways to maximize resources include the following:

✓ Carry in person only a small amount of cash; money in your pocket tempts you to spend and earns no interest. Keep only the minimum required balance in your checking account to avoid charges, and put the balance in savings or an investment account.

✓ Deposit into a savings or an investment account a certain amount each month for your long-term goals and for emergency expenses.

✓ If you know you will be getting a refund on income taxes, file your income tax forms no later than February 15. If you know you will have an amount due, file your forms to meet the April 15 deadline.

✓ Pay all bills before they are due to avoid any finance charges and to establish or maintain a good credit rating.

✓ Mark on your desk and pocket calendars the dates to pay bills: one week before the due date. Mailing the payment seven days in advance (a) allows enough time for it to reach the destination on time and (b) allows your money to earn interest in your bank account for the maximum length of time.

✓ Inquire about possible grants, loans, and scholarships for which you might qualify; apply for them.

✓ Talk with an investment counselor about the form of investment that will reap the highest return for the amount of risk you are willing to take, the length of maturity (time at which bond or note is due), and the possible need of having to access money in the event of an emergency.

What is your local bank that could provide you with investment advice?

✓ If you depend on parents or others for financial support, keep them informed about your academic progress as well as your financial status. Express thanks; do not take financial assistance for granted as though it were expected. People generally are more willing to help students who are appreciative and who demonstrate responsible behavior.

College students typically do not have much excess money. Implementing a plan to maximize resources, however, will set the foundation for future savings and investments.

Minimizing and Reducing Expenses

You can minimize and reduce expenses by practicing thrift, applying your intelligence, and disciplining yourself. Among the countless ways to lower expenses are the following:

🔍 *Enrollment Fees* Register on time or early; avoid late registration fees. If you decide to drop a course, do so at the earliest opportunity. The earlier you process a drop slip, the higher a percentage of refund you can get.

🔍 *Books* Shop for textbooks. Used books cost less than new ones and can be purchased at low cost from a former student of the course; be sure it is the book listed for the course. Get a receipt with the option to return any book within the first two weeks of class should the book not be required.

How could you learn about companies that are replacing their computers?

🔍 *Computer Equipment* If you need a computer and printer, you can purchase a good used one (though not the latest deluxe model) quite reasonably from a company that is replacing its computer system. Watch the ads, and make telephone inquiries. Some companies will give away equipment for income tax advantages.

Where could you shop for used clothing or factory outlet bargains?

🔍 *Clothes* Build your wardrobe around basic colors with interchangeable items. You can be fashion conscious and have a sizable wardrobe of name brands at a fraction of the retail price by shopping at next-to-new shops and factory warehouse outlets. Check for flaws or spots as well as for wear at the hem, under the arms, on pocket edges, and on the collar. Brand new items might be missing only a button or a belt, which can be replaced reasonably.

🔍 *Utilities* You can save utility costs by keeping windows and doors closed to save heat or air conditioning costs. Turn off lights in rooms not being used.

🔍 *Telephone* Make long-distance phone calls during the hours of the lowest rates (night time, weekends, and holidays) for some carriers. If you are calling outside your time zone, place calls to the east before 8 AM your time; place calls to the west after 5 PM. You might purchase a phone card, which offers the most reduced rate though you must enter extra access numbers.

✂ *Airfare* If you are planning to fly home or to a vacation spot, call several travel agents and check the Internet as well as the airline directly to get the best price on an airline ticket. In many cases you can get a more reasonable coach fare by staying over a Saturday night, flying on certain days of the week, making your reservation at least twenty-one days in advance, or scheduling a night flight (if one is available).

✂ *Food* Dining out is more expensive than buying groceries and preparing meals at home, especially for two or more people. Limit the number of meals eaten away from home, and choose moderately priced eating establishments. Before going to the supermarket, make a list of items you need and stick to it. Avoid frivolous items.

✂ *Auto Insurance* To minimize the rate, (a) be a defensive driver and avoid accidents, (b) maintain good grades to qualify for a preferred status, (c) do not drink before driving, (d) choose a higher deductible amount, (e) choose just one insurance company for both auto and home-owners coverage if applicable, and (f) check into the option of a rebate for no claims within so many years.

✂ *Speed of Driving* Slow down. Driving 55 mph burns 15 percent less gas per mile than driving 65 mph.

✂ *Parking Permit* Buy a parking permit and park in the designated lot(s) rather than in metered or illegal parking spaces. Get to the parking lot early to find a good parking place.

✂ *Housing Contracts* Carefully read your housing contract so you know the terms and conditions. If you have to withdraw from college or cancel the contract before the expiration date, follow the procedures explained in the contract. When you do leave, clean the unit and meet all conditions to get your full deposit refunded.

✂ *Meal Plans* If you purchase a meal plan, eat the number of meals covered by the meal ticket. Skipping "paid for" meals costs you double—the price of the meal and the health consequences of lost nutrition.

✂ *Student Discounts* Carry your student ID card at all times. Inquire about a student discount for eating establishments, college events for which there is a fee, subscription rates, professional memberships, and other businesses you patronize.

Which of the local restaurants offer student discounts?

✂ *Self-Serve Choices* Shop at discount stores and service stations that offer self-service (lower prices) in lieu of full service (higher prices). Bag your own groceries, pump your own gas, and use bulk cleaning services.

✂ *Paying Bills* Pay your bills on time to avoid finance charges at high interest rates and a resulting bad credit rating—words of caution that cannot be overemphasized.

✂ *Fines* Return library books on time to avoid book fines; drive within the speed limit to avoid speeding tickets; and park legally to avoid parking fines. Unpaid fines will encumber your academic records and probably will prevent you from registering for the next term.

Which local theaters offer student discounts and/or free tickets for volunteer ushering?

✂ *Concerts and Theater Productions* By volunteering to serve as an usher, you can attend symphonies, concerts, and theater productions free or at a reduced rate.

Additional ways of saving money are limited only by your creativity and ingenuity. Practicing thrift can enhance your feeling of self-worth both psychologically and financially.

Adjusting Your Standard of Living

When financial resources fall short of expenses, your choices typically are to borrow more money and work fewer hours, to work more hours and take fewer course hours (thereby extending your graduation date), or to adjust your standard of living (sacrificing some conveniences and luxuries). You might consider these options:

- *Housing* Choose less expensive housing or share the expenses with a roommate (or add one more to the group).

- *Automobile* Drive a used car or an economy model. The reduced cost will lower or eliminate car payments, and insurance premiums will be lower.

- *Computer Equipment* Instead of owning equipment, use a campus computer lab. You will not have the expense of or responsibility for service calls and repairs.

- *Entertainment* Engage in free or low-cost pleasures: hikes, bike rides, budget movies and rush-hour specials, bird watching, fishing, nature walks, and library visits.

- *Telephone* Order only basic services, and use a phone card. Instead of calling long-distance, send e-mail messages or write letters. Cell phones and LAN lines usually have reduced or free minutes on nights and weekends. If you have a phone that keeps track of the minutes, limit the length of your calls according to the maximum minutes allowed yourself.

These sacrifices are all for the short term to lessen the financial burden of college. The sooner you get a degree, the sooner you can earn a higher salary to support a more luxurious lifestyle.

Exercise 2 Developing a Budget Plan

Review the tips for maximizing resources, minimizing and reducing expenses, and adjusting your standard of living. In the left margin write *To do* next to the ideas you plan to follow. Then make realistic adjustments to the figures in Exercise 1 and develop a budget plan:

a Go to Exercise 1, and review the second column—*Anticipated & Actual Expenses*. In the right margin (next to the figures) write the expenses of your budget plan for the next six months. Total the column.

b Review the first column in Exercise 1—Available Financial Resources. To the left of the figures write any changes in financial resources you plan for the next six months. Total the column.

c Subtract the smaller from the larger total. Describe the changes since Exercise 1.

d Using the accompanying Budget form (Figure 2), make several photocopies. Prepare a budget plan for the next six months.

e Figure your estimated expenses for the next month and prepare a monthly budget plan on the Budget Worksheet in the Personal References section at the end of this text.

Figure 2—Budget

BUDGET		
Year _____	**Six Months** _____ **to** _____	
Resources	**Budgeted**	**Actual**
	$	$
Total Resources	$	$
Expenses	**Budgeted**	**Actual**
Total Expenses	$	$
Difference between Budgeted and Actual	$	

■ Understand Credit Principles and Terms

Your financial plan should include establishing credit and using credit cards carefully. A history of credit worthiness must be established before a financial institution will lend you money or extend credit.

Establishing Credit

To build a sound credit history:

What is the phone number or e-mail address of your local bank to obtain your account balance?

▶ Pay bills promptly.

▶ Maintain a savings account and a checking account without overdrafts (bounced checks).

▶ Be a dependable employee at a steady job.

▶ Apply for a credit (charge) card at a local store or bank.

The cost of credit varies, so shop for the most economical rates. Check on (a) the annual membership fee and (b) the interest rate on an unpaid balance. To find the lowest-interest credit card, visit http://www.bankrate.com. Use of a credit card will not cost anything if you:

▶ Choose a company that does not charge an annual membership fee.

▶ Pay your balance in full by the due date (saving any interest or finance charges).

Minimizing the Cost of Credit

Some people use credit to expand their purchasing power—paying a minimum balance plus an interest charge each month. Comparison shopping is important to find credit at the lowest cost. Before choosing a credit card issuer, consider getting answers to these questions:

1   What is the *annual percentage rate (APR)*? Is it fixed, or will it change with market conditions? The APR is the *finance charge*, the interest charge on an outstanding credit card balance; it is expressed as an annual rate, such as 18 percent. Is interest calculated on the average daily balance, the previous balance before this billing period, or an adjusted balance that takes into account payments you have made?

2   Is the preset credit limit high enough to meet your purchasing needs?

3   What is the grace period? The *grace period* is the period in which you can make new purchases without paying interest; usually it is twenty to twenty-five days. If you have an outstanding balance at the beginning of the new billing cycle, you will not benefit from the grace period. Pay off your balance in full each month to maintain the grace period and to avoid having finance charges. Not all cards have a grace period.

4   Does the lender require credit life, disability, or accident insurance? Are you already adequately covered by other insurance?

5   Is the card widely accepted? Does the card offer any special benefits?

Read the credit or loan agreement carefully (including the fine print), and be sure you understand the terms. Be cautious of special offers to students. To minimize credit card costs:

❑ Pay off your balance in full each month to maintain the grace period and to avoid paying interest. If you have $1,000 in a savings account at 3 percent interest, you will earn a little over $30 in one year. Using that $1,000 to pay off $1,000 on an 18 percent card will save you $180.

❑ If you need cash, charge a purchase to your credit card rather than take out a *cash advance* (a loan in the form of cash billed to your credit card). Cash advances are more expensive and should be obtained only for emergencies.

❑ Keep track of the dates you mail payments and how much credit you have left. Though the card may not have an annual fee, other fees might be assessed:

   Late fee—when payments arrive after the due date
   Over credit limit fee—if you charge more than your credit limit
   Lost card replacement fee—if your card has been lost/stolen more than once

❑ Pay the maximum each month. The more you pay each month, the less time it will take you to pay off the debt and the less interest it will cost you. Making just the *minimum monthly payment* (smallest amount you can pay and still be a cardholder in good standing) is the most costly way to pay off your balance.

You will receive many credit card offers—both by mail and in person as you shop. To establish a good credit rating, open no more than one or two credit or charge card accounts. Then manage your credit accounts carefully.

Checking on Your Credit Record

Credit bureaus keep records of credit habits to assist businesses and lenders assess the credit worthiness of applicants. You might check your credit bureau records for accuracy. Information on a credit report includes the names of credit cards you carry, the stores at which you shop, your personal loans, names of people or businesses who have inquired about you, and credit card or financial mistakes you have made.

If you have been denied credit, employment, or insurance within the last sixty days, you may obtain a free copy of your credit report from one of the major credit-reporting companies. Otherwise, you may purchase a copy of your credit report for approximately $10.

Equifax	Experían	TransUnion
Phone 1-800-685-1111	Phone 1-888-397-3742	Phone 1-800-888-4213
http://www.equifax.com	http://www.experian.com	http://www.transunion.com

When you request your credit report, include this information: your first name, middle initial, and last name (including Jr, Sr, etc); your spouse's name (first name, middle initial, and last name); your home address and any address within the previous two years; your Social Security number; your date of birth; and your legal signature.

If you discover inaccuracies, write to the credit bureau and describe the error(s). The bureau is required to reverify the information or remove it from your file. If negative information is accurate, it must remain in your file. You can, however, write a letter of explanation to be kept in your file. Negative information is kept for seven years.

Exercise 3 Applying Credit Principles

List the charge or credit cards you use and the last three months' bills and payments:

Credit Card	Three Months Ago Amount Due / Paid		Two Months Ago Amount Due / Paid		Last Month Amount Due / Paid	
_____	$_____	$_____	$_____	$_____	$_____	$_____
_____	$_____	$_____	$_____	$_____	$_____	$_____
_____	$_____	$_____	$_____	$_____	$_____	$_____

For ALL accounts:

Total the finance charges (if any) for the last three months. $_____
What is the total of unpaid balances on the most recent statements? $_____
What are your goals in establishing credit and in reducing or minimizing costs?

_____
_____

Based on your review of these items, do you need to make adjustments in your financial planning? _____ If so, describe:

_____
_____
_____
_____
_____

Apply for Financial Assistance

Many financial assistance programs, categorized as need-based aid and merit-based aid, are available to help meet the costs of higher education. Most federal aid and state aid programs are offered on the basis of financial need. Scholarships, awarded on the basis of merit and/or need, are offered through departments and organizations of your college.

Your eligibility for need-based programs can be determined only after your family financial status had been evaluated. To apply for aid, you must fill out the Free Application for Federal Student Aid (FAFSA) form, which is available from the financial aid office on campus. Among the federal need-based programs are the following:

Where is the financial aid office? What are its hours?

▶ Pell Grant

▶ Perkins Loan

▶ Stafford Loan

▶ Federal Supplemental Educational Opportunity Grant (SEOG)

▶ Work-Study

Grants are financial aid you do not have to pay back. *Work-Study* lets you work and earn money to help pay for college. *Loans* are borrowed money that you must repay with interest.

To qualify for federal student aid programs a student must:

Where is the student employment office?

▶ Have financial need

▶ Have a high school diploma or General Education Development (GED) certificate

▶ Be enrolled or accepted for enrollment as a regular student working toward a degree or certificate in an eligible program

▶ Be a United States citizen or eligible noncitizen

▶ Have a valid Social Security number

▶ Make satisfactory academic progress

▶ Sign a statement of educational purpose and a certification statement on overpayment and default (both found on the FAFSA form)

▶ Register with Selective Service if required

Applying for Financial Aid

Student financial aid depends upon the financial strength of the parents as well as the student's own resources. All need-based aid is awarded according to a formula established by the federal government. The formula evaluates income, assets, family size, and other measures of financial strength.

The FAFSA form, used to apply for federal and state financial aid, is available in December from the financial aid office. To be considered for all financial aid programs, submit the application between January 1 (earliest date possible) and February 28 (to meet the March 31 deadline in plenty of time). *You must reapply for federal aid each year.*

After mailing your application, you can expect notification that your FAFSA was received in approximately four to five weeks. The acknowledgment will include your Student Aid Report (SAR). Read the information carefully and follow its instructions; then send all pages of the SAR to the financial aid office.

Eligible students can expect to receive an award letter, stating the types and amount of assistance that can be offered, in late May. You must complete and return the award letter to the financial aid office to confirm your acceptance of the award(s).

For the most successful results, follow these suggestions from the financial aid office:

❑ Start early. Each year reapply by February 28 to receive financial aid for the summer or fall term. If you wait until the March 31 deadline, choices are fewer.

❑ Receiving aid for the fall term does not apply for summer; you must apply separately for summer aid.

❑ Read and follow the procedures given in the instruction booklets. Ask questions about anything that is not clear.

❑ Complete your federal income tax return (and have a copy of your parents' income tax return) before you fill out the FAFSA form.

❑ Contact the financial aid office to monitor the progress of your application. After filing the application, check every two or three weeks until you receive the SAR. After returning the SAR, check every few weeks until your award letter arrives.

❑ If your address or name changes, notify the financial aid office immediately so you will not miss any important communication.

❑ Before making a decision to drop a class or to withdraw from college, see your academic advisor and a financial aid officer. Be sure you know the consequences. The reduced credit-hour load could affect your financial aid. Audited classes do not count toward financial aid.

❑ Make an appointment with a financial counselor if an unexpected situation arise, such as loss of income or unexpected medical expenses.

Applying for Scholarships

Scholarships are designed to recognize and reward students for academic performance and leadership abilities. They are an incentive for students to continue excelling in college. Scholarships cover all or part of the required student fees (tuition and student services). Typically, students must be enrolled full time to be eligible.

In the department of your major, for which scholarships might you be eligible?

The administration of scholarship money is done by the financial aid office, but the selection process is done by the respective department, college, or campus organization. To obtain a scholarship application form, go to the department or college of your major or to the organization sponsor.

Exercise 4 Getting Financial Assistance

1 Obtain information about the financial assistance that is available.
   • For financial aid, go to the financial aid office.
   • For scholarship money, go to the department of your major or the campus organization.
2 Fill out an application form; follow the directions carefully. Note the deadline dates.

■ Express Appreciation for Financial Assistance

No doubt you are grateful to those who are helping support your financial needs while you are in college. Your family (parents, spouse, or grandparents) might be sacrificing some personal needs or pleasures to help pay for your college education. If you are employed, your employer might allow you to work on a flexible schedule (giving you time off work to study for exams or complete projects) or to study when there are pockets of free time.

Many individuals, organizations, and companies provide scholarships to college students. Knowing the value of a college education, they contribute to educational advancement (including scholarships) instead of giving money to charities.

Financial supporters of your education deserve more than your oral thanks; they deserve a special thank-you letter.

Exercise 5 Saying Thanks

Write a special letter of appreciation to the person or organization that has helped to pay for your education.

✍ Be specific in explaining how the financial support or scholarship money was used.
✍ Give a progress report on your college education experience.
✍ Take an interest in the person or organization by asking questions and making comments about their activities and event.

Sign your letter. Use a window envelope or address a plain envelope. Stamp and mail it.

Solve This Case—Financial Resources Versus Expenses

Terry is a college student who rents a three-bedroom house ($800 a month), which is shared with another student. The third bedroom is used as an office or study room, in which each has a computer and printer. Terry works at a convenience store from thirty to thirty-five hours a week to earn enough to meet car payments on a 2004 sports car and the insurance premiums. Expenses that have increased during the last few months are the result of maintaining a long-distance relationship (240 miles away)—long-distance calls to home, driving home every other weekend, and entertainment (Saturday night dinner and movie).

Financial resources are falling short of meeting expenses, and the term grades of a 16-credit-hour load are in jeopardy of meeting a 2.50 GPA minimum requirement for the academic program.

1 What are major choices Terry could consider?

2 How could Terry reduce expenses to lessen the financial burden of college?

My Reflections Journal

Respond to three of the following questions for this week's journal entry, answering in one to two paragraphs each. Using your computer, you may either print the pages and turn them in on paper or e-mail the pages to your instructor. Ask your instructor which method he or she prefers.

1 What are the biggest challenges in maintaining a budget plan?

2 How do you feel about your use of credit cards and your credit history?

3 How is your college education being financed? What percentage of your expenses is paid by your family? What percentage is paid by you from your savings and/or employment?

4 Are you receiving any financial aid—work-study employment, scholarship, or other?

5 Upon having read and discussed this chapter, what do you plan to continue doing as good practices? What changes do you plan to make in managing money?

Website Practice Test

On the website at http://www.casadyenterprises.com/collegeedgebook/practicetests.htm you can access a practice test to check on your understanding of the chapter concepts. You may print the results of this self-test to review before taking the respective in-class exam.

Key to Self-Assessment—Assessing Money Management Awareness
1—b, 2—b, 3—a, 4—b, 5—a, 6—a, 7—b, 8—b, 9—a, 10—a

EXPLORING DIVERSITY

Objectives

Upon completing this chapter, you should be able to:

- Define and use terms related to diversity correctly

- Expand your global perspective

- Appreciate diversity within the nation

- Be aware of services offered for students with disabilities

- Be aware of different sexual orientations

AN INVIGORATING ASPECT of higher education is the diversity on campus, which gives you an opportunity to grow intellectually, emotionally, spiritually, and socially. As children, your circle of familiar faces included your family, neighborhood, and elementary school classmates. In high school your circle began to enlarge—perhaps through work experience, travel, and a larger school district. Unless your parents' work required moving to various parts of the nation or world, your circle of familiarity probably remained somewhat small.

In college your circle becomes larger. You meet people who differ in age, gender, race and ethnicity, sexual orientation, physical ability, culture, and socioeconomic status. *Diversity* refers to the differences among people. Understanding diversity means recognizing and appreciating the differences among cultural groups, neither looking down on them nor being critical of them, while valuing their contributions to society.

Various departments offer courses that focus on diversity issues. Until you enroll in such courses, this chapter might expand your global perspective and broaden your view.

■ Define and Use Terms Related to Diversity Correctly

Discussions about diversity typically include the following terms, which sometimes are used inappropriately. To establish a foundation for accurate and tactful communication, you might find it helpful to review these basic terms and definitions.

Bisexual A person emotionally, physically, and/or sexually attracted to members of the same sex as well as to members of the opposite sex.

Cultural Group A group of people who share certain behaviors, beliefs, history, language, and values. Cultural groups may be based on religious beliefs, gender, physical abilities, ethnicity, institutional affiliation, and so forth.

Culture The customary beliefs, social norms, and material traits of a racial, religious, or social group.

Discrimination The act of denying opportunities, resources, or access to a person because of his or her group membership.

Ethnic Group A large group of people who have common ancestry and who share language, religion, and other cultural patterns. Many ethnic groups exist within each racial group.

Ethnocentrism Belief in the inherent superiority of one's own ethnic group and culture.

Gay The common and accepted term for homosexual males.

Heterosexual A person primarily attracted to members of the opposite sex—emotionally, physically, and/or sexually.

Homosexual A person primarily attracted to members of the same sex—emotionally, physically, and/or sexually.

Lesbian The common and accepted term for homosexual females.

Multicultural Having to do with various distinct cultural groups.

Nationality The status of being a member of a nation (by birth or naturalization).

Prejudice Conscious or unconscious negative action, belief, judgment, or opinion about another social group without knowledge of or examination of the facts.

Race A subgroup of people with distinguishable physical characteristics that are genetically transmitted.

Racism A conscious or unconscious action, belief, or thought that shows superiority over or discriminates against a person or group because of their particular race.

Stereotype A preconceived or oversimplified generalization (attitude, judgment, or opinion) about an entire group of people without regard for their individual differences. Although stereotypes may be complimentary, often they are negative and prejudiced.

Transsexual A person with an overwhelming desire to become a member of the other sex; a person whose sex has been changed externally through surgery.

Transvestite A person who dresses in the clothing of the opposite sex for psychological reasons.

■ Expand Your Global Perspective

Imagine the world's population (according to the Mid-2000 World Population Census reported in January 2004) scaled down to a college of 1,000 administrators, faculty, staff, and students. In the campus community of 1,000 people there would be 606 Asians (60.6 percent), 131 Africans (13.1 percent), 120 Europeans (12.0 percent), 52 North Americans (5.2 percent), 86 South Americans (8.6 percent), and 5 Oceanians (0.5 percent).

By the year 2005 one-third of Americans will owe their employment to foreign trade, and multinational corporations will control one-half of the world's assets. More than 90 percent of those entering the work force will belong to groups traditionally considered minorities. You will improve your marketability as a graduate if you can communicate effectively with people in other countries—composing international correspondence, speaking at least one other language, and adjusting to cultural differences.

Reviewing Research Findings

A recent survey (by Mona Casady and Lynn Wasson) of international companies was conducted to determine their communication practices and screening strategies when hiring new employees. These international businesses had customers, suppliers, branch offices, and/or business associates in at least one country outside the United States. The 120 companies that provided information during a telephone interview represented thirty-nine of the fifty states. Among the findings were the following:

- The major countries or regions with which U.S. international companies communicate are (in order of frequency beginning with the highest) Great Britain, Canada, Japan, Australia, Germany, Mexico, Middle East, South America, and France.

- College graduates who can speak and write a foreign language have a competitive edge in the job market.

- Written communication (in printed format) should be concise, simple, and free of slang.

A collaborative study conducted by the author and business communication classes in 2004 involved 118 interviews of international people (students, professors, and friends) representing forty-four countries. Major findings of interest include the following:

- *Impressions of the United States* People from other countries are most impressed by the friendliness of Americans, the career opportunities and job availability, the variety and quality of food, the freedoms enjoyed, the living conditions, a sound economy, available activities and entertainment, open mindedness and ability of different cultures to coexist, and the quality of higher education. The most frequently cited negative impressions of Americans are ethnocentrism and prejudice against international people, bland food and numerous fast-food restaurants, materialistic values (too money conscious), and weak family structures.

- *Cultural Differences* The biggest adjustment for people coming to the United States is the change in diet. Other major cultural challenges include dress attire and style of clothes, the educational system, religion (many denominations and practices), the standard of living (large homes and more cars), weather differences, and drinking laws.

- *Communication Barriers* Slang, jargon, and clichés are primary causes of confusion in international communication. English as a second language is difficult to learn. Accents differ and cause difficulty in word recognition. The double meaning of words is confusing. On the telephone and in person, some people speak too fast. Body language is difficult to read.

Where is the study away or student exchange office?

Many colleges offer study abroad and exchange programs to expand students' global perspective. The International Student Exchange Program allows students of its member campuses to study in more than forty countries around the world. Students pay the tuition, room, and board fees at their home institution; they are provided with the same benefits at the host institution.

Learning the Customs and Courtesies of Other Countries

Imagine living with an exchange student or studying in a foreign country. In preparation you would study the country's history and culture, including its way of greeting people. As a guest, you would want to know the typical customs and basic courtesies of your host or hostess. Following are some cultural norms for different countries. Of course, these might not be reflected in each citizen of the country, for all people are individuals.

England Handshakes are reserved for formal occasions. Except for young people and close friends (who may be addressed by first name), appropriate titles (Mr, Mrs, Miss) should be used. Telephone ahead before visiting at someone's home. Good manners are admired: Men often stand when women enter the room and open doors for women. Extra touching, such as backslapping or putting an arm around a new acquaintance, should be avoided.

Canada Though customs and courtesies vary somewhat across the country, Canadians are more reserved than Americans. Standards of etiquette are formal and pronounced: compliment the host and hostess on the meal, write a thank-you letter promptly, and leave or send a gift (flowers are appropriate). The best greetings are a firm handshake and a sincere *Hello*. Use direct eye contact, but avoid overusing physical gestures.

Japan The traditional greeting is a bow. Guests should bow as low and as long as the other person (but not lower). With a formal introduction by a third party, address people by name and title; use first names only among family and friends. Remove your shoes before stepping into a Japanese home. Emphasis is on modesty and reservedness. When eating from a bowl, hold it up at chest level (instead of bending down to it). Chewing gum or yawning in public is impolite.

China Punctuality and proper etiquette are important, as well as dignity, patience, and respect for Chinese customs. Avoid touching, slapping on the back, or shaking hands. A slight bow and a brief handshake are appropriate. After dinner the guest of honor is the first to depart, and people leave shortly after the meal is finished. Compared to Americans, the Chinese are more reserved and shy, and the speaking distance between two people is greater.

Germany More reserved and formal than Americans, Germans address acquaintances by their titles and last names. The most common greeting is a handshake. Visitors may present flowers to the host or hostess. Guests stand when the host or hostess enters the room and remain standing until the host offers a seat again. Men stand when a woman enters the room. Talking with hands in the pockets is disrespectful. Pointing a finger to one's head is considered an insult.

Mexico Either a gentle handshake or a nod is an appropriate greeting; longtime friends may embrace each other. Close acquaintances may greet each other by kissing on the cheek. People stand close to each other while talking. After a meal guests should stay to visit a while before leaving. An appropriate gesture for *No* is moving the hand left to right with the index finger extended and the palm facing outward.

Saudi Arabia Person-to-person meetings are preferred to communication by phone or mail. Since they have a relaxed sense of punctuality, Saudi Arabians may not be on time for appointments. A souvenir item from one's country is an appropriate gift to present after the first or second visit. Expressing too much admiration for anything a host owns can cause the person to feel obliged to give it to the admirer. The left hand is used for private matters, the right hand for public matters. Thus, people do not use the left hand for eating or for giving anything. To expose the soles of the feet to others is considered rude.

Where is the international student services office?

Where is the office of multicultural student services?

Knowing the basic courtesies and customs of other countries is important as you expand your global perspective. Whether you are a guest of an international acquaintance or host, you want to act appropriately and communicate effectively.

Most colleges have international as well as multicultural student services. International student services provide assistance to international students, which includes orientation programs and help with matters relating to immigration and naturalization. The office of multicultural student services provides academic guidance, cultural programs, a resource center, and social activities to promote diversity and cultural awareness. Students are provided information about campus resources and are linked to other support groups on campus.

Exercise 1 Expanding Your Global Perspective

Interview an international person (student, faculty or staff member, friend, employer, or co-worker). Ask the following questions; then ask other questions of interest to you.

1 Name of person interviewed_____

2 Country of origin _____

3 Official language of the country _____

4 What does the person like most about being in the United States?
_____

5 What is most difficult about speaking and writing the English language?
_____

6 What are the major cultural differences (language, dress, food, time consciousness, relationships, values and norms, beliefs, sense of space, and work habits/practices) between that country and the United States?
_____
_____

7 What has been the biggest adjustment to living in the United States?
_____
_____

8 Who has helped you the most to feel welcome and at home here?
_____

9 In what ways was this person helpful and kind?
_____
_____

■ Appreciate Diversity Within the Nation

Within our nation we have the opportunity to grasp and to appreciate what diversity represents. The primary dimensions of diversity are age, ethnicity, gender, physical ability, race, and sexual orientation. Secondary dimensions of diversity are educational background, geographic location, income, marital status, military experience, parental status, religious beliefs, and work experience.

The U.S. Bureau of the Census reported on November 1, 2000, the percentages of racial groups that constitute our resident population as shown in Figure 1. Because Hispanics and Latinos may be of any race or a combination of races, they are not distinguished in Figure 1.

The revised standards by the federal statistics system have five main categories of race: American Indian or Alaska Native (1.0 percent), Asian (3.6 percent), Black or African American (12.3 percent), Native Hawaiian or Other Pacific Islander (0.1 percent), and White (75.1 percent). Additional categories are Some Other Race (5.5 percent) and Two or More Races (2.4 percent). The 2000 Census was the first census that allowed people to identify themselves as members of more than one race.

Figure 1—Graph of Percentages of Racial Groups

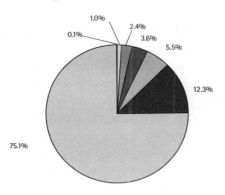

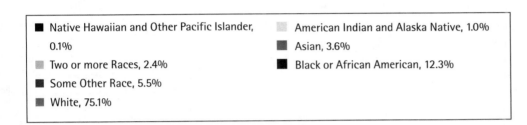

Each racial group includes many ethnic groups. Some writers and speakers combine the topics as *Racial and Ethnic Groups* or *Race and Ethnicity*. Much of what we know about American racial and ethnic groups is based on differences between groups. Within each ethnic group people share a common ancestry and generally the same language, religion, and other cultural patterns.

Learning About Major Ethnic Groups

Ethnicity or origin, as defined by the Census Bureau (http://www.census.gov/Press-Release/www/2001/raceqandas.html), is "the heritage, nationality group, lineage, or country of birth of the person or the person's parents or ancestors before their arrival in the United States. People who identify their origin as Spanish, Hispanic, or Latino may be of any race."

In the United States the five main ethnic groups are European Americans, African Americans, Hispanic Americans, Asian Americans, and Native Americans. A brief introduction to each includes some historical and cultural information.

European Americans The majority of our nation's population are descendants of immigrants from Germany, Ireland, England, Italy, Scotland, France, Poland, The Netherlands, Sweden, Norway, Russia, and Wales (listed in order of highest to lowest percentage). WASP (White Anglo-Saxon Protestant) refers to Protestant Americans whose ancestors came from England, Scotland, and Wales.

Most being from England, white Anglo-Saxon Protestants have a strong influence in our society. Because they settled the colonies, the English have had a dominant role in establishing the English language, English laws, and Protestant religions. Competition from the Irish, Germans, and Italians has challenged Anglo-Saxon dominance. Successful leaders from these countries have made their mark in business, education, politics, and professions.

Hispanic Americans According to the July 2002 Census, Hispanic Americans (also called Latinos) comprise 13.4 percent of the population—constituting the largest minority group in the United States. Over twenty separate nationalities are represented in the population. Hispanic Americans originate from Mexico, Puerto Rico, Cuba, South America, Central America, and combinations of other ancestries. These ancestries include the Spanish, Native Americans, Europeans, and to some degree Africans. The exact count is unknown; because though most Hispanic Americans are legal residents, many have entered the country illegally.

Mexicans first became citizens in 1848, when the United States purchased or won what would become Arizona, California, Colorado, Nevada, New Mexico, Texas, and Utah. Immigration, spurred on by Mexico's population growth and economic problems, has been the driving force in recent years. Puerto Ricans first became citizens in 1917, after Puerto Rico became a U.S. territory. Since the 1950s many Puerto Ricans have immigrated for job opportunities. Cubans started migrating heavily to Florida in 1959 when their country became Communist.

Speaking Spanish as the primary language, almost half the Hispanic Americans are unable to speak English. Lack of proficiency in English is an obstacle to getting good jobs. Improved formal education at the high school and college levels is a leading goal.

African Americans African Americans (black Americans) comprise 12.7 percent of the population (as of July 2002) and are the second largest minority group in the United States. Their history traces back to the arrival of indentured servants in 1619. Soon afterward many African Americans were brought here as slaves to work on cotton, tobacco, or sugar-cane plantations. Slavery ended during the Civil War in 1865, but segregation and discrimination still were practiced with intensity.

The Civil Rights Act (1964) sought to end racial segregation and began to improve many opportunities for African Americans. The act prohibits segregation and discrimination in various facets of society, including employment, schools, public facilities, housing, hotels, and theaters. Although gains have been made in major educational, political, and economic areas, African Americans still face challenges in our society.

Though many differences exist among African Americans, sociologists note several cultural tendencies. Public behavior may be emotionally intensive and expressive. A strong sense of community is supported by a high regard for family and religion.

Asian Americans Asian Americans are the fastest-growing (by percentage) minority ethnic group in the nation. Yet the percentage is smaller than that of African Americans and Hispanic Americans. With ancestry that can be traced to more than twenty different countries, the largest groups are Chinese, Japanese, Filipinos, Koreans, and Vietnamese.

The first groups to come to the United States were the Chinese (in 1849 during the gold rush on the West Coast) and the Japanese. In search of better economic opportunities, they initially were willing to work for low wages. Soon they began to operate businesses and to buy their own farms. Despite the challenges of discrimination, Asian Americans appear to be among the most prosperous minorities in the United States.

In spite of a wide range of differences in language, social class, and national history, Asian Americans share some cultural norms. They share a strong loyalty to family and community, an emphasis on educational attainment, and a strong work ethic.

Native Americans Native Americans initially were called Indians because Christopher Columbus mistakenly thought he had landed in India when he came to North America. Native Americans now have a formal relationship with the U.S. government that has been established by the Constitution and certain treaties, court decisions, and statutes. According to treaty obligations, the U.S. government provides for their health, education, and general welfare.

Native Americans continue to struggle to maintain sovereign rights protected by treaties. Politically, economically, and educationally, they remain one of the most disadvantaged groups in the nation. To preserve their cultural heritage, Native Americans place heavy emphasis on teaching their youth the native language, crafts, history, and religious ceremonies of the respective tribe.

States with the largest Native American population are Oklahoma, California, Arizona, and New Mexico. The tribes with the highest number of members are the Cherokees and the Navajos; each has over 200,000 registered members. Of the more than 300 Native American tribes, however, most have fewer than 10,000 members.

The poem "Diversity" shares a message of appreciation and tolerance for differences in those around us.

The Diversity Creed

Where would you go to learn more about other cultures and ethnic groups?

I believe that diversity is a part of the natural order of things—as natural as the trillion shapes and shades of the flowers of spring or the leaves of autumn. I believe that diversity brings new solutions to an ever-changing environment and that sameness is not only uninteresting but limiting.

To deny diversity is to deny life—with all its richness and manifold opportunities. Thus, I affirm my citizenship in a world of diversity and with it the responsibility to:

- *Be tolerant. Live and let live. Understand that those who cause no harm should not be feared, ridiculed, or harmed—even if they are different.*

- *Look for the best in others.*

- *Be just in my dealings with the poor and the rich, the weak and the strong; and whenever possible to defend the young, the old, the frail, and the defenseless.*

- *Avoid needless conflicts and diversions, but be always willing to change for the better that which can be changed.*

- *Seek knowledge in order to know what can be changed, as well as what cannot be changed.*

- *Forge alliances with others who love liberty and justice.*

- *Be kind, remembering how fragile the human spirit is.*

- *Live the examined life, subjecting my motives and actions to the scrutiny of mind and heart so to rise above prejudice and hatred.*

- *Care. Be generous in thought, word, and purse.*— Gene Griessman

"The Diversity Creed," by Gene Griessman, PhD. http://www.presidentlincoln.com

Using Respectful Terms

When referring to people who fall under the category of one of the diversity groups, we should use terms that designate mutual respect and appreciation. See Table 1 for appropriate terms.

Self-Assessment: Assessing Diversity Awareness ✔

The following paired statements represent opposite ends of a continuum. For each entry put an X in the 9 that represents where you fit on the continuum of cultural diversity.

I gravitate toward others who are like me.	❑	❑	❑	❑	❑	❑	❑	I gravitate toward others who are different from me.
Everyone is the same, with similar values and preferences.	❑	❑	❑	❑	❑	❑	❑	Everyone is unique, with differing values and preferences.
I feel more comfortable with some groups than others.	❑	❑	❑	❑	❑	❑	❑	I feel equally comfortable with all groups.
I do not have stereotypes about other groups.	❑	❑	❑	❑	❑	❑	❑	I have stereotypes about other groups.
Newcomers to our society should adapt to the rules.	❑	❑	❑	❑	❑	❑	❑	Our society should change the rules to adapt to newcomers.
I am irritated when people do not speak English.	❑	❑	❑	❑	❑	❑	❑	I am understanding when people do not speak English.
My choice would be to chair a homogeneous committee.	❑	❑	❑	❑	❑	❑	❑	My choice would be to chair a multicultural committee.
On a team project I am task focused and do not waste time chatting to build relationships.	❑	❑	❑	❑	❑	❑	❑	On a team project I begin by building relationships and then get to the task.

Draw a line to connect your ❑s. The closer your line is to the right-hand column, the greater is your awareness about diversity-related issues.

For the following list check the cross-cultural actions that annoy or frustrate you.

- ❑ No eye contact
- ❑ Coming late to class, appointments, or group meetings
- ❑ Standing too close when talking
- ❑ Refusing to shake hands
- ❑ Soft, limp, weak handshake
- ❑ Calling you by name inappropriately or not calling you by name
- ❑ Not contributing to conversation and/or not asking questions

Table 1 Respectful Terms to Use

WHEN REFERRING TO	USE	INSTEAD OF
People from other countries	International people; refer to the country or city of origin	Foreigners
Biracial people	Biracial people	Mulattoes
Black people	African Americans, Caribbean Americans, black people, people of color	Negroes, minorities, colored
Asian people	Asian Americans, Japanese, Chinese, Koreans, Pakistanis, and so forth; people of color	Minorities, orientals
Pacific Islanders	Pacific Islanders, Maoris, Polynesians, etc; use island name—Cook Islanders, Hawaiians; people of color	Asians, minorities
American Indians	American Indians, Native Americans; name of tribe—Cherokees, Iroquois, Sioux; people of color	Minorities
Hispanics, Latin American people	Hispanic Americans, Latinas/Latinos, Chicanas/Chicanos; use country of national origin—Chileans, Cuanos, Puerto Ricans; Hispanics; people of color	Minorities
White people	European Americans; use country of national origin—German Americans, Irish Americans, Polish Americans; white people	Anglos, WASPs, Caucasians
Differently abled	Developmentally disabled, physically disabled, physically challenged	Crippled, handicapped
Blind people	People who are blind; visually-impaired	The blind
Deaf people	People who are deaf; hearing-impaired	Deaf and dumb, deaf-mute
Wheelchair user	Wheelchair user	Confined to a wheelchair
People with mental retardation	People with mental retardation; developmentally delayed	Retarded, idiot, moron, slow, simple
Gay men and lesbians	Gay men, lesbians	Homosexuals
Older adults	Older adults, elderly	Geriatrics
Younger Adults	Younger people, young adults	Kids, yuppies

■ Be Aware of Services Offered for Students with Disabilities

Where is the disability services office?

Whether you have a disability or know students with disabilities, you want to be aware of the support services provided by your college. Assistance is available to students with hearing impairments, mobility impairments, visual impairments, learning disabilities (such as dyslexia and dyscalculia), head injuries, chronic illnesses (including AIDS/HIV, diabetes, epilepsy, and psychological disabilities), coordination impairments, and speech impairments. On the college level, the responsibility for getting assistance from campus support services and for informing professors about a disability rests with the student.

Being Eligible for Support Services

To be eligible for services, students must:

1 Have a disability that substantially limits one or more major life activities (hearing, seeing, learning, talking, walking, and so forth).

2 Have documentation for or are perceived as having an impairment (an example would be disfiguration caused by severe burns).

3 Demonstrate that the requested services are necessary for participation in college programs.

Any service the college provides for all other students must be provided for any student with a disability. Examples include field trips, tutorial services, and the shuttle system. If a service is free to other students, it must be made available at no cost to students who have a disability. On the other hand, the college is not required to create a new service only for students with disabilities.

Communicating Effectively

In talking with people who have a disability, remember they are human. Speak directly to them, and be considerate if they need extra time to say or do something. Do not talk down to them. Here are suggestions for specific situations:

Hearing Impaired Get the person's attention by waving your hand or tapping him or her on the shoulder. Speak clearly and slowly, but do not shout or exaggerate lip movements. Use simple words and keep sentences short. Provide a clear view of your face and mouth so the person can read your lips. If the person cannot understand after you have rephrased your message, write it on paper.

People Who Are Blind Using a normal tone of voice, introduce yourself and others who are with you. When beginning a conversation, address the person by name so he or she knows you are talking to him or her. Ask the person if he or she wants assistance. If so, allow the person to take your arm (rather than your taking hold of the person's arm). Warn the person of steps, curbs, and inclines in the path. Use specific terms such as *left* and *right*. Offer seating by placing the individual's hand on the arm or back of the chair. Do not pet a guide dog. Walk on the side of the person away from the dog.

User of Crutches or a Wheelchair Allow the person to keep the crutches or wheelchair within reach. Consider distance and weather conditions when giving directions. Ask the person if he or she wants assistance (being supported by the arm if on crutches or being pushed in the wheelchair) before you do so. Do not hang on a person's crutches or lean on a wheelchair; you would be getting too close to the person's body space. To converse with someone in a wheelchair, sit or squat so your heads are parallel.

Exercise 2 Using Acceptable Terms

For each of the words to avoid, write an acceptable and recommended term:

AVOID	ACCEPTABLE AND RECOMMENDED TERMS
Handicapped person	_____
Confined to a wheelchair	_____
Simple, slow	_____
Deaf-mute	_____
The blind	_____
Crippled	_____
Retarded	_____

■ Be Aware of Different Sexual Orientations

In college you meet, attend classes with, work with, and are taught by a diverse group of people. Sexual orientation is one of many ways in which people differ. Educated persons with appreciation and respect for diversity are expected to communicate effectively with everyone, including those of a different sexual orientation.

Inappropriate behavior and conversation typically result from being biased, judgmental, and uninformed. As a result, many gay and lesbian people hide their sexual preference and do not tell others (come out).

Professional associations are helping to inform society about sexual orientation. In 1973 the American Psychiatric Association determined that homosexuality is a way of life; it is not an emotional or mental illness. According to the American Psychological Association, trying to change the sexual orientation of a homosexual person is unethical.

Exercise 3 Handling a Diversity Issue

Assume you are chair of the program committee of a student organization on campus that is planning a Valentine's Day social event. Each member is being invited to bring a special guest. One member suggests having a couples game. Another has an idea for a competitive game involving men versus women. You are aware of members in your organization who are gay, lesbian, and single (heterosexual but without a partner or guest). Your diverse membership is comprised also of those who have dietary restrictions, including those who are diabetic and who are vegetarian.

1 How would you lead the discussion to conclude with activities that would be enjoyable for all members and guests?

_____

_____

2 Identify two types of activities that would be appropriate for this social event.

_____

3 What refreshments (food) would you order?

_____

_____

At the close of this chapter you might be interested to know about exemplary service on behalf of groups that suffer from diversity issues. Perhaps you will be inspired to do something special for someone who faces challenges in our society.

Raul Yzaguirre is president of the National Council of La Raza, a Latino organization of 3.5 million people that works to improve education, employment, health care, and immigration policy for Spanish-speaking people. Once a fisherman off the Texas coast, he now is a major voice in U.S. policy.

Robert Moses, a civil rights activist and math teacher, directs an algebra project that teaches low-income high school students the skills they need for college. Each week he flies from his home in Massachusetts to a Mississippi high school, where he trains high school graduates to teach algebra to their younger peers.

Jody Williams is the Founding Coordinator of International Campaign to Ban Landmines, an assembly of 1,400 nongovernmental organizations that formed an alliance to ban landmines. She is the force behind the 1997 Mine Ban Treaty that bans trade and manufacturing of landmines; governments are required to dig them out of the ground.

Dean Kamen, an inventor who holds more than 150 patents, was moved when he observed a man struggling to get his wheelchair up a curb. He invented the self-balancing iBOT, which

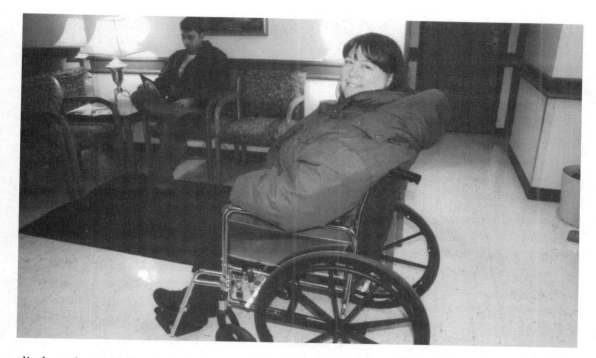

climbs stairs, moves at a runner's pace, and rises up on its rear wheels so the occupant is elevated eye-to-eye with standing people.

Your global perspective and appreciation for diversity within our nation no doubt has expanded. As you continue your lifelong learning venture, may you continue to value the unique characteristics and contributions of people who are different from you.

Solve This Case—Who Are These Great Leaders?

After reading each paragraph synopsis, identify the internationally known leader:

LEADER #1 Born at the time of slavery, he became one of the most influential black leaders and educators of his time. To encourage black people to get a practical education, he founded the Tuskegee Institute (Tuskegee, Alabama), a vocational school for black people. His strong belief in the mutual progress of blacks and whites qualified him to serve as an advisor to congressmen, governors, and presidents. His rise to national prominence was described in his autobiography, *Up from Slavery.*

LEADER #1 Born in the Ukraine, she emigrated to Wisconsin in 1906 and then emigrated to Palestine in 1921. Founder of the State of Israel, she served as its fourth prime minister from 1969 to 1974. During her administration she worked for a peace settlement in the Middle East. At the outbreak of the fourth Arab-Israeli War, she resigned her post (1974) but remained a strong political figure until her death in 1978, when it was revealed that she had suffered from leukemia for twelve years.

LEADER #1 Born in 551 BC and orphaned at an early age, he was China's most famous teacher, philosopher, and political theorist. Largely self-educated, he was deeply disturbed by the social conditions of his time. Dedicating his life to social reform, he based his teaching upon ethics and he emphasized sincerity. His teachings were compiled by his students after his death in what is known as the *Analects,* which became the foundation of the social lifestyle in China, Korea, Japan, and Indochina.

My Reflections Journal

Choose two of the following questions to discuss in your journal entry, writing one to two paragraphs about each. Using your computer, you may either print the pages and turn them in on paper or e-mail the pages to your instructor. Ask your instructor which method he or she prefers.

1 Do you have a friend or an associate of a different race or ethnic group? If so, how has this person influenced your awareness of diversity?

2 Describe a situation in which you were treated differently than others of a group. What were your feelings?

3 Having explored diversity through reading, discussing, and doing activities of this chapter, will you approach diversity issues differently in the future? How?

4 Are you a member of a "diverse group"? If so, what have been its effects on your beliefs and practices?

Website Practice Test

On the website at http://www.casadyenterprises.com/collegeedgebook/practicetests.htm you can access a practice test to check on your understanding of the chapter concepts. You may print the results of this self-test to review before taking the respective in-class exam.

PREFACE TO PERSONAL REFERENCES

Dear Student

Over the years one of the positive comments I have received from many of my first-year students is "Thanks for having us keep a reference manual; I still use it." Because the reference manual worked so well for my students, this edition includes a major focus on the creation of your own Personal Reference Manual. The manual will not be filled out at the end of a chapter or the end of the book. Instead, it is an integral part of the text, which will be developed as you read through each chapter of the book.

You will be cued to fill in the Personal References worksheets, located at the end of the book, by questions that appear in the margins throughout the text. This will provide an immediate application of the materials and will allow you to customize your book. The process of filling in the worksheets in this Personal References section will not only provide you with a comprehensive manual of your campus; it also will lead you to discover all the resources—both on and off campus—that will contribute to your success at college. Upon completion of your Personal References, you can remove the entire section and place it on a shelf close to your desk for reference throughout college.

My peer leaders (sophomores, juniors, and seniors) maintain a reference manual that includes all these pages. They like having all the pages in one section (rather than positioned throughout the textbook) so they can find the information easily and quickly. At the end of the term they report how helpful it is to have this handy guide that customizes the textbook for their individual needs.

You will use your Personal References all the years of your college experience. As you begin to fill in the forms and tables, think about what you will encounter as a freshman that you will use in the last year of college. Be careful as you construct it so the foundation supports your specific needs as the years evolve.

Best wishes for an enjoyable and successful college experience.

Mona Casady

Personal References of _____

Table of Contents

Academic Advisor

Name _____

Professional Title_____

Department _____

Office Location_____

Office Hours _____

Office Phone _____ E-Mail Address _____

DATE OF APPOINTMENT   *NOTES ON DISCUSSION AND ACTIONS*

_____   _____

                         _____

_____   _____

                         _____

_____   _____

                         _____

_____   _____

                         _____

_____   _____

                         _____

_____   _____

                         _____

_____   _____

                         _____

_____   _____

                         _____

_____   _____

                         _____

Budget Worksheet

BUDGET		
Year _____ **Month of** _____		
Resources	*Budgeted*	*Actual*
	$	$
Total Resources	$	$
Expenses	*Budgeted*	*Actual*
Total Expenses	$	$
Difference between Budgeted and Actual	$	

Calendar of the Term

MONTH	SUNDAY	MONDAY	TUESDAY	WEDNESDAY	THURSDAY	FRIDAY	SATURDAY

Campus Organizations

Organization 1_____

Person contacted _____ Phone _____

1 Purpose and goals_____

2 Standard meeting times_____

3 Frequency of regular meetings _____

4 Minimum expectations or responsibilities of a member_____

_____

5 Major activities_____

6 Cost of annual dues $_____ Other costs_____

7 When new members are accepted_____

Organization 2_____

Person contacted _____ Phone _____

1 Purpose and goals_____

2 Standard meeting times_____

3 Frequency of regular meetings _____

4 Minimum expectations or responsibilities of a member_____

_____

5 Major activities_____

6 Cost of annual dues $_____ Other costs_____

7 When new members are accepted_____

Campus Resources

RESOURCE OR SERVICE	BUILDING	BLDG ID & ROOM	DIRECTOR'S NAME	TELEPHONE
Academic Advisement Center				
Notes				
Academic Skills Center (Reading, Studying)				
Notes				
Athletics Department				
Notes				
Audiovisual Equipment				
Notes				
Bookstore				
Notes				
Bursar				
Notes				
Campus Recreation				
Notes				
Career Services				
Notes				
Chaplain or Campus Ministries				
Notes				
Commuter Services				
Notes				
Computer Services/Help				
Notes				

RESOURCE OR SERVICE	BUILDING	BLDG ID & ROOM	DIRECTOR'S NAME	TELEPHONE
Copy Center				
Notes				
Counseling and Testing Center				
Notes				
Dean of Students				
Notes				
Disability Services				
Notes				
Employment Office (Students)				
Notes				
FAX Machine				
Notes				
Financial Aid Office				
Notes				
Health & Wellness Center				
Notes				
ID Card Office				
Notes				
International Student Services				
Notes				
Judicial Programs				
Notes				
Learning Diagnostic Clinic				
Notes				

RESOURCE OR SERVICE	BUILDING	BLDG ID & ROOM	DIRECTOR'S NAME	TELEPHONE
Library Services				
Notes				
Math Center				
Notes				
Multicultural Resource Center				
Notes				
Multicultural Student Services				
Notes				
Parking Administration				
Notes				
Physical Fitness Center				
Notes				
Postal Services				
Notes				
Records Office				
Notes				
Registration Center				
Notes				
Residence Life & Services				
Notes				
Safety/Security/Transportation				
Notes				
Student Activities				
Notes				

RESOURCE OR SERVICE	BUILDING	BLDG ID & ROOM	DIRECTOR'S NAME	TELEPHONE
Student Union				
Notes				
Study Away/Student Exchange				
Notes				
Telecommunication Services				
Notes				
Tutorial Services				
Notes				
Veterans Services				
Notes				
Writing Center				
Notes				

Career Planning Worksheet

Name of career services center/office _____

Location _____ Phone # _____ Office hours _____

Director _____ E-Mail _____

Career counselor _____ E-Mail _____

Cooperative ed/internships director _____ E-Mail _____

Findings of Self-Assessment:

Categories of People and Code   *Disciplines Being Considered and Code*

_____ 1st Place _____

_____ 2nd Place _____

_____ 3rd Place _____

Career guidance and other self-assessment software available:

_____   _____

_____   _____

Resources available: Website addresses:

_____   _____

_____   _____

Career Day/Fair—Date, Time, Place: _____

Classmates

COURSE	CLASSMATE	TELEPHONE	E-MAIL ADDRESS	NOTES

College Catalog Information

1 Primary mission of the college: _____

2 College *Catalog* website address: _____

3 College's mailing address: _____

_____

4 Cost of tuition per credit hour: $_____

5 Cost of student services fees: $_____ Services they cover: _____

_____

6 Where to go to get a transcript: _____ Is a fee charged? _____

7 What minimum GPA is required for a student to be in good standing? _____

8 What GPA would result in a freshman being suspended? _____

9 What is the last date to drop a class without having to get the instructor's grade?

_____ (No–Penalty Drop Date)

Mark it on your Calendar of the Term.

10 To be classified as a sophomore, how many credit hours must be earned? _____ cr hrs

11 What is the minimum academic load to have full-time student status

during a regular term? ____ cr hrs

during a summer term? ____ cr hrs

12 Who receives a midterm grade report at your college? _____

13 What are the withdrawal procedures of your college? _____

14 What are the minimum total credit hours required to earn a bachelor's degree? _____ cr hrs

15 What is the minimum overall GPA required for graduation? _____ GPA

Computer Facilities

DESCRIPTION	BLDG _____ ROOM _____	BLDG _____ ROOM _____	BLDG _____ ROOM _____
Computers			
Printers			
Software/Programs			
Days and Hours of Operation			
Phone Number			
Type of Users Served			
Kind of Special Paper to Buy			

Goals Worksheet

My life's mission is to _____.

Major Long-Term Goals Ranked in Order of Priority

1 _____ (High)

2 _____

3 _____

Obstacles to overcome in order to earn the bachelor's degree:

_____

_____

Plans to overcome obstacles:

_____

_____

Term Goals Ranked in Order of Priority

1 _____(High)   4 _____

2 _____   5 _____

3 _____   6 _____

Health, Wellness, and Recreation Facilities

FACILITY LOCATION	ACTIVITIES AVAILABLE	COSTS INVOLVED	CALL TO RESERVE	LOCKER AVAILABILITY	CHECK-IN REQUIRED

Learning Style Worksheet

Are you left brain or right brain dominant? _____

How does this impact your learning preferences, strengths, and weaknesses?

_____

_____

Identify your learning styles. For each, cite your own characteristics that lead you to believe you are one type of learner:

Factual versus Analytical _____

_____

Participative and Dependent versus Competitive and Independent _____

_____

Visual versus Auditory versus Kinesthetic _____

_____

Where to go for formal tests:

Office   _____   _____

Test(s)   _____   _____

Cost   _____   _____

What techniques do you use if you have to function in a way that does not conform to your dominant learning style? Refer to the Adjust to Teaching Styles section.

_____

_____

What memorization techniques might you try? _____

_____

Living Agreement

- Alarm clock wake-up _____
- Time to use bathroom _____
- Wearing each other's clothes _____
- Use of each other's supplies _____
- Meal preparation _____
- Kitchen clean-up _____
- Laundry _____
- House cleaning _____
- Quiet hours for studying _____
- Lights-off hours for sleeping _____
- Use of computer equipment _____
- Radio, TV, and stereo time _____
- Phone messages _____
- Phone bills _____
- Rent and utility bills _____
- Appliance rentals _____
- Visitors of same sex _____
- Visitors of opposite sex _____
- Child care _____
- Lawn care _____
- _____ _____
- _____ _____

Date _____

Signatures _____   _____

Off-Campus Resources

RESOURCE OR SERVICE	NAME	ADDRESS	CONTACT PERSON	TELEPHONE
Aerobic Exercises				
Notes				
Bank/Investment Representative				
Notes				
Clothes				
Notes				
Computer Equipment & Software				
Notes				
Insurance Agent				
Notes				
Office Supplies				
Notes				
Pharmacy				
Notes				
Planned Parenthood				
Notes				
Rape Crisis/Victim Center				
Notes				
Restaurants				
Notes				
Theaters				
Notes				

RESOURCE OR SERVICE	NAME	ADDRESS	CONTACT PERSON	TELEPHONE
Vitamins/Minerals/Herbs				
Notes				
Worship Place				
Notes				
Yoga Classes				
Notes				
Notes				
Notes				

Study Groups

COURSE NAME _____

   Day(s) to meet _____   Time(s) to meet _____

   Place _____   Remember to bring _____

Members of Study Group

Name	Phone Number(s)	E-Mail Address
_____	_____	_____
_____	_____	_____
_____	_____	_____

COURSE NAME _____

   Day(s) to meet _____   Time(s) to meet _____

   Place _____   Remember to bring _____

Members of Study Group

Name	Phone Number(s)	E-Mail Address
_____	_____	_____
_____	_____	_____
_____	_____	_____

COURSE NAME _____

   Day(s) to meet _____   Time(s) to meet _____

   Place _____   Remember to bring _____

Members of Study Group

Name	Phone Number(s)	E-Mail Address
_____	_____	_____
_____	_____	_____
_____	_____	_____

Teacher Information

COURSE		TEACHER INFORMATION						
PREFIX & NO	SEC NO	NAME AND DEPARTMENT	OFFICE LOCATION	OFFICE HOURS	OFFICE PHONE	E-MAIL ADDRESS	DEPT SECR PHONE
		Notes:					
		Notes:					
		Notes:					
		Notes:					
		Notes:					
		Notes:					

Term at a Glance

MONTH	MONDAY	TUESDAY	WEDNESDAY	THURSDAY	FRIDAY

INDEX

in note taking, 81
in research, 188, 189
Overload permission, 110

P

Paraphrases, 191
Parasitic STDs, 150
Parliamentary procedures, 262-263
amendments, 262
debate, 262
motions, 262-263
voting, 262
Participative/dependent learners, 60
Pass/not pass regulations, 110
Pauk, Walter, 81
Peale, Norman Vincent, 12
Periodicals, research with, 188
documenting, 191-192
Personal growth and development,
139. See also Wellness
Personal profile, 17
Peterson's Job Opportunities, 238
Physical fitness
campus resources for, 10
Physical wellness, 138
Plagiarism, 172
Portfolios, developing, 248
Prejudice, 282
Prerequisites, 110
Presentation software, 162, 167
Priority setting, 39-54
Probation, 108
Problem solving, 67-69
Procrastination, 52
Programming languages, 163
Promises, keeping, 231
Proofreaders' marks, 207
Protocols, Internet, 169
Proving, in essay questions, 99
Psilocybin, 147
Pubic lice, 150, 151
*Publication Manual of the American
Psychological Association,* 191
Public speaking, 210-213

R

Race, 282
Racism, 282
Rahe, R H, 126
Rape, 154 See also Sexual assault
Reading textbooks, 74-75
Realistic disciplines, 232
Recite, 81
Record, 81
Records, database, 170
Records management system, 8

Recreation and leisure
groups for, 210
time management and, 45
Reference materials
library, 176
for regular work, 7
Registration
fees for, 107
planning next term's, 117-119
Relationships, 215-230
conflict resolution in, 225-226
human relations skills, 215-230
leadership and, 227-229
Relaxation techniques, 128-129
Repeat policies, 110
Research
documentation of, 191-192
Internet, 169-171
library, 175-193
photocopies in, 190
steps in, 181
Residence halls, 4
Responsible behavior, 141-157
alcohol and, 143-146
drugs use and, 147-149
personal safety and, 154-155
sexual assault and, 154-155
sexually transmitted diseases and,
149-153
tobacco and, 146-147
values and, 156
Résumés, 241-242
Review
in essay questions, 99
of notes, 82-83
Revision of writing, 202
Rewards, 53
Rohypnol, 148
Roll call voting, 262

S

Safety, 155
Saudi Arabia, customs of, 285
Scabies, 150
Schedules
changing class, 109
efficient, 117
homework, 52
for large projects, 52
month/week at a glance, 48,
50-51
personal, 18
planning efficient class, 51
procrastination and, 52-53
term at a glance, 46-47
weekly, 48-50
Scholastic honors, 110-111

Search engines, 169
See You at the Top (Ziglar), 215
Self-concept, 10-14
building a healthy, 12-14
overcoming negative influences
and, 11-12
personal profile and, 13
recognizing strengths in, 11
Self-Directed Search, 232-234
Sensing vs intuition, 61
Sentence completion questions, 96-97
Service groups, 212
Sexual assault
date-rape drugs and, 148
definition of, 154
precautions to avoid, 154
what to do after, 154-155
Sexually transmitted diseases, 149-152
communicating with partner, 153
reducing risk of, 149, 152
sexual behavior and, 152-153
signs and symptoms of, 150-152
types of, 150-151
Sexual orientation, 293
Short-answer questions, 96-97
Sleep, 136-137
Smoking, 146-147
Snacks, 134
Social correspondence, 28
Social disciplines, 233
Social wellness, 138
Software, 161-163
application, 162, 163-167
communication, 163-164
customized, 162
database, 166-167
graphics, 165-166
operating system, 162
presentations, 167
programming languages, 163
spreadsheet, 166
windowing, 162
word processing, 164-165
Speaking, public, 210-213
Speaking rates
in speeches, 211-212
vs listening rates, 79
Special collections, library, 180
Speeches
delivering, 211-212
following up after, 212-213
preparing, 210-211
Spell checking, 206
Spiritual wellness, 139
Spreadsheets, 166
Stereotypes, 282
Stimulants, 147

SUNDAY	MONDAY	TUESDAY	WEDNESDAY	THURSDAY	FRIDAY	SATURDAY

SUNDAY	MONDAY	TUESDAY	WEDNESDAY	THURSDAY	FRIDAY	SATURDAY

SUNDAY	MONDAY	TUESDAY	WEDNESDAY	THURSDAY	FRIDAY	SATURDAY

SUNDAY	MONDAY	TUESDAY	WEDNESDAY	THURSDAY	FRIDAY	SATURDAY

SUNDAY	MONDAY	TUESDAY	WEDNESDAY	THURSDAY	FRIDAY	SATURDAY

SUNDAY	MONDAY	TUESDAY	WEDNESDAY	THURSDAY	FRIDAY	SATURDAY